Praise for *Code Talker*

"From Guadalcanal through Bougainville to Peleliu, Nez relates a riveting tale of jungle combat and his personal struggle to adapt to civilian life following the most cataclysmic war in our nation's history. Gripping in its narrative, *Code Talker* is history at its best."

—Colonel Cole C. Kingseed, U.S. Army (Ret.), coauthor of *Beyond Band of Brothers: The War Memoirs of Major Dick Winters*

"A fascinating inside look at one of WWII's most closely guarded secrets . . . This is an important book, a previously untold piece of our history." —Marcus Brotherton, author of *Shifty's War*

"One of the hallmarks of a true war hero is that they never think of themselves as one. Another is that they often go to the grave without telling their stories. Fortunately for us, WWII Navajo code talker Chester Nez has finally told his, along with coauthor Judith Schiess Avila. With humble beginnings on the checkerboard of New Mexico, Mr. Nez's values were cultivated of the ground on which people walked. Later, in the midst of war, we can feel his struggle to reconcile those values with what he confronts moment to moment on the battlefield. History books can list facts about the Navajo code talkers, but they will never be as true as Mr. Nez's firsthand account. *Code Talker* is memoir at its best!"

—Karen Fisher-Alaniz, author of *Breaking the Code*

"You don't need to be a fan of World War II literature to appreciate this memoir . . . a fascinating melange of combat in the Pacific theater, the history of the Navajo people, and the development of a uniquely American code that remained unbroken by the Japanese throughout the war and classified until 1968. . . . Packed with Nez's one-of-a-kind experiences that secured his remarkable—and rightful—place in American history."

—The Associated Press

"A remarkably affecting first-person account of the Navajo Marines who served their country with distinction through some of the worst battles of the Pacific theater." —*The Washington Times*

"Readers will be captivated by stories of Nez's childhood and his days as a Marine." —*PW Annex Reviews*

"There's lots of detail of personal effort, suffering, and boredom, summoning the true flavor of the war and a portrait of those who made a valuable contribution to the war effort . . . Accessible and compelling, this is recommended for general readers as well as World War II history buffs." —*Library Journal*

CODE TALKER

CHESTER NEZ

with Judith Schiess Avila

BERKLEY CALIBER, NEW YORK

BERKLEY BOOKS
Published by the Penguin Group
Penguin Group (USA) Inc.
375 Hudson Street, New York, New York 10014, USA
Penguin Group (Canada), 90 Eglinton Avenue East, Suite 700, Toronto, Ontario M4P 2Y3, Canada
(a division of Pearson Penguin Canada Inc.) • Penguin Books Ltd., 80 Strand, London WC2R 0RL,
England • Penguin Group Ireland, 25 St. Stephen's Green, Dublin 2, Ireland (a division of Penguin
Books Ltd.) • Penguin Group (Australia), 250 Camberwell Road, Camberwell, Victoria 3124, Australia
(a division of Pearson Australia Group Pty. Ltd.) • Penguin Books India Pvt. Ltd., 11 Community
Centre, Panchsheel Park, New Delhi—110 017, India • Penguin Group (NZ), 67 Apollo Drive,
Rosedale, Auckland 0632, New Zealand (a division of Pearson New Zealand Ltd.) • Penguin Books
(South Africa) (Pty.) Ltd., 24 Sturdee Avenue, Rosebank, Johannesburg 2196, South Africa

Penguin Books Ltd., Registered Offices: 80 Strand, London WC2R 0RL, England

The publisher does not have any control over and does not assume
any responsibility for author or third-party websites or their content.

Copyright © 2011 by Chester Nez
Cover design by George Long
Cover photos: Chester Nez and the code talker medal courtesy of Brian Leddy; tank #BJTF75 © The
Print Colledctor / Alamy; aircraft #BFNTX7 and beach landing #BFNN11 © The Art Archive / Alamy
Book design by Laura K. Corless

PUBLISHING HISTORY
Berkley Caliber hardcover edition / September 2011
Berkley Caliber trade paperback edition / August 2012

ISBN: 978-0-425-24785-3

The Library of Congress has catalogued the Berkley Caliber hardcover edition as follows:

Nez, Chester.
Code talker / Chester Nez, with Judith Schiess Avila.
p.   cm.
Includes bibliographical references and index.
ISBN 978-0-425-24423-4
1. Nez, Chester.   2. Navajo code talkers—Biography.   3. World War, 1939–1945—Cryptography.
4. World War, 1939–1945—Personal narratives, American.   5. World War, 1939–1945—Participation,
Indian.   6. United States. Marine Corps—Biography.   7. Marines—United States—Biography.
8. Navajo Indians—Biography.   I. Avila, Judith Schiess.   II. Title.
D810.C88N49   2011
940.54'5973092—dc23
[B]
2011023701

PRINTED IN THE UNITED STATES OF AMERICA

10 9 8 7 6 5 4

Penguin is committed to publishing works of quality and integrity.
In that spirit, we are proud to offer this book to our readers;
however, the story, the experiences, and the words are the author's alone.

This book is dedicated to the 420 World War II Navajo Marine code talkers—men who developed and implemented an unbreakable communications system that helped ensure the American defeat of the Japanese in the Pacific war.

When the war ended, other combatants were free to discuss their roles in the service and to receive recognition for their actions. But the Marines instructed us, the code talkers, to keep our accomplishments secret. We kept our own counsel, hiding our deeds from family, friends, and acquaintances. Our code was finally declassified in 1968, twenty-three years after the war's end.

This book may be my story, but it is written for all of these men.

May they and their loved ones walk in beauty.

FOREWORD

by Senator Jeff Bingaman

The memoir that follows is the most recent example of courage from Chester Nez. Long ago, he and his fellow Navajo code talkers were brave enough to leave the homes they loved to support a country that often spurned them. With intelligence, skill, and courage they were a significant factor hastening the Allied victory in the Pacific.

Employing the Navajo language for secure communication was a masterstroke that was successful only because Navajos themselves were recruited to serve as Marine Corps Radio Operators. Using the Navajo language, they developed and transmitted the code, which proved unbreakable. When the war was over, they continued to protect the code—and their part in the victory—until it was declassified twenty-three years after the conclusion of World War II. Deemed TOP SECRET for decades, it is appended to this memoir.

Only in 1968 did their contribution become known. In 2000, the Congress of the United States, in an effort to recognize and honor the heroic contributions of the code talkers, authorized that the Congressional Gold Medal be struck in their honor. In July 2001, in the Rotunda of the Capitol, the presentation was made, and long-delayed thanks expressed.

Chester Nez, one of the twenty-nine original code talkers, offers this memoir of his American life before, during, and after World War II. It is a treasure, and so is he.

Jeff Bingaman
United States Senator for New Mexico

Senator Bingaman and Senator Daniel Inouye of Hawaii sponsored the "Honoring the Navajo Code Talkers Act" in 2000.

CODE TALKER

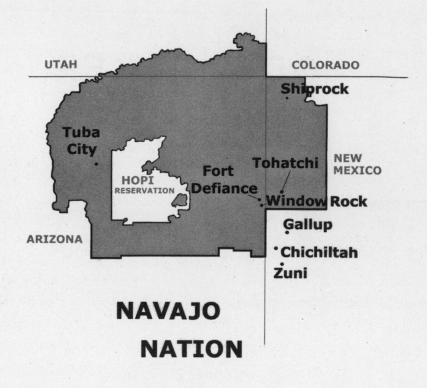

UTAH COLORADO

Shiprock

Tuba City

NEW MEXICO

HOPI RESERVATION

Tohatchi

Fort Defiance

Window Rock

ARIZONA

Gallup

Chichiltah

Zuni

NAVAJO
NATION

PROLOGUE

"I'm no hero." Chester Nez chuckles. "I just wanted to serve my country."

I just wanted to serve my country. To appreciate that remark, you need to know a little modern Native American history. In Chester's home state of New Mexico, Native Americans were still denied the vote when he volunteered as a Marine in World War II. Nevertheless, the military called upon Chester and fellow Navajos to devise a code that many analysts believe assured the United States' defeat of Japan in the Pacific war.

Chester, eighty-six years old when I met him, now ninety, is the only living "original" code talker. These were the twenty-nine men who first devised the famous Navajo code and took it into battle against the Japanese.

I try to picture this soft-spoken man in battle, an image that is always elusive. Instead I see the vast expanses of his grandmother's land in New Mexico, with Chester, a tiny figure in the sunbaked landscape, herding sheep. Or I see the little boy who, at boarding school, was punished for speaking his native Navajo language, the very language that led to the famous code.

When Chester, his son Mike, and I first met, we did not know that we'd create this book. An interview was what Chester and Mike had in mind. But talking for a couple of hours wasn't enough. I have never been in the military, and I am not Navajo. I did not know what to expect. So, like a fisherman I cast my questions into vast unknown waters and pulled in an assortment of remarkable narratives. I first learned about Chester's role as a World War II code talker. The saga of the devastating war, over before I was born, captivated me. Then, hearing of his childhood in the Checkerboard Area in New Mexico, where a difficult life made him strong, pulled me back even further into a rich history. Everything began to fit together, each piece a necessary part of the whole.

After thinking about it for a couple of days, Chester agreed to let me write his biography. But early on he expressed some concerns. What if his story wasn't long enough to fill a book? He hadn't done any more than so many other men, so why were we writing about him? What if he forgot something important, or remembered something incorrectly? What if his story wasn't exciting enough?

Readers of this memoir will realize—I hope—that Chester's fears soon proved baseless.

Chester grew up on the Checkerboard. His family's land sat side by side with spreads owned by Anglo-Americans, Hispanics, and other Navajos, not far from the huge Navajo Nation—commonly called the Navajo Reservation—that straddled the borders of Arizona, New Mexico, and Utah, and bordered on Colorado.[1] Life in the Navajo Nation was difficult when Chester was a child. Life on the Checkerboard was even more difficult.

"We could go for three or four days without eating," Chester recalls. "Everything always comes last to the Checkerboard. My sister Dora's house is wired for electricity, but she still has no power. They say it is coming soon."

---

1 Archives.gov. In 1942, during the early months of the United States' involvement in World War II, the Navajo Reservation covered twenty-five thousand square miles.

That was in 2007. Dora's house is located on the Checkerboard land where Chester grew up. She died in 2008, still with no electricity.

The account of Chester's life is important because it tells of a people whose deeds have too often been overlooked. I believe this is the first book to tell of the full life experience of a code talker who grew up as most Navajos then did—herding sheep, attending boarding school, eking out a day-to-day living. This is significant. In *Code Talker*, the memoir of World War II Navajo Marine Chester Nez, Chester takes a close look at his childhood, a childhood that, in broad strokes, represents the formative years of an entire generation of Navajos. *Code Talker* examines the courage and spirit that imbued the Marines in World War II who developed and utilized the famous, unbreakable Navajo code. In doing this, it highlights a significant contribution made by an indigenous culture. The multifaceted Navajo language enabled that code to be developed, demonstrating how the diversity that defines our nation—diversity of color, of background, of language—contributes to our strength.

There are some things Chester remembers that don't jibe completely with history as read in a textbook. That is to be expected, especially concerning the wartime events experienced by the code talkers. The code talkers were such a well-kept secret that their very existence was classified for twenty-three years following the close of hostilities in World War II. In 1968, when their contributions to the war effort were finally declassified, their history was available to be recorded for the first time. Much of this history relied on memories that were nearly a quarter of a century old.

This is Chester Nez's saga. We record here his recollection of events. Where his memories diverge from accepted history, his memories take precedence. We have worked hard to accurately depict the wealth of information Chester remembers.

Also, some of the practices and events that Chester recalls diverge somewhat from traditional Navajo practices. We have striven to footnote these divergences throughout the book, but once again, we have recounted things as Chester remembers them. It is impossible to neatly label and codify the customs of the Navajos, now numbering more than a quarter-million people. Divergence is inevitable.

As our interviews progressed, I began to write. But something *was* wrong. It wasn't Chester; it was me.

I'd finished Chester's biography before I realized that his story wasn't mine. It was his. Chester is alive, and this book needed to be his memoir, not a biography written by someone else. So I listened to the tapes again. By then we had recorded more than seventy-five hours.

The calm, modest voice on those tapes reminded me that, traditionally, Navajos are private people. They don't seek praise or applause when one has simply done his duty. In the telling of his story, Chester's desire is simple: he hopes that those readers who are not Native American will appreciate and understand something outside their own experience, and that those who are Native American will find a source of pride in their heritage.

I listened. Chester's voice was strong, his multifaceted story riveting. Here it is.

Judith Schiess Avila
May 2011

CHAPTER ONE

Guadalcanal Invasion

November 4, 1942: Approaching Guadalcanal

Nothing ever dried. My damp combat uniform chafed at the back of my neck. Water ran down my forehead and into my eyes. A trickle meandered down my back as I stood on deck in the dark. The railing of the transport ship dripped with rain, but in the tropical climate, its wet surface was warm to the touch. The ship rolled slightly in the South Pacific waters, a constant unsettling movement that, just weeks ago, would have made me queasy. But my stomach held steady.

Born to the Navajo Nation, now a Marine—Private First Class Chester Nez—I'd never even seen the ocean before enlisting.

It was good, being able to sail without feeling squeamish. I tried to concentrate on that, and not on where I was heading. But thoughts seeped into my brain like seawater. Like other traditional Navajos, I'd always believed in the "Right Way." Balance must be found, not only between individuals, but between each person and his world. My hands gripped the rail. The ship's steady progress brought me inexorably closer to Guadalcanal. For three months, battle had raged there. How could I find any balance in that?

I reminded myself that my Navajo people had always been warriors, protectors. In that, there was honor. I would concentrate on being a warrior and on protecting my homeland. Within hours, whether in harmony with this world or not, I knew I would join my fellow Marines in the fight.

Belowdecks, machine guns, earthmovers, and other heavy equipment filled the ship's belly. The items we were likely to need first had been packed last so that they would be easily accessible upon landing. Aircraft carriers had preceded our troop ships, carrying dive-bombers to blast Guadalcanal's beach prior to the Marine landing.[1] The transport ship I sailed upon was accompanied by destroyers, cruisers, battleships, and additional transports.

I squinted. A battleship was barely visible through the gloom off the port side of my transport. A shiver—pride? relief?—ran through me. Battleships and aircraft carriers were the largest vessels in the U.S. fleet. On the huge ship's deck, I caught glimpses of a triple gun turret, wielding guns that fired sixteen-inch-diameter shells. Its dark bulk appeared and disappeared in the predawn murk.[2]

We thirteen code talkers traveling with the fleet were late-arriving members of General Vandergrift's 1st Marine Division. Several regiments of the 2d Marine Division sailed with us in the transport ships. Our briefing had told us that the capture of Guadalcanal, an island in the Solomon chain off the northeast coast of Australia, was the first stepping-stone to an eventual attack on Japan. At Guadalcanal, the Japanese enemy waited.

---

1 The dive-bombers were designed for descents of sixty degrees from horizontal.

2 Acepilots.com: The USS *South Dakota*, a battleship that fought in the Battle of Guadalcanal, had a standard displacement of thirty-five thousand tons and a length of 680 feet. It carried a main battery of nine guns arranged in triple turrets. The guns launched sixteen-inch-diameter shells. A secondary battery of sixteen five-inch-diameter guns was fixed amidships.

I could have stayed in high school, I thought. Maybe I should have. But, as a warrior, how could I ignore the fact that my country had been attacked?

I'd volunteered for the Marines just seven months before, in April 1942, only a few months after the Japanese strike against Pearl Harbor, Hawaii. Until joining up, I had never left Navajo land, except for a few hours en route to boarding school. My wiry frame barely met the Marines' minimum weight requirement of 122 pounds, but I knew I was strong. I straightened and shoved trembling hands into my pockets. I was a man now.

The ship would not reach Guadalcanal for a couple of hours. I walked below several levels to the mess hall, where the taut faces of the other twelve code talkers aboard ship greeted me. We were all dressed the same. Our combat uniforms were a gray-tan color, a bit grayer than the color now commonly called khaki. They consisted of a short jacket and trousers, with a darker brown T-shirt. We carried a poncho that reached almost to our ankles. We had been issued two pairs of thick socks, supposed to keep us from developing blisters on the march, and two sets of underwear. Our helmets were a tan-gray color with a cloth covering that had blotches of faded green, tan, and dark gray. Those blotches helped them blend in with the terrain—camouflage, the Marines called it. Our boots, boondockers, were made of thick leather. They came up to just above our ankles.

I liked the smell in the galley area, although lots of Marines complained about it. I guess I'll always be drawn to the aroma of cooking food, after spending my early years in boarding schools where I was never able to eat what I wanted, when I wanted, or as much as I wanted. We lined up and joked with the guys who were serving, asking them to give us plenty of chow. Sometimes we got slabs of steak too big for a dinner plate. We placed our trays, loaded with sausage, corned beef, steak, and scrambled eggs, on a long, narrow counter and stood to eat. Every time the ship pitched or rolled, the trays slid, moving from one guy to the next and back again. We'd wait for our own tray to slide back, then resume eating.

As I raised my coffee cup, Charlie Begay jabbed a sharp elbow into my ribs. "Hey, Chester. Sure could use a beer right now. How about you? Pabst Blue Ribbon or Budweiser?"[3]

I chuckled. While in San Diego, on liberty from Marine basic training, we men had frequented bars, wearing our uniforms so we wouldn't get thrown out like other Native Americans did. Many of us had never had a drink before joining the Marines.

"Budweiser," I said. "Always Budweiser." I laughed and resisted the urge to switch from English to Navajo. "That place in San Diego. The Slop Chute, enit?" I glanced around at the other code talkers. "Wish we were there instead of here."

English came easily now, ever since boarding school when we were kids. My fellow code talkers and I knew the white people's words, but among ourselves we generally spoke in Navajo. Because of our mission, we didn't do a whole lot of moving around the ship or mingling with the other Marines. Instead, we gathered together on shipboard, practicing our code. Always practicing.

All thirteen of us men had had a hand in designing the secret code, together with nineteen other Navajo Marines, back in the States.[4] Recruited for our fluency in both Navajo and English, we'd been locked in a room after basic training and told to develop a secret military language using our native Navajo. Now each man was determined that the code would guarantee an American victory over the Japanese in the Pacific.

"Jackass." I laughed. "Whose idea was 'jackass'?" The Navajo word for "jackass"—spelled *tkele-cho-gi* in our code phonetics—stood for the

---

3 Budweiser was introduced in 1876; Pabst Blue Ribbon in 1893.

4 The "Original Twenty-nine" volunteers were joined by three other Navajo Marines, both in developing the code and in taking it into battle.

English letter *J.* I looked around at the smooth, young faces of my friends. They all grinned. Whose idea had that been?

The white man's military had accepted us as tough Marines. Hardened by the rigors of life on the reservation or the Checkerboard Area, we often outperformed our white peers. In basic training, Marine sergeants bragged about the prowess of Platoon 382, the Navajo recruits. And our code was part of a bold plan to take the Pacific islands back from the dominant Japanese.

Cutting through endless ocean toward my first battle, the code's proving ground, my twelve buddies and I studied and restudied the entire vocabulary of two-hundred-plus words. All of us were fluent, yet we all continued to practice. We could afford no doubts, no hesitation. Accuracy and speed were a matter of life and death.

We practiced transmitting messages among ourselves and to code talkers on other ships. The new language became solid and unshakable, embedded in our minds as firmly as childhood memories. We transmitted, deciphered, and responded to messages almost without hesitation. We were ready. We hoped.

I smiled to myself, thinking about the shipboard radio operator who'd heard the strange code and warned his commanding officer that the Japanese had broken into U.S. communications. Apparently, officers on the flotilla of ships around us compared notes, wondering if communication security had been breached. They shut down all U.S. communications in order to isolate the Japanese transmissions. They heard only silence.

When communications resumed, we Navajos started transmitting again. We relayed information about the landing craft and the groups of personnel who would populate each craft for the imminent landing on Guadalcanal.

Not even our shipmates knew of our secret communications mission. But several of the admirals had been informed of the code developed by thirty-two[5] Navajo Marines. I guess they finally realized that what they were hearing was that code. Forbidden to divulge this new secret weapon, they simply spread the word to other high-ranking officers that a group of Native Americans had joined the Marines. And the United States Marines were speaking Navajo.

We Navajo men moved belowdecks to the barracks area. We stood around in a random group. One man, probably Eugene Crawford, said a prayer for all of the Marines about to land on the Japanese-held island. Speaking Navajo, he asked that all would survive, of course knowing how unlikely that was. I'm sure the other men added their own silent prayers, like I did. I talked to the Old Man upstairs, asking for protection.

The Marine brass encouraged prayer. I wasn't sure whether they really believed in its power, or whether they were like baseball coaches who observed every possible superstition. But they approved of our praying.

Four or five miles north of Guadalcanal, everyone gathered on deck in the rain. I looked around at my fellow code talkers and wondered whether my face was as tight as theirs. A couple made jokes in Navajo, ribbing the rest of us. The laughter was muted.

The 2d Division Marines and we late-arriving 1st Division Marines were briefed on what to expect in the water and on the island when we landed. I promised myself I would be brave. But the air vibrated with apprehension.

A chaplain addressed us, reciting a blessing. I held the small buckskin medicine bag my father had sent and said my own silent prayer. *Give me courage. Let me make my country proud. Please protect me. Let me live to walk in beauty.* Around me the other Navajos seemed to be doing

---

5 The history books all say twenty-nine, but I prefer the figure thirty-two since Ross Haskie, Wilson Price, and Felix Yazzie also helped immeasurably in the development of our code. Ross and Felix invaded Guadalcanal with us.

the same, each hoping to "walk in beauty" again in their native homes in Arizona and New Mexico.

After the chaplain spoke, a high-ranking officer—either a colonel or a general, I can't remember which—stepped up to address us. I nodded at Roy Begay,[6] my partner for the landing, and tried to smile. My tall friend, a skinny frame masking his strength, smiled back, but his expression looked forced. Though we'd been friends since boarding school, I had never seen good-humored Roy look so scared.

The officer talked straight. "I hate to say this," he said, "but I guess we all know that some of you will not return from this battle. Some of you will never see your families again." He cleared his throat, hesitating. Then his voice took on strength and determination. "Always remember, you are defending both your country and your families. The Japanese attacked your land, your home. And now you will make your country proud."

Despite the peril we faced, the officer then tried to put us at ease, tried to help us understand what lay ahead on Guadalcanal. He spoke like a father talking to his son. "It's okay to be scared," he told us. "It would be foolish not to be scared. And you men are anything but fools." He hesitated again. "Just remember your training."

We all nodded.

I can do this, I thought. I pinched some corn pollen from my medicine bag, touched my tongue, my head, and gestured to the east, south, west, and north, then tucked the bag back into the pants pocket of my fatigues.

When the officer stopped speaking, I walked off by myself. One of my buddies called my name, but I kept walking, pretending not to hear.

---

6 Roy is listed as one of the original twenty-nine code talkers, but for some reason, the literature I've read on us does not show him as one of the thirteen landing on Guadalcanal that November. However, he was definitely with us. Our mission was so secret that many records were classified, and after 1968 (when the code was declassified) reports of specific events often depended on fallible memories.

I thought about my father and grandparents, my younger sister, Dora. I pictured the dazzling sun of New Mexico and wished I could feel its dry warmth baking my skin. I thought of the air there, so pure and clear. I whispered a prayer of beauty:

In beauty all is made whole.
In beauty all is restored.

I thought about what I was to face, wondering whether I'd be one of the men to die. It was five o'clock in the morning, November 4, 1942, the most terrifying day of my life.

We approached the northern shore of Guadalcanal. Gray tones of daylight revealed black smoke drifting thick over the island. I offered silent thanks to the Navy's pilots who had bombed the enemy, hoping to drive them away from the shoreline where we Marines planned our landing. We drew closer, and the battleships in our flotilla let loose. The roar of huge weapons made our ears ring. Shells, sixteen inches in diameter, plowed into the beach.

As we drew closer, the black smoke, brought in on a heavy, slow wind, settled on my skin, and the sharp smell of explosives stung my nose. I saw a helmet floating in the water. I tried not to look too closely, not wanting to see whether it was American or Japanese.

My buddy Roy and I watched as the first wave of men, laden with gear, climbed down heavy nets to their landing craft. It must have been around eight-thirty in the morning by then, but everything was gray with rain and smoke.

"We can do that," said Roy quietly. "Nothing to it."

"Ouu," I said in Navajo, biting the word off like the English word *oat. Yes.*

Of course we had practiced landing: the climb down the rope nets, the rifle, the grenades, our packs jammed full of the necessities of war. But this time enemy fire tore into the water and ricocheted off the ship. Men cried out—wild, startled shouts. Our legs trembled and hands shook. Nothing was the same.

We code talkers did not disembark in the dangerous first assault wave. Apparently, Marine command deemed our mission too critical. As we looked on, the landing boats filled, forming a circle offshore and waiting until all the craft in the first wave were manned. Then the shelling from our ships moved up from the beach to the hills, and the boats hit the island all at once.

It will get better, I told myself, *once we're in the Higgins boat, once we're moving.* But everyone in my landing crew, the third wave, looked real worried.

I remembered our briefing. The Japanese were winning in the Pacific. Our fleet in Pearl Harbor, Hawaii, had been the one deterrent to Japan dominating virtually all of the Pacific islands. And now that Pearl Harbor had been crippled, the Japanese were clearly dominant. The United States had no bases on islands other than Hawaii. Bases and airfields, both needed for refueling craft and provisioning troops, were critical if the United States was to eventually attack the island monarchy of Japan.

The United States' strategy was to conquer the Pacific islands one at a time, thus becoming the commanding force in the area. So, three months before, on August 7, 1942, the 1st Marine Division—without us code talkers—landed on a very different Guadalcanal. Back then only 2,200 Japanese occupied the island. Most were not soldiers, but construction workers building an airfield.

That first landing of the Marines met with little resistance from the construction workers. But Japanese forces reacted quickly, planning an air attack to be launched within two hours of the U.S. landing. A volunteer Australian "coastwatcher" sent warnings to the U.S. military one hour ahead of the Japanese attack. The Japanese sank an American transport that carried supplies for the troops. Under heavy enemy fire, Admiral Fletcher withdrew his three aircraft carriers, despite protests by Rear Admiral R. K. "Terrible" Turner, who was in charge of moving ammunition and provisions ashore to supply the U.S. fighting men.

Prior to the night of August 8 and early morning of August 9, the Japanese Naval base at Rabaul, six hundred miles to the northwest of Guadalcanal, launched every available warship. They arrived at a strip of sea separating Guadalcanal from the Florida Islands to the north, an area nicknamed "The Slot" by U.S. troops, in the dark early hours of August 9. The U.S. fleet was caught off guard. The Japanese sank two of the five Allied cruisers that sat off Guadalcanal's north shore. The cruisers' role was to protect transport ships which supplied the Marines on the island. They held crews of upward of one thousand and, depending on their class, varied over a range of sizes. The loss of a cruiser was devastating.[7] Two more Allied cruisers were so badly damaged that they were abandoned. The fifth cruiser, USS *Chicago*, sustained sufficient damage to put it out of action.

Two American destroyers were also badly damaged. Originally a class of ship designed to destroy torpedo boats, destroyers carried both torpedoes and depth charges. They utilized these weapons in attacking larger ships. Destroyers were small and inexpensive to build, at least when compared to cruisers and battleships. The destroyers acted as scout ships for the fleet.[8]

In the dark, the Marines on shore couldn't be sure what was happen-

---

7 AcePilots.com. World War II Baltimore-class cruisers displaced 13,600 tons, had a length of 673 feet 5 inches, a beam measuring 70 feet 10 inches, a draft of 20 feet 6 inches, and a speed of 33 knots. Armaments consisted of nine guns that launched 8-inch-diameter shells, twelve guns launching 5-inch-diameter shells, forty-eight 40-millimeter antiaircraft guns, and twenty-four smaller, 20-millimeter, antiaircraft guns. They carried two aircraft and a crew of 1,142. (Thanks to Stephen Sherman.)

8 Ibid. The Fletcher-class destroyers displaced 2,100 tons, had a length of 376 feet 3 inches, a beam measuring 39 feet 8 inches, a draft of 13 feet, a speed of 36 knots, and a crew of 273. Armaments were five 5-inch-diameter guns and ten 21-inch-diameter torpedo tubes, as well as eight depth charges.

ing. They prayed that the fireworks meant the ships belonging to the Land of the Rising Sun were sinking. The poetic name "Land of the Rising Sun" was how the Japanese referred to their homeland, especially in relationship to their rival, China, whose huge landmass was located just west of Japan. Of the two countries separated by the Sea of Japan, the Japanese got the sun first.

Given the heavy U.S. Naval losses, "Terrible" Turner had no choice. He withdrew his transport ships along with the unarmed commercial merchant vessels, carrying unloaded supplies and military equipment, that had been recruited to serve the Allies. The next morning those men on Guadalcanal realized they were left exposed, with no air cover and no reserve provisions of food and ammunition. It was a devastating blow for a group of fighting men who had tried to convince themselves that their country was invincible. The battle, dubbed the Battle of Savo Island, was the worst Naval defeat endured by the United Sates in 130 years. And the Japanese had lost no ships.

Deprived of much-needed food and ammunition, the Guadalcanal operation, originally code-named Operation Watchtower by Allied brass, became known among the fighting men as Operation Shoestring. Despite their lack of Naval support, and despite the fact that the Japanese—who controlled the seas around Guadalcanal—delivered reinforcements of men, food, and ammunition, the hungry Marines used every bullet and drove the enemy from the airfield. They hung a banner that announced UNDER NEW MANAGEMENT, and in two weeks they completed the work begun by the enemy, christening Henderson Field on August 20, 1942, in honor of Major Lofton R. Henderson. Henderson, a dive-bomber squadron leader, had been killed at the Battle of Midway, the westernmost of the Hawaiian Islands, the previous June.

Assault troops trained to attack and capture a position, not to occupy it, the Marines, nevertheless, held on. They lacked the weapons and ammunition required to defend their position on the airfield, but somehow they lasted until reinforcements and supplies finally arrived. Meanwhile, they knew that their Henderson Field would soon provide a landing place for fighter planes and, after that, larger bombers—like the B-25 and the B-17 Flying Fortresses.

But the Japanese did not let go of Guadalcanal. Their war strategy depended upon the Guadalcanal airfield as a supply base. The enemy persisted in defending the remainder of the island, bringing supplies and reinforcements from Bougainville, a large island to the northwest. Enemy ships maneuvered "The Slot" in the dark of night. These night attempts at resupply became known as "The Tokyo Night Express."

By the end of the third week of August, approximately one thousand Japanese reinforcements, fighting under Colonel Kiyono Ichiki and eager to kill for their emperor, had landed at Taivu, situated twenty miles east of the American-held beachhead near Lunga Point. These men, expecting an easy victory, were defeated by Major General Alexander Vandergrift's 1st Marine Division. In mid-September, Japanese Major General Kawaguchi landed with six thousand more Japanese troops. They, too, were defeated by American forces, at the Battle of Bloody Ridge, just south of Henderson Field, on September 13.

By mid-October, the Japanese had delivered twenty thousand soldiers to the island, including a full division of the Japanese 17th Army, led by Lieutenant General H. Hyakutake.

When we code talkers arrived in early November to join the 1st Marine Division in battle, the brutal fighting had already taken heavy tolls on both sides.

Our Higgins boat swung out over the water and was lowered by a crank mechanism with chains fastened to bow and stern. We scrambled down the rope net, hands and feet flying over the holds. The ship moved on the waves and I swung toward and away from its metal side, holding on for dear life. The rope I clung to smelled strange, a mixture of oil and hay chaff. I tried to remember to grip the vertical lines and step on the horizontal, at the same time making sure I didn't overtake the man below me. At the bottom of the net we dropped into the waiting Higgins boat. Then an armlike mechanism unsnapped the fore and aft chains, and we formed a circle with other boats, waiting for all of the landing craft in our assault wave to be manned. Finally we started for shore, with the boats fanned out so we wouldn't bump into each other.

We men in the landing craft sat mute. The Higgins boat pitched steeply in the surf as we approached shore. Nearly flat-bottomed, with a rectangular shape and only a four-foot draft, the boat was able to pull up close to the beach. Although the craft was open on top, a metal armor plate along the sides made it partially bullet-resistant.[9] Roy and I rode side by side. Roy's good-natured features had frozen in a blank expression.

When we neared the beach, a Marine unlatched the ramp that formed the bow of the boat. The hinged ramp opened, and we rushed down into chest-deep water, holding our rifles above our heads in the continuing rain. Japanese artillery shells exploded around us. Noise roared, continuous, like the clamor of an enraged crowd. Sharp punctuations—individual explosions—added to the din. Bodies of Japanese and American soldiers floated everywhere. I smelled death, as bullets sliced into the water. Blood stained the tide washing onto the beach.

A Marine floated nearby, his sightless blue eyes staring up at a foreign sky. I had spoken with him only moments before entering the landing craft. He'd been in San Diego at boot camp when I was there, but in a different platoon. I didn't even know his name. My body went cold. My throat tightened up, and I struggled for breath. My eyes burned with unshed tears. After that, I did my best not to look at the faces of the dead.

---

9 www-cs-faculty.stanford.edu. Higgins boats were also called LCVPs (Landing Craft, Vehicle, and Personnel). Their length was 36 feet 3 inches, beam 10 feet 10 inches. Displacement, when unloaded, was 18,000 pounds. Speed was 9 knots. They carried two machine guns and could deliver thirty-six fighting men, fully combat-equipped, to shore.

With heavy seawater filling our boots and dragging against each step, Roy and I forced ourselves to struggle forward. *The killing fields. Our baptism.* The word the drill instructors had used in basic training kept running through my head. *Baptism. Baptism. Baptism.*

Navajo belief forbids contact with the dead, but we waded through floating bodies, intent on not becoming one of them. *Close your mind,* I told myself. I tried not to think about all those dead men, their *chindí* violently released from this life. *I am a Marine. Marines move forward.* I tried to make myself numb.

We pushed bodies and parts of bodies aside, some looking more like raw beef than the limbs of human beings, fought our way forward, and finally fell gasping on the beach.

Onshore, we attempted to find our assigned unit. Japanese fighter planes—Zeros—flew overhead in a formation that echoed the V-formations of Canadian geese. The Zero no longer dominated Allied fighter planes as it had in the first months of the war, but those bright red disks, sun symbols, on the underside of its wings sent a chill down my spine. I knew those enemy planes carried machine guns, cannons, and bombs.

We found General Vandergrift, who assigned us to Signal Officer Lieutenant Hunt. Following Hunt's orders, we moved to the tree line on the edge of the beach and hauled small folding shovels from our backpacks. Making ourselves as small as possible, crouching at the tree line, about 150 yards from the surf, we performed our first battle duty: digging foxholes. Every feverish thrust and twist of the shovel brought us closer to crude shelter from land-based bullets, but nothing would protect us from the bombs and bullets dropping from the sky. Enemy fire exploded around us from every direction. Rainwater filled the holes as we dug.

"All those bodies in the water," I said to Roy.

"Yeah?"

I stabbed my shovel deep into the sand. "We didn't really have a choice."

"No."

I tossed the shovelful of sand. Neither of us needed to say more. It was good, having Roy with me. Roy understood.

I was lucky to be partnered with Roy. He was a really good man, serious as can be about our code work. Some of the code talkers joked around a lot, probably to relieve the constant tension. But Roy and I were temperamentally well suited to each other. The gravity of our code work kept us both pretty solemn, although we appreciated a good laugh when it was provided by one of the other men. Roy was superb with the code. He and I, we never once let each other down.

We tested our radio equipment, with me cranking and Roy speaking into the microphone. Roy nodded. *Good.* Our TBX radio was unique, a wireless system that generated its own electricity via the cranking motion. Our only wires were the ones connecting the headsets and microphone to the crank box. Other modes of communication used on the islands, both radio and telephone, depended upon the wiring, which was strung by Marine communications men. Our TBX could pick up radio stations, the news, but we weren't allowed to switch to that. We had to keep communications open for coded messages.

That first night, Roy and I crouched in our foxhole, side by side but facing in opposite directions, so my knee was pushed against Roy's shoulder and vice versa. The water crept nearly chest-high. Heavy drops fell like bullets, causing the water in the foxhole to splash. We two desert boys had heard tales of rain like this.

I bumped Roy's arm with my knee. "Remember in boarding school? The white man's Bible," I said. "All this rain."

Roy chuckled. "Yeah. Noah and the flood."

"*Ouu.* Noah." I hesitated. "I'd volunteer to board his ark right now."

Although we were supposed to take turns in our foxhole sleeping and keeping lookout, neither of us slept. Gunshots sounded in intermittent bursts, tearing through the dark, soggy night. Blue-white artillery tracers streaked across our field of vision—enemy artillery shells. Our own shells had red tracers. I couldn't yet distinguish between the sounds of Japanese and American gunfire, but the colors were immediately evident.

In the heavy murk, I tried to picture myself back home in sunny New Mexico.

"Do you think we'll be scared like this all the time?" Roy asked, his voice breaking.

I answered simply, "Yes."

Roy sighed. "I'm going to pray," he said.

Hot tears burned my eyelids, and I noticed that Roy wiped at his eyes with both fists.

"You and I, we're going to get through this," I said.

Roy just nodded.

I moved my lips, making no sound.

Lord, please help me.

I switched to a traditional Navajo prayer.

In beauty I walk.
With beauty before me I walk.
With beauty behind me I walk.
With beauty around me I walk.
With beauty above me I walk.
With beauty below me I walk.

Prayers were a comfort for me. They gave me confidence. My prayers brought me back home to *Chichiltah,* and I walked with the sheep in the place whose name meant "Among the Oak Trees." I could picture it so clearly. The view from Grandmother's land was beautiful in all seasons. Patches of bright green in spring, with the new buds on the oaks and scrub oaks. Masses of silver-green in summer, with the chamisa and sagebrush growing as tall as a small adult. Splashes of gold and red in autumn, when the oak trees changed color. Red and white in winter, the snow deep and nourishing over the brick- and tan-colored soil. And a powerful sky watched the changing seasons, turquoise blue and studded with stark white clouds—a view you drank in like cold water on a sweltering day.

When I arrive home after this war, I promised myself, *my father will be happy to learn how the Navajo language helped the troops. My family will be proud of my part in developing the top secret code.* I just had to make it through, so I could see *Chichiltah* again.

I smiled, remembering the sheep and goats, the sound of their bells. The baby sheep and goats wore jingle bells, and the adults a kind of small cowbell, nothing too loud, just enough noise to reveal their location if they wandered off. I loved the sound, like soft chimes in the dark. Maybe, if I concentrated, I could block out the gunfire and hear, instead, the bells.

CHAPTER TWO

Sheepherding, Back on the Checkerboard

Mid-1920s

The smell of Auntie's coffee and the bleat of a lamb woke me well before sunrise. Opening my eyes to slits, I looked for Old Auntie. Was she still angry? Yesterday my older brother Coolidge and I had lagged behind the herd, playing with our slings. We got in trouble with Old Auntie.

Ah! There she was, piling juniper branches onto the campfire. Her form etched a black shadow against the dark gray of the landscape. *Shimá Yázhí* ("auntie" or "little mother") hummed as she worked. She must be in a better mood.

I turned and stared up into the dark. The sky arched above me, decorated by First Man and First Woman with familiar groupings of stars. The rain had stopped. Lying still, I savored the aromas of earth, wet piñon, and sagebrush. The comforting smell of damp wool and the fragrance of juniper sticks burning in Auntie's fire told me that all was as it should be. I breathed quietly, not wanting Old Auntie to know I was awake. In a few minutes I'd get up and start chores.

I hadn't heard the owl last night. That was good, because the previous night its screeching had awakened us. If the owl followed us, it meant there was trouble—even death—brewing, and we'd have to find a medicine man to set things straight. I'd been born in winter, and this was my sixth spring, but I already knew the importance of the "Right Way." Things must be in balance.

Even before sunrise, I could picture the wide-open country, thousands of unfenced acres, that surrounded me. The land spread out like a random-patterned blanket. Piñon, juniper, and oak trees stretched in dense, intermittent bands. Occasionally, the delicate blue-green foliage of cedars interrupted the yellower green of their relatives, the junipers.[1] In the open areas, silvery chamisa sprang up in the rust-colored earth. Cactus, too, thrived: many-branched cholla and flat-lobed prickly pear. Yucca plants, with sharp, swordlike leaves and spectacular white flower clusters, stood like soldiers. And over everything stretched the sky—at times boiling with thunderheads, at others a bottomless inverted lake of pristine blue. The sun ruled supreme, making its powerful presence known nearly every day.

"*Shimá Yázhí,*" I said, "I'm awake."

"Me, too," said Old Auntie's twelve-year-old sister.

My two older brothers, Charlie Gray, in his early twenties, and Coolidge, in his teens, rolled out of their bedrolls. Uncle, Auntie's late-twenties brother, just a couple of years younger than Old Auntie, stirred and stretched under his sheepskin blanket.

"Hang your blankets to dry," said Auntie, her voice commanding.

Maybe she is still angry, I thought. A sheep bleated softly. The goats

---

1 The names "juniper" and "cedar" are often used interchangeably. Only certain varieties of juniper, with a bluer, more delicate foliage, are actually considered to be a type of cedar (although not a "true cedar," which is of genus *cedrus* not *juniperus*). Juniper and cedar bark was often used as diapers by the Navajo, after it was rubbed and crushed to soften it.

and sheep were my best friends. We always named the babies, and they responded to their names. Sometimes, when my aunt was mean, my sister Dora and I hid in the cornfield. Dora, whose Navajo name, *Binishíít Baa*, meant "woman who fights a battle in a circle," was a good companion. When we felt lonely, the sheep and goats always made us feel better. Especially the kids and lambs that followed us around, just like dogs.

Old Auntie hoisted the heavy sheepskin water bag and poured water into the empty coffee can that she used to cook breakfast. The herd always found shallow, scattered water holes when it was on the move, but we *Diné* (the People) wanted clean water. We carried drinking water from our well at home when traveling with the sheep and goats. I'd watched Grandma make that water bag, stripping the wool, oiling the leather with animal fat to make it waterproof, then stitching the thick material. It had taken a week.

I stood and shook my blankets, the bottom one soft and the top one slick to shed rain or snow. A lamb, no more than a few weeks old, jumped at the sudden flapping. Last night's shower, a soft, female rain, had lasted for only a short while, barely dampening the bedding. I hung the blankets over a tree limb to dry, along with the sheepskins on which I'd slept the previous night.

I pulled a shirt on over my head. I slept in my shorts, a hodgepodge of patches and mends. The soles of my feet had thick calluses that enabled me to walk over rough ground without pain. I preferred to go barefoot in the warmer months.

Auntie frowned at me but grabbed a pinch of corn pollen from the pouch worn around her neck. She touched my tongue and head with the pollen derived from our tribe's staple food. Then she held her pinched fingers out to the east, south, west, and north, the morning blessing.

"*Betoli,* milk a couple of the ewes and fill this bottle." Auntie handed me a Coke bottle. "Don't spill any."

Betoli, my "traditional" name, meant "light complexion" in Navajo.[2] I belonged to my mother's clan, the Black Sheep (*Dibé-lizhiní* or *Dibé-tizhiní* in Navajo). Navajo clan affiliations are passed down through the mother, not the father. Decisions involving me were made by the clan. I had heard Father offer opinions, which were considered respectfully. But I knew the clan was responsible for the final verdict when considering any problem involving me and my brothers or sister.

I did as told, first washing the manure from the teats of two sleepy ewes. The manure assured that their lambs did not nurse until the humans wanted them to. Then, leaning my forehead against the warm flank of the first sheep, I mimicked what I'd heard Old Auntie say as she milked.

"Don't worry. I'll leave some milk for your lamb."

I milked both ewes into a small pail, pouring the milk carefully into the soda bottle. When I looked around, Old Auntie was still busy at the campfire. I placed the bottle of milk on the ground, not too close to the fire, so Auntie wouldn't knock it over in the dark. That would anger her for sure.

Grabbing the small pail, I approached a female goat. While I petted her head she nuzzled against me, content. After a while I reached for a teat and bent to squirt milk into the pail. I raised the pail to drink.[3] I loved goat's milk, although it was really better after it had been boiled. My eyes squinted as the sharp milk hit my tongue. Boiling gave the milk a milder flavor, although it didn't always get rid of all impurities. Once I found a bug—I think it was a louse—gorged on milk till it was about ready to pop, in the boiled milk pail. Still, I preferred the sharp goat's milk to the cow's milk provided at the trading post.

---

2 Although it is customary in many Navajo families to address one another by kinship terms (i.e., "my son" or "grandfather") rather than by given name, when I was a child my family addressed me as *Betoli*.

3 Normally, we would milk the goat into a pail and strain the milk through a flour sack, then boil it to pasteurize it. When out with the herd, we sometimes drank the fresh milk as described here.

I walked over to Old Auntie. "Is there any goat cheese left?"

"Just a little. I'm saving it for later. But breakfast will be ready soon."

Auntie took the soda bottle filled with sheep's milk and fitted a nipple onto the top. She fed a lamb whose mother had abandoned her, holding the bottle with the nipple facing downward and tugging it gently, causing the lamb to suck noisily. It was unusual for a ewe to ignore her lamb, but fairly common among the goats and kids. So we always kept a couple of soda bottles and nipples on hand.

I laughed, watching the hungry little animal. Despite her mother's neglect, she was thriving. She'd adapted well to the bottle.

The others joined us, and we six gathered around the campfire, a source of warmth and orange-tinged light in the still-dark morning. We ate the breakfast Old Auntie had made—blue cornmeal mush and goat's milk. The herd was already restless, and just before sunrise it would be on the move, so we ate quickly in the wavering light cast by the fire.

That day we would follow the three hundred sheep to a new grazing area, where we'd stay for a few days before moving on. Ewes and lambs made up our herd, along with a few goats and kids. The eight rams belonging to Grandmother, *Shimásání* (the old mother), were corralled until mating season. The really young lambs and kids were corralled separately, and didn't accompany the herd until they were strong enough to keep up. When we had newborns in the herd—in the spring—we brought the mothers back to nurse them at night or nursed them by bottle. Later, when Grandmother's herd more than tripled in size, the logistics became quite complicated.

The sheep were placid and easy to care for. Even so, Old Auntie wanted us to be on constant alert. The twenty goats who also accompanied the herd were more lively than the ewes. Traditionally, Navajos had a lot of respect for sheep, and not so much for goats, although they were certainly cute and fun when they were babies. At any rate, combining sheep and goats was a common practice. The two species blended well.

After breakfast, we all helped Auntie pack bedrolls, the remaining food, and the heavy water bag onto the big brown "sheep horse." This horse lived on the range with the sheep and carried the items necessary for us *Diné* to survive.

Snow, a white eighty-pound dog, stood alert at one side of the herd. Five other dogs took up their posts around the fringes. Then my two aunties, my uncle, my two brothers, and I moved out with the animals. We walked through deep grass, never worrying about our flocks having enough to eat. Other Navajo families shared the range, with no fences to keep anyone out.

After grazing in one place for two or three days, Grandma's herd moved on to new grass. I knew that the constant movement was good for the safety of the livestock. Predators did not gather in any one area, knowing where to find the animals.

We followed the sheep. The day grew warm and quiet. A straggler headed toward a clump of juniper. I glanced at Old Auntie. She nodded, then watched me throw a small rock out beyond the lamb, turning her back in toward the rest of the herd.

A gray shadow flashed off to my right. Coyote? The hated animals often lurked among the thick piñon and sagebrush. I stood absolutely still and waited, then carefully bent down and picked a stone, fitting it into the rubber of my inner-tube slingshot. Young Auntie held a coffee can filled with rocks at the ready. The noise of the rocks, when the can was shaken, would scare a coyote. But I heard and saw nothing.

Just as I turned back to the herd, the sharp cry of a kid rang out. A coyote had grabbed the baby goat by the leg, pulling it into a clump of sagebrush. My heart beat fast as I aimed the slingshot, heard it thud, then charged toward the fracas. Young Auntie shook the coffee can, creating a racket. Old Auntie yelled and plunged from across the herd. Three dogs raced over, barking and growling. The coyote dropped its prey, running with its tail between its legs.

The mother goat and I reached the kid before Auntie did. It cried piteously. Four punctures marked its leg. Blood flowed freely.

"Good," said Auntie, when she arrived. "The blood will clean the wound." She examined the leg. "It's not bad. He can walk."

I stayed close to the kid and his mother as we continued our trek. Coyotes posed a serious threat to the lambs and kids, and sometimes even to the older animals. And any animal lost to a coyote was a double loss. Not only was the wool (or in the case of a goat, the milk) gone, but the meat as well. Even if our dogs recovered the carcass, no self-respecting Navajo ate meat killed by the devil coyote. Everyone knew evil people came back as coyotes after they died.

The scared little goat kept up with the herd. As the few scattered remnants of rain clouds evaporated, a turquoise-blue sky arched over us. The temperature in the early part of the "moon of large plants"—the white man's month of May—rose to the midseventies. Life was good.

Some days we covered between fifteen and twenty miles on foot. That day we walked eleven miles or so, stopping to build camp on a slight rise in the shade of a piñon grove. Snow, the big sheepdog, selected the rise that day. He, like his six humans, preferred to watch the sheep from above, keeping an eye out for danger and stragglers.

I scratched behind the big dog's ears. "Good boy."

Snow, like all of the dogs, herded by instinct. Every morning he approached the sheep, eager to be moving. On the days when we stayed put, Snow climbed a rise and watched, ever alert.

There was time before dinner. I walked to the horse, turned back once to Snow. "Stay," I said. I pulled my toys from the load lashed to the back of the sheep horse.

My sling, different from the slingshot I had used on the coyote, was made from the tongue of a shoe, cut off when Grandma wasn't looking. Two holes on either side of the tongue allowed a string to be attached. I returned to the rise, sitting near Snow, placed a pebble on the shoe tongue, and wound the sling over my head like a cowboy's lasso. *Slap!* The pebble hit the trunk of a dead tree, bounding back and startling Snow.

"What are you doing, *Betoli*?" shouted Old Auntie. "You'll alarm the sheep."

I shoved the sling into a frayed pocket and pushed my toy car around in the dirt. "Barooooommmm, barrrrroooomm!"

The car had wheels made from empty spools of thread. Windows had been carefully cut into a rectangular cardboard matchbox from the trading post, creating the car's body. Red dirt—now dry and powdery despite last night's rain—puffed out from the car's wheels.

The baby goat who'd been attacked by the coyote ran up to me and rubbed his head against me. He wanted to play. A good sign. The kids and lambs had sweet personalities, and they recognized me as a friend. I rubbed the little goat's head. Then I gently pushed him back toward the herd.

I stowed my car and leaned against the trunk of a piñon, thinking. Like always, I tried to picture Mother's face. Mother, *Shimá* in Navajo, had died a couple of years before, when I was young, too small to remember her. And there were no pictures to show me what she had looked like. But I felt sure she had been very beautiful.

Father, *Shizhé'é,* who had some training as a medicine man, had cared for Mother when she was dying. He built a lean-to for her about a mile and a half from our home. My younger sister, Dora, and I could not visit. Father didn't want us to be upset. And if death came, our absence kept us from following the dead person into the next world. This danger— that the deceased's ghost or *chindí* might lead the living away—led to the tradition of moving the seriously ill away from their primary home and, especially, the children. Even so, I knew that something was very wrong.

Only a few weeks after Father built the lean-to, my mother died. And after her death, one-year-old Dora, our older brothers, and I were not allowed to attend the burial.

According to tradition, the grave was dug by the oldest males in the family. Adult female relatives stayed with the dying person and prepared the body, but did not go to the grave. And while my father and grandfather dug the grave, tradition forbade them to speak to each other. Grandfather, the oldest male relative, stripped to just a breechclout and placed my mother into the ground. Afterward, they told no one where the grave was. My family observed the customary four days of mourning, during which no one left home or received visitors.

Father combined his livestock with Grandma's animals. In the Navajo matriarchal society, motherless children always stayed with their maternal grandmother. Father stayed, too.

Grandma ran the everyday living, making it all look so easy.

We lived on Grandmother's land, in a "summerhouse" made from juniper and oak branches. Today called the Checkerboard Area, our land butted up against spreads owned by both Navajos and non-Navajos, creating a diversified patchwork. It sat near the Navajo Nation, or the Navajo Reservation, that overlapped the border between Arizona and New Mexico. The sections belonging to Navajos, although separate from the Navajo Nation proper, were considered "allotments" held in trust for the families that lived there.

The Navajo name for my home was *Chichiltah*, "Among the Oak Trees." Between Gallup and Zuni, New Mexico, Grandma's house sat among red rock cliffs in a box canyon with a ravine in the bottom and a well just off center, near the ravine. Oak trees provided shade in summer. The sheep and goats loved the plentiful acorns.

Everyone worked hard, and no one spoke about Mother's last days or her death. But my family frequently talked about her life. The Navajo language has no word for actual death. They use the word *ádin*, which, roughly translated, means "no longer available." So Grandma and Father talked about how Mother had helped out with the sheep or tended a sick goat. We talked about her as though she was still there, just "unavailable."

"Betoli." Coolidge's whisper pulled me from my thoughts about *Shimá*.

My older brother placed a finger across his lips. *Quiet.* Then he pointed by raising his chin and twitching his lips toward a tree limb above my head.

I squinted. The dark, sleeping form of a porcupine lay draped in a crook of the limb. My pulse raced. Porcupine meat was delicious.

"Take that branch," said Coolidge, pointing with his thumb to a fallen bough, "and try to kill it quick."

Coolidge climbed the tree, placing each foot carefully. I bent to grab the broken limb from the ground. Coolidge shook the branch where the porcupine lay, and the startled animal fell. One quick club with the limb killed the prickly critter. I silently thanked the spirit of the porcupine for allowing us to catch him so easily.

Coolidge singed the quills from the furry body over Old Auntie's cook fire and dug a pit. He cut a few branches from a dead piñon, broke them into small pieces, and placed them in the pit, stuffing small juniper twigs and dry leaves in as kindling. The dry branches burned readily, requiring only one match. While waiting for them to burn down to coals, Coolidge dressed the porcupine, removing the entrails and splitting the breastbone to fold the animal neatly open. Meanwhile, I collected more branches, placing them over the hot coals already in the pit.

"A big one." Coolidge's eyes shone. Porcupines sometimes grew to the size of a small sheepdog. He placed the porcupine carefully, split side down, on the branches, then covered it with more branches. When the fire burned down, he threw dirt over the coals and built a final fire on top.

As the aroma of porcupine fat whetted our appetites, the sun set, splashing orange and pink across the western sky. Sheep bunched up for the night, some lying down and others grazing close by. The moon would be full. A full moon encouraged the flock to wander. I spread my blankets close to the sheep. After dinner, the first watch would be mine.

I smiled to myself. Like my uncle, who was a grown man, I cared for the sheep. Some days I sensed that my siblings and I were a burden to

Old Auntie and Grandmother. But, as a sheepherder, I was able to help. That made me proud.

Auntie called us all to dinner, and we ate thick tortillas with goat cheese. The porcupine would cook all night, with Coolidge waking to restart the fire two or three times. But, meantime, the soft, white goat cheese had a wonderful flavor, sharp and clean. I ate every bit of mine, then licked my fingers.

Auntie tapped me on the shoulder. "Where's that goat the coyote tried to kill?" she asked.

I separated the kid from the other animals in the herd, pulling it toward Auntie. The mother goat followed.

"Here he is." I peered down at the little goat's back leg, where it had been bitten. "It's not bleeding anymore."

Auntie stroked the kid's back and examined its leg in the fading light. "I'll make a poultice while the fire is still burning," she said. "Get me some sage."

Younger Auntie went for sage, returning with an armful of the silvery-leafed plant. Old Auntie pounded the sage with a rock, poured a bit of water into a can, added the sage, and heated it over the fire. She let it cool a bit, then applied the mush to the goat's leg, wrapping it with strips of cloth to hold it in place. "By morning he'll be much better," she said.

I fell asleep that night to the aroma of roasting porcupine. In the morning we'd have a delicious breakfast, with meat that tasted much like pork. Old Auntie would be in a fine mood, after the hearty breakfast.

CHAPTER THREE

The Great Stories

Mid to Late 1920s

I sat by a snapping winter fire, surrounded by family. Moving in closer to the blaze, I turned my back to the heat for just a moment. Then I turned forward again, my eyes focused on Father. My eyelids wanted to close after a long day of work, but excitement kept them open. It was story time.

Before dark, we had talked with the Holy People about crops, livestock and the need for rain. Now stars blinked in the black sky above us. I waited, eager. In Navajo life, everything has a story, narratives that are significant both in ceremonies and in everyday life.

"The *Diné* roved over the land to find food for their sheep," Father said quietly.

"The four sacred mountains protected them, outlining a huge hogan that the Holy People had made safe for the *Diné.*"

Any Navajo who left those familiar boundaries had to prepare himself with prayers and blessings. Mount Blanca, the White Shell Mountain, represented the east and marked the northeastern corner of the safe area. It stood near Alamosa, Colorado. Mount Taylor, the Turquoise Mountain, at Grants, New Mexico, represented the south and marked the southeastern corner. The San Francisco Peaks, also called Abalone Shell Mountain, near Flagstaff, Arizona, represented the west and marked the southwestern corner. And Mount Hesperus, Obsidian Mountain, in southwest Colorado represented the north and marked the northwestern corner.

Father grew silent, and Grandmother, after waiting politely to see whether Father would continue, took up the thread of the story. "The Navajo language played an important role in the creation of the world. At the dawn of creation, four Navajo words were spoken."

I knew the words by heart: *'adinídíín* (light), *nahasdzáán* (earth), *tó* (water), and *nitch'l* (air).

"As these words were spoken," Grandma continued, "the sun, the earth, the oceans, and the air that we breathe appeared." She took a deep breath. "The spoken Navajo words could not be separated from the physical sun, the actual earth, the oceans and air. Speaking our language created the world, and the creation of the world made our language."

I had carried water to the shelter that day from Grandma's spring. Grandma coughed. Her throat sometimes became parched in the dry winters. She stood to get some water from her shack or "summerhouse," and Father continued.

"The first *Diné* emerged into our world—called the 'glittering fourth world'—from three underworlds," he said. "They used a reed to travel between worlds. Gods set the four sacred mountains in place. Coyote, the trickster, helped First Man and First Woman to fling the stars into the heavens."

I held my breath, knowing what came next.

"But soon, monsters began to roam the earth, killing the *Diné*."

We all listened, eyes round.

"Then, Changing Woman, who grew up in New Mexico, married the Sun."

"Did she grow up near here?" asked Dora.

"Not too far," said Father. He cleared his throat. "The Navajo people prayed to the Gods, asking them to slay the monsters. The Gods at first replied that the monsters were also their children. But, after marrying the Sun, Changing Woman had twin boys. The twin sons of Changing Woman visited their father, the Sun. He gave them lightning bolts—the bow and arrow—as weapons against the monsters. The twins slew each monster, and the corpses turned to stone. The stone formations created by the dead bodies of the monsters can still be seen. They lie along the area bounded by our sacred mountains."

I loved this story, and listened carefully every time to be sure that the *Diné* were properly saved from the monsters. The weapons used had been the first bows and arrows. My elders told this story only during winter, hunting season. Since the bow and arrow were associated with thunder and lightning, you didn't talk about them in summer, the season of thunderstorms.

I listened carefully as Grandfather took up the *Diné*'s more recent history. The arrival of first the Spanish, then other Europeans, shrunk the native lands, pushing the *Diné* and other tribes into smaller and smaller territories. Now most lived on the reservation.

When Grandfather was silent, I waited, then looked at Grandmother. Her coughing had subsided. "Will you tell us about the Long Walk?" I asked.

"Ah. That is my mother's story. Yes, I will tell you."

She wrapped her blanket around broad shoulders and sat up straight. My great-grandmother had been very brave. I sat absolutely silent, not wanting to miss a word. A branch snapped somewhere nearby in the cold.

Grandma looked up at the sky, its stars gloriously visible in spite of the blazing campfire. After several moments, she spoke. "The *Diné* fought against the white settlers, trying to keep the land that had always been ours. This land had been given to us by the Holy People. Since the very beginning of time, our people had lived within the land bounded by the four sacred mountains.

"But soldiers pulled our ancestors from their land. A famous white man, Kit Carson, burned Navajo crops, uprooted our trees, killed our livestock, and warned all Navajos to surrender and gather together at Fort Defiance, Arizona. Anyone who did not go to Fort Defiance would be hunted down and captured or killed." She sighed. "My mother, with the others, was forced to march three hundred fifty miles from Fort Defiance to Fort Sumner in New Mexico."[1] Grandma ran a heavily veined hand over her hair and continued. "My mother has told me this. The old, the sick, women, children. All had to go."

Grandma again pulled her blanket more closely around her, as though insulating herself from the story she told. The golden light from the fire played over her face.

"The walk took twenty days, and along the way, hundreds died. If someone got sick, they were killed by the soldiers. If a pregnant woman stopped to have her baby, she was killed. Anyone who tried to help her was also killed. If someone collapsed from thirst or hunger, he was killed.

"More than eight thousand *Diné* eventually made it to Fort Sumner. My mother was lucky. She was young and healthy.[2] But many of her friends and family died at the fort. The *Diné* were held near Fort Sumner in a place called the Bosque Redondo. A large number of Apaches were held with the *Diné*. There were too many people. The soil was not good for crops, not like the soil in our homeland of the four sacred mountains. And the water was bad. It made the people and the animals sick. There were no herbs for healing. There were not enough trees for firewood. The

---

1 This happened in 1864. Fort Defiance became a boarding school in Arizona, the one I eventually attended. Fort Sumner is located in the Bosque Redondo area of eastern New Mexico.

2 She was approximately thirteen in white men's years.

white man could not provide enough food or enough shelter[3] for all of the people they had imprisoned."

She turned and looked from me to Dora and to the other children. Her dark brown eyes were solemn.

"Every Navajo knows of these injustices. Many suffered and many died along the way to Fort Sumner. We remember this time as the 'Long Walk.'"

The Long Walk became a pivotal part of our oral tradition, and it is still discussed today as one of the great tragedies of Navajo history.

But the Long Walk gave us Navajos a sense of shared history and a feeling of kinship that we might not otherwise have developed. It contributed to our feeling of being one people—the *Diné*—the Navajo Nation.[4]

After returning from Fort Sumner in 1868, some families moved back to what is now the reservation proper, but others found plots of land near the reservation, building dwellings and raising sheep and goats. My family was among these latter settlers. The plots, geographically separated from the reservation, became the Checkerboard Area.

The Long Walk was history that I learned of but would never see. I would personally witness the second great Navajo tragedy, the Great Livestock Massacre.

But first, I had a private battle to fight—boarding school.

---

3 Nathan Aaseng, *Navajo Code Talkers*, p. 7. An estimated two thousand *Diné* died in captivity from disease and hunger.

4 Ibid., p. 9. Aaseng mentions this feeling of solidarity.

CHAPTER FOUR

Shipped Off to Boarding School

Late 1920s

I slashed at chamisa bushes with a juniper stick. In the ninety-degree heat, sweat dripped into my eyes, but I wiped at it with the back of my free hand, hardly noticing. There were bigger problems to ponder. Dora and I were going to boarding school.

I picked up my pace, trotting. Now that I was in my eighth summer, I never really thought about the constant motion, following the sheep. I just kept up with the herd like any adult, without noticing the miles that disappeared under my feet.

A wad of sap clung to a tall piñon. I slowed to pull the sticky mass free.

Turning to Young Auntie, I held it out to her. "Here. Take some."

She took a portion of the sap, grinned, and popped it into her mouth, chewing it like gum. I chewed the remainder. The sap was already softened from the heat, and it tasted fresh. *Will they have piñons at school?* I looked off into the distant purple-red mesas, and squinted at the blazing sun. Not a cloud in the sky. Not a fence to be seen. Sheep and goat bells jingled softly. And I knew Father and Grandma waited for us. How could we leave them?

"The government wants Navajo children to learn English," Father had said.

But what about herding the sheep? The livestock assured our family's survival. People on Navajo land needed little money, but the animals were important. Grandfather and Grandmother got almost anything the family needed by trading rugs, mutton, and wool. Few adults had jobs that paid wages.

Father, however, worked full-time for the Mexican man who owned the local trading post, a place for business and for social gatherings. The man, nicknamed "The Thundering Mexican" because of the way he galloped around on his horse, was good to us Navajos. He grew wheat, corn, and other vegetables, and gave nice perks to my family. He helped Father, who already owned horses, to buy a wagon. And Father had come home with treats from the trading post—huge wheels of cow cheese, not as sharp as goat cheese but still tasty, and old inner tubes for making slingshots and other toys.

The Thundering Mexican became a trusted acquaintance. He suggested to Father, who had kept Dora and me, his youngest children, at home, that we should attend school. Government pressure was inevitable, said the Thundering Mexican, if we weren't sent voluntarily.

"Wouldn't you like to go to school? Learn English?" Father had asked us.

Sitting just outside Grandma's summerhouse, we looked at each other. I wondered whether Dora could see the same dread in my eyes that I saw in hers. My brother Coolidge already attended school. And Coolidge was surviving.

I spoke up first. "If you think we should."

"Good. It's settled, then." We knew that Grandmother must have already agreed, or Father wouldn't have broached the subject. So, a verdict had been reached. After the corn was harvested, we would go.

Every night, before falling asleep, I thought about leaving home. In *Chichiltah,* I had a sense of belonging, of being where I should be. School was part of the white man's world. I tried, but couldn't begin to picture what it would be like. As the month of "big harvest" drew to a close, I dreaded being separated from my family.

But a thought slipped quietly into my head, then grew noisy: *I need to learn English. What if I want—or need—to leave Navajo land someday?* Knowledge of English would be crucial.

I knew English was a language that involved reading and writing. Not like Navajo. The Navajo word for school meant both "to count" and "to read." I liked the idea of learning to read and write. That desire drew me toward the mysterious concept of school. I decided I had to at least give it a fair shot.

The day came. We left in the month of "Small Wind"—October—that year. Dora and I climbed into the back of the local missionary's Model T Ford truck. The missionary had agreed to drive us to kindergarten in Tohatchi, New Mexico. I scooted over close to my little sister in the truck bed, making room for several other children. Their shoulders pressed against mine. I sensed their fear.

Piñons and junipers whipped by. I heard my sister murmur softly, "Dora."

The missionary had just assigned us "English" names.

I smiled at Dora. "Chesssster," I said, the sibilance of the unfamiliar name hissing between my teeth.

We arrived at the Tohatchi boarding school well after midnight. The school, made of rough stone, nestled into the foothills of the Chuska Mountains. There were four dormitories, one for the older boys, one for the older girls, and one each for the younger boys and girls. The school was a single large building. The dark hid the shabbiness of the school that first night.

Instead of using the name of our clan, the missionary told the school administrators that "Nez" was Dora's and my last name. *Nez* meant "very long" or "very tall" in Navajo. It came from Father, D'ent Nez, who was a very tall man. *D'ent* meant "the man," so *D'ent Nez* meant "the tall man." The name had been given to him when he registered on the reservation.

It was odd that the school preferred to use Father's name, not the familiar maternal clan names used by us Navajos.

We were fed milk and one thick cracker, about the size of a small woman's palm. Not much of a meal after the daylong journey. I yearned for some mutton or tortillas, or for corn cooked over the campfire.

"I'm still hungry," I said, pushing my empty plate away.

Dora quickly swallowed the last of her cracker.

"Time for bed." The matron, speaking English, pulled me by the arm.

We received no more food that night.

And the food got no better and no more plentiful. Dora and I ate every scrap on our plates, licking our fingers and pressing them onto stray crumbs to pick them up. We arrived at each meal hungry, and left still hungry. We looked for food in the trash pile out back of the school, sometimes finding crumbs or things like spoiled fruit. We wolfed anything that was remotely edible, spoiled or not. Both of us were slim when we arrived at school, but we grew skinny. We felt hungry, always. And we missed our family.

The lack of food took its toll. When Dora and I went home for a visit, we told older brother Coolidge about how hungry we were. One look at our skinny frames and sunken cheeks told our brother and the rest of our family that we weren't getting enough to eat.

"You're not going back there." Coolidge's eyes flashed. "You'll come to Fort Defiance with me."

Grandmother and Father agreed, and we two youngest Nez children returned with Coolidge to the all-Navajo school in Fort Defiance, Arizona.

En route to Fort Defiance, we again bumped along in the missionary's Model T truck. Deeply rutted wagon and horse trails served as roads. I gripped a flour sack tightly in one fist. There was no place to stop for food along the route, so we carried lunch in the sack—fried bread, some mutton, tortillas. I wondered whether it would be the last good food we ate before finishing out the year at boarding school.

The missionary stopped his truck. "Time for a break."

He gave each of us a few sips of water from a canvas water bag that hung over the grille of the vehicle.

Dora looked at me with round eyes. The air-cooled drinking water was thrillingly cold, almost like ice water.

"I hope the food will be better at this school," I said quietly.

Dora nodded.

We climbed back into the truck. *Is it the right thing, going off to another school?* Uncertainties chased around in my brain, but I knew that Father and Grandmother expected me to do my best.

Around midnight, we arrived at Fort Defiance. Cloaked in dark, the dormitories and school building loomed foreign, forbidding. Dora gripped my arm.

I smiled down at her. "It will be okay." My doubts had given way to a calm determination to succeed in this alien place.

Colonel Sumner, a Union commander in the Civil War, had built Fort Defiance in the early 1850s. The outpost was designed as a stronghold for United States soldiers stationed in the western territories. From Fort Defiance they were ordered to quash Navajo uprisings. It was at Fort Defiance that Kit Carson gathered the *Diné* for one of the darkest episodes in their history, the Long Walk to Fort Sumner.

Years later it became a government school for Navajo children, one designed to rid them of the "burden" of their culture and traditions.

Looking back from today's perspective, many former students feel the fort was a bad place for a school. They had bad dreams because of the many deaths and the bodies buried there.

On my first day at school, I lined up with the other boys. Tears streamed down many faces. The first order of business: a mandatory haircut.

Hair fell in piles. I awaited my turn, hands squeezed into fists as I watched the shearing. I figured there must be some mistake. We Navajos believe in witchcraft. Cut hair and fingernail clippings should be gathered and hidden or burned. Such things could be used to invoke bad medicine against their owner. People should not leave parts of themselves scattered around to be picked up by someone else. Even the smallest children knew that.

I looked around. Stern people herded boys into the shearing room. They spoke only English, and I spoke only Navajo. How could I make them understand?

Hair continued to fall, the strands all mingling together. My hair was shoulder length, black as a raven's wing. I was pushed toward the chair, and I climbed up, gritted my teeth, and closed my eyes as the barber worked. When I opened them I was shaved nearly bald. Not even the best of medicine men could separate my hair from the black piles growing around me.

Dour Indian matrons—non-Navajos, but still Indian—watched. Their hawklike eyes stabbed fear into the heart of any child who contemplated protest. I shuddered, looked around at all the baldy kids. *What will happen now?* Who could guess at the consequences of this total disregard for safe hygiene?

Each child was treated for lice. Then medical exams were performed. The doctor poked and prodded at us as though we were sheep.

The school issued uniforms—one-piece, navy-blue suits that buttoned or zipped up the front. I had brought my own clothes with me, but the matrons confiscated them. This, too, worried me. Like any personal object, clothes could be used in a manner similar to hair, as a device for placing a curse on someone.

I looked down at the new uniform. I didn't feel like myself. I looked around at the others. Everyone looked the same. A little boy near me struggled to fasten the unfamiliar uniform buttons. I bent down and helped him.

"Like that," I said in Navajo. "Now you try the others."

"Quiet! English only!" The dark eyes of a matron bored into me. "English, or you'll be punished."

I wonder what she said?

When the little boy still couldn't fasten his buttons, I did it for him. "You can practice later." I whispered the words, guessing that maybe my speaking had angered the matron.

We new arrivals were given a tour of the school. Four red-brick dormitories, placed in a square, housed the students. One of the buildings was three stories high. That one, a beautiful building, sheltered the older girls. The other three dormitories—one each for the older boys, the younger boys, and the younger girls—rose to only two stories. But they all looked huge to us kids who'd been raised in hogans and summerhouses.

The cafeteria sat across a sidewalk from the dormitories, and a short way down the sidewalk was the school. Government employees shared the large, two-story school building. A smaller school, farther down the sidewalk, provided classes for the youngest children.

A trading post, located off school property, but near the edge of the campus, sold candy and toys. And the fields around the school were cultivated with vegetables. These were harvested, and they became ingredients in our meals.

Boys were told not to speak to the girls. Students were allowed to enter some areas, like the living areas and classrooms. Other sections of the campus were out of bounds, and our guide—using hand gestures and helped by an older student who translated the warnings into Navajo—warned us to stay away.

At home I had gone everywhere and spoken to everyone. It seemed odd that at school, certain places were forbidden and speaking to the girls was prohibited.

We boys climbed up to our dormitory room on the second floor of the boys' residence hall. I looked down the long row of beds, all arranged side by side. I had never slept in a "white person's" bed, except at school in Tohatchi. Windows covered one entire wall of the dormitory. It was a long drop to the ground from where I stood.

That first night, the boy in the bed next to me woke in the middle of the night screaming.

"What's wrong?" I asked him in Navajo.

The little boy shivered, although the night was warm. "Terrible dreams," he told me. "Dead men. Indian warriors. And white men, too."

An owl—always a bad omen—perched on a lamppost outside the dormitory. Eerie hoots stirred the still night. We two boys looked at each other, eyes popping. Then we lay back in bed, looking straight up at the ceiling, trying not to move.

The next night, as I climbed into bed, the spirits of dead warriors stood vivid in my imagination. I lay awake, not daring to close my eyes.

Many children had bad dreams in this strange place that had once been a frontier fort, a place of death. The boys in my dormitory were all ten years old or younger. I hated to see them cry. Several other boys and I tried to calm their fears.

I wished my brother Coolidge slept in the next bed. But the older male students had been divided into two groups, eleven through eighteen and over eighteen. They lived in a different building. Like me, most of the other Navajo children had begun school at the age of seven or older. Some were even eleven or twelve. So there were quite a few boys over the age of eighteen, even though Fort Defiance School stopped at sixth grade. Still, there were no older boys in my dorm and no adults to comfort us children after our nightmares.

Older boys. At home I knew which kids were older by the way

they looked, how tall they were, and how strong. Time, back home, was marked by the change of seasons, not by a calendar. I, like most of the children, had not known my birthday or my age. The school obtained birth dates from the records of the Bureau of Indian Affairs at Crownpoint, in northwestern New Mexico. I learned, at age eight, that I was born on January 23, 1921.

I brushed one hand over my hair, feeling the unfamiliar bristles. I had been at Fort Defiance School for several days. I did my best not to do anything wrong, but since I knew no English, it was difficult to figure out the rules.

I addressed a boy, using his Navajo name.

The matron struck me on the back of the head with her open palm. "English only."

"Wood, uh . . . Wood," the little boy whispered to me, pointing at his own chest with his thumb.

"Woodrow," snapped the matron, giving the boy a shove.

The "English" names assigned by the school were made from sounds unfamiliar to us children. Luckily, I had the already familiar name the missionary had given to me. Other kids had a more difficult time with the foreign words that felt wrong in their mouths. But these were now their names. When asked for their new names by a teacher or matron, they struggled to remember. Punishment was immediate for those who forgot.

The half-Laguna matron gestured and spoke to a man dressed in dark-colored overalls. He carried a flat-shaped metal box and wore a belt with various tools hanging out of it. The matron's voice grew hard, and she pointed in the direction of the bathrooms. This matron was half white. The other woman who watched over the young boys in my section of the school was full-blooded Pima. I couldn't decide which one I feared and disliked most.

The kids passing the Laguna-and-white matron gave her and the tool man a wide berth. Still, one stepped too close, and she grabbed him—quick as a snake—by the back of his uniform.

"What's your name?" she asked.

I froze in place, watching the exchange.

The boy looked down at the floor. "Uh, uh . . . Theo . . ."

"Theodore, you idiot." The matron swatted him across the face. "Theodore." She pushed the boy away.

Gulping down tears, he scurried down the hall after his classmates. She turned to me. "What are you looking at?"

I yelled, "Chester," at the top of my voice, then whipped around and followed the others before she could grab me. *She always picks on the littlest ones,* I thought.

The knowledge of constant danger sat lodged in the pit of my stomach like a rock. I tried my best to answer questions correctly, but never knew when a matron would strike. They watched, their dark cold eyes waiting for us to make a mistake, to do something wrong. I was always afraid.

Snow fell softly outside the dormitory windows. Loud whispering came from two beds away. Navajo. I'd been caught speaking Navajo three days before. The Pima matron brushed my teeth with brown Fels-Naptha soap. I still couldn't taste food, only the acrid, bitter taste of the lye soap.

Teachers at the school were encouraged to be strict, and the smaller children were frequently targeted by slaps or kicks. But the lingering taste of the soap was worse than either of those punishments.

"Why do you think the matrons are so mean?" the small, high voice, speaking in Navajo, asked from a bed to my right.

"The teachers are mean, too," said someone on my other side. "And we'll be sent home if we complain."

"I'd like to go home," another voice said.

"It isn't right, though. They're really mean," said a fourth voice in the dark.

I thought about how well I'd been treated at home by my father and grandparents. They never hit me when I was bad. They explained to me that what I was doing was wrong, and said that I should stop. It didn't seem right that the matrons—Indians themselves, although not Navajos—mistreated us, their fellow Indians.

With the snow growing deeper outside, I remembered the "string game," played with my aunties and brothers. The string game honored Spider Woman, who taught the *Diné* to weave. Complex patterns formed when string was "woven" back and forth between our fingers. As the string was carefully passed from one participant to another, the patterns grew more elaborate. The game was played only in winter, just as hunting stories were told only in winter.

I wrapped up in my blanket. I thought about autumn in *Chichiltah*, a golden time, my favorite, when corn was harvested. At the end of a long day, Father often made a kind of basket of barbed wire, filled it with corn, and roasted it over the fire. Lying on that cot at Fort Defiance, I almost tasted the sweetness of the yellow kernels.

When I concentrated, I heard the soft chime of sheep bells. After the long winter, in early spring, they returned the sheep to Grandma's shelter and corralled them to be sheared. It was then that their wool was the fullest, and as the weather warmed, the sheep wouldn't need a thick coat.

We tied the sheep so they wouldn't move and get cut, then used manual shears, starting at the shoulders, and tried to get the wool off all in one piece. Grandma and my aunties then pulled any twigs and debris from the wool and sprinkled it with white clay sand. They let it dry for at least a week, because it contained oils that would make it difficult to work with. Next they carded the wool, using two flat paddles with metal spikes. These were worked against each other, kind of like combs, and the wool was pulled so the fibers all ran in one direction. That was hard physical labor. Next the carded wool was spun into yarn using a spindle, which is a wooden stick with a flat disk near the bottom. The spindle was twirled in one hand, and the carded wool was fed onto the spindle with the other hand. The fibers stuck together, making yarn. The disk at the bottom kept the winding wool from falling off the spindle.

Washing with yucca suds came next, then drying, then dyeing. With dyes made from plants, the wool had to be dipped many times to get a good color. With commercial colors, which were available from the trading post, one application was enough. Some wool was dyed red, some black, some brown. Combining those colors with undyed white wool, the women designed and wove rugs with wonderful patterns.

The looms were made from four sticks, two vertical and two horizontal. The coarsest wool was used to make the vertical strands for the rug or blanket, and finer wool was used to make the design. They used a big wooden comb to pack the horizontal wool down, giving the end product a tight weave. Auntie and Grandma kept busy with the task all winter.

Great-Grandmother had been an especially fine weaver. The trading post owner judged the quality of the rugs with an expert eye. He traded goods the family needed, like coffee, flour, or salt, for rugs. He trusted his customers, and gave products on credit, keeping a ledger of what was owed. When my family didn't need any products from the trader immediately, he exchanged woven goods for aluminum coins, or "chips," in twenty-five-cent, fifty-cent, and dollar denominations. These were stamped with the name of the trading post. My family used the post "money" when they needed it—for rope or sugar, candy or saltines, or dozens of other things the trader sold.

Under the cover, I pressed a cold foot against my leg for warmth. At home, I had warm clothes that Grandma and my aunties made for me. From big squares of sheepskin they made shoes, folding the fur on the inside and wrapping it around my feet, securing it with twine. My winter pants and shirt were also sheepskin. Wet sheepskin, beaten with rocks and rubbed with sticks, grew soft. Then, as with the water bag, animal grease applied to the leather side of the skin made it water-repellent. The cozy clothing had thick, warm wool on the inside.

I shivered. I couldn't wait for summer break.

CHAPTER FIVE

Bullies and Religion

Late 1920s, Early 1930s

Rain streamed down the dormitory windows, showing no signs of letting up. The weather had warmed a bit, and plants had begun to grow, but we probably wouldn't get to go outside all day.

Pretending disinterest, I watched the two older boys who'd been called to the dorm to babysit. The matrons always left for the weekend. When it rained and we couldn't go outside, we smaller boys were at the mercy of our older schoolmates. Despite the strict discipline at school, or perhaps because of it, many bullies had sprung up among the school population. The teachers and administration usually ignored them, apparently preferring to stay out of their way in a safe classroom or office.

The taller of the two boys commanded, "Line up." He gestured with two hands. "Both sides."

We scuttled to the sides of the room, our heads hunched into our shoulders.

The empty middle of the room seemed huge. Tall Boy grinned at his friend. He tossed him a baseball, keeping one for himself. "Cross over," he said quietly.

We raced, protecting our heads with our arms. The very smallest cried as they stumbled across the room. Both big boys fired baseballs at us, cheering when they hit their targets.

I dodged and aimed a stare, sharp as a blade of yucca, at one of the boys. I'd never been hit. I hated to see the smaller children cry, but I didn't dare help them. We'd played this game before, and the bullies attacked anyone who tried to help.

Someday, when I'm big, I'll pay them back.

I stood under the steady flow of the shower, the matron watching to be sure I got clean. Water puddled at my feet. I remembered carrying water by bucket at home in *Chichiltah. A waste. All this water.*

Standing under the warm flow, I yawned, although the five-thirty wake-up was no problem for me. At home I often got up earlier than that. While the matrons were waking any stragglers I'd made my bed. At home I slept on the ground. Life at school, if you only considered the amenities, was much softer than life on the Checkerboard.

I soaped what was left of my hair and rinsed it, turning to glance at the frowning matron. She gestured for me to hurry.

As I pulled on my uniform, I hoped there wouldn't be a fight in the cafeteria that morning. The normal breakfast—oatmeal and prunes—wasn't bad. But leaving the cafeteria . . . That was another story entirely.

The older boy and girl sitting at the ends of the rectangular table-for-eight finished their oatmeal. Before they could reach for my bowl, I wolfed the remnants of my cereal and placed dish and spoon on the table. The three younger girls sitting across from me did the same. But one of the two boys on my side of the table didn't finish soon enough. The big girl glanced to be sure the dining room attendants weren't watching and grabbed his last prune.

Although the older two were there to make sure we younger ones ate, they generally snatched anything they wanted from the smaller students' plates.

A male monitor at the side of the room gave a hand signal, and we put our utensils down and stood, leaving dishes and trays on the table. Another signal told us to exit the cafeteria. I, along with the other boys my age, lined up quickly at the boys' door. But not quickly enough. The eleven- to eighteen-year-old boys were already there, and the eleven- to eighteen-year-old girls were at the girls' door. They'd all smuggled out dishes and leftover oatmeal, flinging them at one another as they exited. Soon we smaller kids became targets, with dishes, utensils, and coffeepots flying through the air. We ducked while matrons and administrators ran into the kitchen, leaving us on our own. Bullies barged into the bakery and stole bread, but the cooks didn't dare intervene.

Later that day, at lunchtime, I lined up single file with the other kids. As we approached the cafeteria, older boys whispered to us behind their hands. "There's meat today. And bread. Make a sandwich and bring it to me."

"Hey!" It was Coolidge, my older brother. He shook his fist at the bullies. "Leave my brother alone."

I smiled and ducked into my place at the table. I ate the mutton and bread that day, leaving none. Normally lunch was pinto beans cooked with a little bacon, so mutton was a real treat.

Coolidge wasn't always there to intervene, however, and I knew that next time I might leave the cafeteria hungry, hiding a sandwich in the kangaroo pocket of my uniform and handing it over to some bigger boy.

Marching back to the dormitory in single file, I was careful to stay right behind the boy in front of me. *No straggling allowed.*

From the dorm, we were called to afternoon classes. I waited while the fourth, third, second, and first graders lined up and marched to class. Finally it was my turn—kindergarten. Both Dora and I had done kindergarten at Tohatchi, but we'd been told that we had to repeat it there at Fort Defiance.

In class I dove immediately into my assigned seat. No one spoke except the teacher. "Sit up straight, arms crossed in front of you," she said, demonstrating the proper posture.

That was usually the way we were told to sit, and everyone in class complied. I glanced over at the kids on the other side of the room. They sat stiff as statues, all trying not to move.

Questions began. The teacher wrote YES and NO on the board, instructing the students to choose one or the other for each answer.

Picture books and pictures taped to the walls helped in the learning process. We children listened, desperately trying to pull some meaning from what the teacher said. I clamped my lips together. As on other days, I volunteered no answers. Anyone who answered incorrectly was punished. It was safer not to volunteer, not to stand out.

But the teacher called on me. "Yes," I said, feeling sure that was the correct response.

Her eyes squeezed into slits, and she slapped a ruler against her palm. "Chester Nez, the correct answer is 'no.' Come up here."

Head hanging, I walked slowly to the front of the class. While the other students sat silent the teacher whacked me across the shoulders with the ruler. *It doesn't hurt that much*, I told myself, squeezing my eyes closed. But I knew it was wrong, trying to humiliate a person in front of his peers. Father would never do such a thing. The other students sat unmoving, knowing their turn at punishment would come soon enough.

"Go back to your seat, and pay attention," the teacher said.

None of the teachers spoke Navajo, and paying attention to the meaningless English was not easy. We'd been warned not to speak to the other children during meals or in class, so we couldn't help each other out with the teacher's questions. Even during free time, in the dormitory or outdoors, English was the only language allowed. Since almost none of the new students knew English, this was an impossible mandate.

In class, if a child dared, he raised his hand for permission to go to the bathroom. Of course, he had to ask in English, so most tried to hold it until after class. We weren't allowed to fidget or to look around at each other. Eyes stared straight ahead. Feet were planted firmly on the floor. Hands and heads remained motionless.

But in order to avoid being hit, we had to learn. Eventually we students began to get the gist—if not the finer meaning—of what was said. And one thing became alarmingly clear: the school planned to erase everything we'd been taught at home.

After the last class of the day, I was ready to vent some pent-up energy. We returned to the dormitory to play inside. We had no indoor toys, so we invented games or played things like hide-and-seek.

Then we marched to a supper of rice or corned beef with cabbage grown on the school's farmland. After eating and escaping the older kids at the cafeteria, we younger boys returned to our dorm. Bedtime was seven-thirty or eight o'clock.

It was a glorious, sunny Saturday. I had made lots of friends my age at school. We all gathered in a group.

After we tired of hide-and-seek, we meandered in a cluster to the trading post. It was down the sidewalk from the small kids' school, just outside the Fort Defiance grounds. We boys had a few coins from doing odd jobs. The same two-story building that housed the older children's school also provided office space for a host of government workers. Coal furnaces heated the building. The other boys and I broke up coal and received ten cents per bucket. Government workers also hired students to chop wood, and when the plumbing broke, we were paid to haul quantities of water to the offices.

At the trading post, Robert Walley and I bought marbles with money we'd earned hauling coal. Robert was one of my closest friends at Fort Defiance.

Outside, one of the guys drew a circle in the dirt with a stick. We all shot marbles, trying to make them land inside the circle while hitting someone else's marble out. After the game, our pockets bulged, and at night, kids crawled around under the dormitory beds looking for dropped marbles.

After Dora and I completed our first year or two, the school began to send a truck at the beginning of the school year to collect us kids from the Gallup area. We met the truck at the Two Wells Trading Post in Gallup, thirteen or fourteen miles from my home in *Chichiltah*. On those back-to-school days, Father loaded me, Dora, and any other local school-bound children into his horse-drawn wagon. Older brother Coolidge always returned to school early, so he wasn't with us. Father brought cold food—roasted mutton or goat, fried bread, and tortillas. At the trading post he fed us, and any other children who arrived, while we waited for the Fort Defiance truck.

When the truck arrived, we labored up into its bed, then turned back to watch the trading post and Father disappear in the distance. Tears washed tracks down dusty cheeks. We dreaded the long time away from our families, and those of us who were returning students felt a mounting anxiety. As each slow mile unwound, we drew closer to the hated discipline at school.

To add insult to injury, before I grew older, the bigger boys who rode with us in the truck bed stole the big bags of food our parents had packed for Dora and me.

My friend Robert Walley took matters into his own hands, deciding one winter that he'd had enough of school. He ran away with a couple other boys. They headed southeast, traveling through Arizona into New Mexico.

I kept up with my studies, but I missed Robert. We usually studied together. And other boys had begun to join us. Our group of boys played together on weekends. Without runaway Robert, and several others in the gang who'd escaped with him, weekends dragged.

I walked over to the trading post. The dimes and nickels in my pocket jiggled against each other. I liked having my own odd-job money. For a long while I stood in front of the candy display. It all looked good. Then—as usual—I chose red licorice. I selected a few marbles, paid for everything, and headed back to the dorm.

That night I paid a dime for a movie, finding a seat between two friends who hadn't run away with Robert. Some school movies were free, but the good ones cost ten cents. This one was a Tom Mix story. Pretty much all the movies were about cowboys defeating Indians. I liked Tom Mix. I also liked Buck Jones and Hopalong Cassidy, both popular movie choices at the school. After watching those movies, some of the little kids planned to be cowboys when they grew up.

A month passed. No Robert.

The boys in my age group were sitting at lunch when—despite the ban on talking—a buzz went around the cafeteria. Navajo police had captured the runaways at their homes, returning them to Fort Defiance. Tired of studying by myself in my dorm room and spending weekends without my good friend, I felt relieved to hear the news.

A hush blanketed the room. No clink of silverware. No sounds of chewing. I looked up from my beans. Robert and the other escapees filed ˋ into the cafeteria dressed as girls. They stood against one wall, their heads hanging, for what seemed like forever. Everyone stared.

I sat like the others, mesmerized by the girls' clothing. And when I went to get Robert that night to study, I was told that the runaways were not allowed to associate with the other students for a month.

Robert hadn't told me about his plans to run away. It was all very secretive. But I would not have joined them, anyway. I'd already seen too many kids humiliated after making a dash for freedom. And I didn't want to leave Dora.

I traipsed through the trees in the school yard, keeping an eye out for the right kind of stick. The day before, I'd shattered my old stick. *There!* The fallen branch was straight, with a curve at the end.

That afternoon my friends—now ten years old—gathered at a vacant field to play hockey. I swung the new stick a few times, getting used to its balance. When twelve boys had arrived at the field, we chose up sides, two teams of six.

We buried a ball in the dirt. Everyone raced in, using their sticks to unearth the buried ball. Each team fought to hit the ball into its opponents' net to earn a goal.

After about an hour of play, a younger boy ran up. "The football pants are here!" he said. Everyone abandoned the game and ran down to the classroom that was used as a locker room. Sure enough, a few new football pants lay spread out on a desk. There was never enough money for full uniforms, so we wore the pants with T-shirts.

Most of the boys at school loved football. We made our own cleats, fastening a kind of tack to the bottom of our everyday shoes. Our helmets, made from a canvaslike material, tied under our chins. The flat devices offered very little protection and were nicknamed "fried bread" helmets. If we got lucky, we made it to the locker room before a game in time to get a set of upper-body protective pads. There weren't enough pads to go around, and we often played pickup games of football without protection.

"Too bad we can't just take them back to the dorm with us," Robert said, looking at the new pants. But rules had to be obeyed, and the first boys to get to the locker room before a game got the gear.

It was a Thursday. Cold. The two-and-a-half-mile trek to church was going to be chilly. And the weather was supposed to get worse. It would be colder by Sunday, when we'd again take that same walk. Church. Thursday and Sunday. Without fail.

Another Robert, Robert Adams, and I arrived at church early and changed into altar-boy vestments. It was my fourth year as an altar boy. I could dress in the vestments, reciting the correct prayers with each item of clothing, in my sleep.

"Do you think there's a connection?" I asked.

Robert raised both eyebrows. "What do you mean?"

"Between Catholic and Navajo."

Robert adjusted the neck of his flowing surplice. "Do you?"

"Holy water and corn pollen. Kind of the same idea," I said.

Robert's forehead furrowed. "I guess."

"Even the sign of the cross—forehead, chest, each shoulder. That's kind of like a blessing with corn pollen."

"Kind of." My friend did not look convinced.

"And what about our creation, speaking the Navajo word for 'light,' and then the sun appeared. In the Bible, God said, 'Let there be light,' and the sun appeared. Same thing."

A look of comprehension dawned on Robert's face, and he smiled at me. "I think you've got something, there."

The government school at Fort Defiance believed we students should all be Christian, specifically Catholic. I've always loved to sing. I sang in the Catholic church choir for three years while attending boarding school. I served as an altar boy for four years.

Boarding school taught me about Christmas, the birth of Jesus. On the big day, each student received a bag of candy and fruit in celebration. And Fort Defiance erected a Christmas tree, a beautiful thing, covered with lights and ornaments. None of us had ever seen one before attending school.

The priests and nuns taught us about Catholicism: the Trinity, saints, and sacraments. The new religion presented new ideas, differing in disquieting ways from the religion we had learned at home. The Navajo Right Way stressed the importance of a life in balance, a respect for all things as part of nature, even rocks and blades of grass. The Catholic Church stood in awe of God's creation of the world, but did not feel the same kinship with nature that we Navajo children had been taught.

The new religious teachings caused many of us to question where we really belonged—in the white man's church or on the reservation with our own sacred beliefs. Torn between two cultures, we were unable to fully embrace either one. We didn't know where we fit. Navajo ceremonies were seen by the nuns and priests as pagan, and the Navajo Holy People were looked down upon. The white clerics had no misgivings about voicing their disdain for the cultural heritage we had brought from home.

The new teachings caused confusion. We students were taught only the white man's way at school and only the Navajo way at home. And each culture saw the other as wrong.

CHAPTER SIX

Building Grandmother's Hogan

Early 1930s

Father led our horse, the odd-looking, stripped-down wagon frame bumping along behind. I trotted beside him. "Look!" I pulled at Father's sleeve and pointed at a tall, straight piñon with my thumb. "That one. Look how straight."

He nodded. "A good one."

I felt good being out with the men and not, for once, facing the disapproval of Auntie. Father and Uncle lifted the long two-handled saw from the wagon frame. They lined up on either side of the tree.

"Move away from the trunk," Father warned me.

Uncle gripped one end of the saw and Father the other. Within five minutes, the twelve-foot tree crashed to the ground. I helped remove the small branches with an ax, and they lashed the long log to the wagon frame. Father had removed the wagon box that morning, so the logs for Grandma's hogan could be carried on the frame.

"Three," said Uncle. "That's enough for this trip."

We turned the horse toward the building site. After unloading the three logs, we headed out in search of more.

I could sense Grandma's pleasure. A hogan was a real home. Grandfather and Grandmother had lived in a rough shelter made from tree branches and logs since before I was born. They stayed in that shelter through all seasons, not moving from pasture to pasture with the sheep and the younger family members. Their home was cold in winter, hot in summer, but Grandmother did not complain. No one had life easy on the Checkerboard.

Nevertheless, Grandfather, Father, and Uncle had decided it was time for Grandma to have a permanent home, a hogan. She chose the site for the traditional one-room dwelling, a slight rise, backed up to the western side of the box canyon where we lived. The project carried an energy with it that made me hum while we worked.

Logs, cut in uniform lengths, would form the eight sides of the hogan. No windows.

"The straight sides will each be the length of a log and will come about this high." Father held his arm out at shoulder level. "Then we will cut the logs shorter and shorter so they step in, making a rounded roof."

I nodded. Of course I had seen hogans before. Lots of them. They made a round, solid shape on the landscape.

We labored for several days. Each log had to be notched so it would fit and hold tightly to adjacent logs. At the center of the roof dome, a hole was left open for smoke. This was the only opening in the new dwelling, other than the door. I dug dirt to fill the chinks between logs and to keep out the cold in winter, heat in summer. More dirt, shoveled onto the roof, provided additional insulation. The doorway, as always, faced east. Wooden hunting bows were hung over the door on the inside and the outside for protection. When everything else was finished, Grandmother hung a blanket—one of traditional design, that she had woven herself—to cover the door opening.

Before Grandma and Grandpa entered the hogan, they sent someone to fetch a medicine man from his home. The family watched as he performed a traditional blessing. I noticed that Father, who had trained for a while as a medicine man before Mother's death, watched with an intent, serious expression.

The man entered the door and moved clockwise around the dwelling, blessing each of the four directions with corn pollen. Then he stepped outside, walking clockwise from the east to the south, west, then north. At each compass point, he again blessed the hogan. Last, he blessed the door.

Life in the new dwelling was now ready to start—in harmony and balance, the Right Way.

Grandma continued to bless her snug home before sunrise each morning. I watched her many times as she walked outside, took a few pinches of corn pollen from a pouch, and made her blessing to the east, south, west, and north, always moving clockwise. The four directions were very important in Navajo belief. East (*ha'a'aah*) was where life began, the sunrise. South (*shádi'ááh*) was where you got warmth. West (*e'e'aah*) had to do with the way you spent your day, what was ahead and behind, also where the sun was carried away at sunset. North (*náhokos*) was where everything was put to rest.

The pollen used in Grandma's blessing was collected at harvesttime, in September. The women in my family harvested the corn and saved the pollen. They shook the corn tassels into a pan or used a rag to remove the pollen. Then they sorted out any impurities—like corn silk. The pure pollen was stored in a jar or a flour sack and, usually, blessed by a medicine man. Medicine men went from house to house in the summer, blessing corn pollen. Only blessed pollen could be used in a medicine bag.

Most families had lots of pollen on hand, but several times I saw Grandma use ash when she ran out. She put a pinch on her shoes, not her tongue. Then she made the blessing. Ash helped Dora and me when we couldn't sleep. It got rid of nightmares. Grandma put ashes from the fire on our arms or our forehead.

In the new hogan, Grandma's cook fire, built right on the dirt floor in the center of the room, was no longer threatened by wind or rain. Eventually, Father hauled a large oil can, with no bottom, from the trading post. The can had a fireplacelike opening. It did double duty as stove and fireplace, sitting in the middle of the hogan. In its lid was a hole, into which Grandpa inserted a pipe. The metal pipe stuck up through the roof, letting smoke exit the room.

Once the hogan was built, I savored the days like today, when the sheep grazed close to home, and we returned at night for dinner. Eating with Grandmother and Grandfather was much better than cooking meager fare over a campfire. As I approached the hogan, I was hit by the full, rich aroma of roasting mutton, Grandma's home-cooked meal.

When I entered, a litter of prairie dogs slept curled up inside, near the cook fire. It was a cool day, topping out somewhere around seventy. Not like the ninety-plus-degree days we'd often endured in summer.

I picked up a prairie dog, stroking its soft back. The little "dog" burrowed against my chest. I offered it some goat's milk, which had been strained through a flour bag and boiled for human consumption. It sucked it from my finger, eating hungrily.

I put the little rodent down and stepped outside. The prairie dog followed, standing with his front paws up, like a little man. When I went back inside, the prairie dog barked bravely at the outside world. Then a real dog barked somewhere off in the distance, and it scampered back inside.

I helped Grandma spread flour sacks that had been ripped open and sewn together in a circular shape. They made a table on the dirt floor. The mutton sizzled over the fire, fat spitting onto the open flames. I could hardly wait to wrap it up in a tortilla and eat it like a sandwich.

When it was finally time for dinner, everyone sat on the dirt floor, with the bowls of food placed on the flour sacks. I looked around at my family, raising my brows at my sister, Dora. She smiled and nodded at me. Everything about the hogan felt luxurious after the makeshift shelters on the trail. There were no books, no electricity, and no plumbing, but we were snug and secure. I reached for a tortilla and rolled some mutton inside.

Oil lamps cast wavering shadows across the single room. Outside, the relaxed nasal bleat of a lamb and the higher cry of a goat let us know that all was well. A puppy's bark, a litter from one of the sheepdogs, rose above the soft whisper of wind in the evergreens. And inside, the almost magical fragrance of burning juniper lulled the family after a hearty meal.

I asked Grandma, "Will you tell us a story?"

A cricket chirped just outside. Grandma looked up at the ceiling, then down at the empty dishes sitting on her burlap table. She turned her gaze to me. "When I was only a girl . . ."

Grandma told us about her childhood. My eyes drifted closed. It had been a long day. In less than a month, school would resume for me, Coolidge, and Dora. I wished that I could stay home and spend the winter with my family. As I drifted to sleep, I pictured snow, deep around the hogan. When I was very young, sometimes my brothers and I stripped naked in the snow, and Father rolled us in a snowbank. This Navajo tradition toughened us children against winter cold. Afterward, we rushed to sit by the fire and warm up. The laughter of my brothers still chimes in my head.

I woke when it was still dark, the remnants of a dream tugging me back toward sleep. With my eyes closed, I reconstructed the dream. It was autumn. Neighbors, aunts, uncles, and cousins had come to stay for several days, maybe even a week or two, bringing blankets and food— fresh and dried meat and canned goods. There would be feasting and storytelling around the fire.

I loved spending days with the sheep and goats, but I also looked forward to the social gatherings. There, stories I knew and loved were told for the hundredth time. With everyone squatting around a big fire outdoors, tales of current events were spun, things like new hogans being built, or animals being sold or traded. We children listened as adults traded stories about weather and crops. The *Diné* had no electricity and no radios. News was spread at these gatherings—things like births and deaths, the price of wool, the amount being offered at trading posts for our Navajo-design blankets and rugs. It was exciting just to think about it.

But I would be back in school by then. A feeling of dread lodged in my stomach. I wouldn't be there when winter came, when the range of the sheep would be limited and they'd stay in the big box canyon surrounding Grandma's home. I wouldn't be there when Father boiled the unhusked corn to feed the animals, and sometimes the *Diné,* too. When snow covered the grass, the livestock would also eat juniper and piñon branches. Along the road to *Chichiltah,* the trees were bare up as high as the sheep and goats could reach. And herders cut branches for their livestock when the animals couldn't reach them on their own.

I turned over, thinking about how snug Grandma's hogan felt. I liked that it backed up to the west side of the canyon, only a hundred yards or so from the steep red rock cliffs that formed the canyon's rim. The cliffs provided the back wall for a sheep corral and also gave shelter to Grandma's home. They helped protect animals and people from frigid winter winds.

CHAPTER SEVEN

Sweat Lodge

Early 1930s

I bathed in the arroyo, where a spring bubbled up to the surface of Grandma's land. The new hogan had no indoor plumbing, and in hot, early September a bucket, used to rinse my hair, made the arroyo into an outdoor tub. The cool water refreshed and relaxed me in the dry summer heat.

I lay back and closed my eyes, letting the sun dry my chest.

Better than the arroyo bath was the cleansing Coolidge, Father, Grandfather, Uncle, and I performed a few days later—a cleansing of both body and spirit—the sweat bath.

Grandma, Auntie, and the younger girls stayed at home. Back then, only males entered the sweat hut. A first sweat bath was a kind of coming-of-age ceremony for a young boy. I think I first went into the sweat hut when I was five. My dad taught me the prayers that must be said and told me where to sit. We prayed not only for ourselves, but for our tribe.

Coolidge, the three men, and I hiked toward the quiet place where the hut stood. The location had been carefully selected. Disturbance there was unlikely.

As we crested a small hill, I glimpsed the compact lodge, built into a wide, flat hole. Years ago, my relatives had dug that foot-deep hole into the cement-hard desert earth. As a result, the structure sat slightly below ground level. Entering it was like entering into the earth's womb.

Poles, their forks joining together at the top like strong fingers, fanned out from a central point in the sweat lodge. This created a round structure that was similar, at first glance, to a hogan. But the sweat hut had no horizontal logs and there was a peak rather than a hole at the center of the roof. The solid roof was needed to hold the heat in. Small branches filled the wide gaps between supports at the bottom of the lodge, and dirt shoveled over the wooden poles provided insulation and strength. Heavy blankets and rugs were piled over the dirt on the outside of the lodge.

That morning, I had helped collect the finest sand from the riverbed, carrying it to the lodge and placing it outside the door. Now Father, Uncle, and Grandfather built a fire outside the lodge. They searched for rocks, especially dark volcanic rocks, and threw them into the fire to heat. Coolidge and I then carried the hot rocks into the sweat hut, balancing them on the fork of a stick. We piled them inside, to the left of the entrance, in a shallow depression, approximately four inches deep.

We and the men then entered the lodge on hands and knees, an act of humility. A special prayer was recited upon entering. We wore just a breechclout. When the entrance blanket lowered, sudden darkness filled the room. I couldn't see the others inside the shelter. Grandfather poured water mixed with sage and juniper over the rocks, and billows of steam rose in the dark lodge—entering deep into our lungs.[1] Aromas of juniper

---

1 Many Navajos took dry sweat baths, utilizing radiant heat from the hot rocks. However, my family poured water over the rocks to create steam. We also employed the medicinal plants mentioned above in the sweat lodge.

and sagebrush filled the small room, the sage smelling much like Vicks VapoRub and having the same effect. Nasal passages opened, and congestion cleared. Father had made medicines from the two plants. Each of us drank some. We smeared the rest on our bodies to discourage things like arthritis or swelling.

I sat at the back with my brother. Hot steam made me groggy, and I wondered how the adult males stood it, sitting so near the steaming rocks. The three men and we two boys filled the compact, heated space.

The men sang traditional songs, celebrating our relationship to the four compass directions. Coolidge and I joined in on the songs we knew, but on many we just listened to the men. Heat grew more intense, like a fever, melting away energy and any thought of the outside world. Sweat streamed down my forehead, stinging my eyes.

Coolidge and I knew we couldn't leave until the adults had finished singing. Only then would the ceremony complete its work, uniting us with the physical world so that nature became a part of our hearts, bodies, and systems. This assured that impurities left us and that we were taken care of from sunrise to sunset and through the nights to come.

After an hour, we emerged, saying an exit prayer. I squinted in the bright sunlight, and late-summer air cooled my body. Standing on a blanket, I splashed sand carried from the riverbed over myself. The sand, fine as powder, didn't stick, but it removed the sweat. No towel was needed.

I felt good. Lighter. A sweat bath was not to be taken heedlessly, and I had prepared carefully, examining my life both at school and at home. I knew I'd entered into the sweat hut with the proper attitude. So I felt sure that the ceremony had provided me with what I sought—protection, strength against bad influences, and a cleansing of the soul.

Many products of the earth were utilized in the bath. Sand, rock, fire, air, water, and wood all went into the building of the sweat lodge or the ceremony itself. We, as participants, created a connection to the earth by utilizing its products. The four principal elements—earth, water, fire, and air—were an honored part of the sweat hut ceremony.

Like all Navajo ceremonies, participants had their own individual reasons for taking part. The benefit gained depended upon the seriousness of the individual partaking in the ritual. Bad thoughts could spoil everything. Only those who threw their hearts and minds into the ceremony, invoking the Right Way, received the fullest blessing.

When I did that, the sweat bath cleaned my soul and everything else in my day-to-day life.

CHAPTER EIGHT

The Great Livestock Massacre

Mid-1930s

The summer day at *Chichiltah* sizzled with heat and expectations. Father and Grandma counted the days and months of summer, making sure they knew when my school resumed in the fall. Hot days filled with freedom raced by, and that back-to-school date would come too soon. But right now I was free again—of teachers, of that heavy feeling that I was about to answer a question incorrectly, and of volatile matrons.

I rattled the fence I'd just mended to test its strength. *Good.* It formed part of the family sheep corral. I stretched and sipped from a canvas jug of water.

The far-off rumble of heavy equipment, a sound not often heard in Navajo country, gave me warning. If I had known what was coming, my heart wouldn't have pounded with eager anticipation. But the sound, and then the sight of a flatbed truck carrying a huge bulldozer, was uncommon—and intriguing. I wiped the sweat from my eyes. What could it be for?

Then in my thirteenth or fourteenth summer, I didn't connect the heavy equipment with any kind of problem. I raced down to the dirt road to watch. Navajo men dismounted from the flatbed. They worked for the Bureau of Indian Affairs, government employees, they said. With a good deal of sarcasm, reservation Navajos called government workers "Washing-done."

Grandmother and Grandfather looked at each other, numb expressions frozen on their faces.

The men drove the heavy-duty bulldozer off the flatbed, down a hastily placed ramp. My family and I watched. The big machine lumbered across Grandma's property, raising clouds of dust. It stopped not far from the hogan. We heard scraping sounds as a huge trench was dug. When the trench was complete—about 150 feet long and four or five feet deep—the men and machine moved to a plot of land inhabited by another family and dug another long hole in the ground. They dug three or four trenches, each on property owned by different neighbors.

Were they preparing for some new ceremony? The workers left with no explanation. I imagined a huge sing with multiple bonfires. But my adult relatives were strangely quiet.

A week or so later, the BIA men returned on horseback. My family gathered at the hogan.

The BIA workers blocked one end of the trench on Grandma's land, leaving the other end open. "You need to round up your sheep and goats," one man said. "Herd them into the trench."

Grandfather's face had turned to stone. "But—"

"Do not protest, Grandfather," one of the BIA workers said, using the polite form of address for a younger man addressing an elder. "Haven't you heard, you'll get thrown in jail?"

My stomach knotted as I helped herd all but three hundred of Grandmother's sheep and goats into the deep trench. The willing, domesticated animals moved readily into the trench through the open end. Then the BIA workers sealed that end. A flammable material was sprayed on the animals, and they were set on fire.

We couldn't believe what we were witnessing. I covered my ears, but could not block the shrieks of the animals, especially the goats, who had a high, piercing cry. The stench of burning wool and flesh filled the normally fresh air.

That night, as I lay sleepless, the screams echoed in my head. Across the hogan, Grandmother and Grandfather cried softly.

Through years of hard work Grandma's herd had grown to around a thousand animals, mostly sheep, with a scattering of goats. The entire family had worked hard to build up our herd, and we were happy and grateful for our healthy animals. In Navajo country, sheep were a measure of wealth. So, despite the Depression afflicting the rest of the nation, my family had worked their way to success. I knew that Dora and I had helped. With the herd reduced by seven hundred head, all those years of labor came to nothing.

I lay in the dark, tears sliding down my cheeks. Many of the animals had been pets, greeting their humans with bleats and head butts. I missed them. And Dora missed them. Those animals deserved respect, not such a terrible death at the hands of cruel men. Finally, exhausted from the terrible day, I fell into a deep sleep.

I woke up feeling groggy, but knowing that something was wrong. Then the stench of burned livestock filled my nostrils. I dressed and went outside. Auntie was already up, working. Together my family performed the tasks necessary to care for our remaining animals. We moved like machines, unable to process what had happened.

Late that night, I again heard Grandmother's and Grandfather's stifled sobs. I overheard their whispered words to each other. They could not imagine how they would make up for their loss.

Father, working at the trading post, learned that families all over the reservation and the Checkerboard were devastated by the massacre of their livestock. Any family with more than a hundred head of sheep and goats was subject to the "reduction." The number of animals killed varied on a sliding scale, depending on how big each herd was. Horses and cattle were also killed, but their deaths were more humane. They were shot rather than burned.

The shocked families warned one another not to protest. There were rumors of arrests.

A historical perspective on the politics of this disaster doesn't soften the blow still felt by the families who were deprived of their livelihood. The program may have been well intentioned, but like many other political decisions, the results proved disastrous.

It was during the Great Depression, and Franklin D. Roosevelt, elected in 1932, was president. His legislative agenda, the "New Deal," initiated many programs and public-works projects designed to help employ the needy. The disastrous livestock reduction might never have occurred if four things had not come together.

First, reservation and Checkerboard land, aggressively grazed by livestock, was less productive than it had been. Sheep were the primary animals raised, and they graze close to the ground, often killing the roots of plants. The dust bowl in the southwestern Great Plains had created a more serious problem than the problems on Navajo land, but still, overgrazing was then under the microscope of public awareness. As John Collier wrote: "The Navajo reservation is being washed into the Boulder Dam reservoir."[1] This government project, begun in 1931, is now known as the famous Hoover Dam.

Second, the overgrazing coincided with a federal New Deal push for a huge park to be created on Navajo land. The proposal, first made in 1931 by Roger Toll, died, but was renewed when Roosevelt was elected. People argued that the park would create jobs, but it would also absorb land needed for grazing Navajo livestock. The National Park Service

---

1 *Survey Graphic: Magazine of Social Interpretation* 23:6 (June, 1934), p. 261. The dam is in Arizona.

decided that the Navajos could continue to live on the parkland, but they would have to retain their "quaint" ways of life, continuing to raise sheep and implementing no improvements. This would do nothing to relieve the already overgrazed conditions. It was driven home to officials that fewer animals would mean fewer demands for grass.[2]

Third, John Collier, the new Commissioner of Indian Affairs, felt pressured to do something to rehabilitate Navajo grazing lands. He opposed the Navajo National Park, but proposed a stock reduction program as the solution to the overgrazing problem.

And fourth, Collier also promised to expand the land area of the reservation in return for the reduction in livestock. He wanted to incorporate lands already used by the Navajo for grazing, making their stewardship official. This would include at least some of the Checkerboard Area. The idea seems somewhat contradictory, since with more land, more animals could be supported, but the land was, by then, so poor that Collier felt a livestock reduction would still be in order.

As planned, Collier's recommendation for reservation expansion lessened the vehemence of Navajo objections to his proposed stock reduction. The stock reduction proposal passed.

The Bureau of Indian Affairs jumped in, employing Navajos to execute the reduction mandate. In an attempt to make up for the diminished income from their liquidated livestock, the government also promised the Navajos an education that would lead to jobs with various New Deal public-works programs.

But then John Collier proposed the "Indian Reorganization Act," a proclamation of "cultural freedom" for Indians which basically proposed to make the various tribes into corporations administered by the United States government[3]. The act was passed by the Pueblos but rejected by

---

2 NPS.com.

3 Frank Waters, *Masked Gods,* pp. 132–133.

the Navajos. Still, Congress passed the act in 1934, leaving the future of the Navajos poorly defined in the eyes of the government.

Once the livestock massacre was completed, with the Navajo sheep population having been reduced from a high of 1.6 million in 1932 to only 400,000 in 1944,[4] the promised geographical expansion failed to take place, although, to his credit, John Collier did fight to obtain more land for the reservation.[5] The proposed national park was also defeated, a small blessing for those who kept sheep and other livestock. Only a few Navajos were given public-works employment. And the education program that was promised—preparing more Native Americans to work on the numerous public-works projects—did not materialize for the members of the Navajo tribe, the tribe that had rejected John Collier's Indian Reorganization Act.

It was odd that in Depression times, the mutton of the slaughtered animals was not preserved as food. Nor were the wool and leather utilized. A small portion of the meat was canned for later use, although the meat from Grandma's herd and neighboring herds was simply destroyed. Three or four years later, some canned mutton was distributed to chapter houses on the Checkerboard and the reservation.

Some Navajo families were paid a pittance for their destroyed livestock, less than three dollars per head of sheep, when the market value vacillated between eight dollars and fourteen dollars per head. Other families were never paid. I am not sure whether my family received any money for their dead animals.

There are historians who suggest that the government's stock reduction program was aimed at making the Navajos less independent and

---

4 Waters, p. 142.

5 Arizona and New Mexico sheep and cattle interests opposed the expansion of the reservation, and legislators from New Mexico and Arizona fought successfully for the bill's defeat.

more dependent upon the "generosity" of the government in Washington, D.C. I don't know about that, but I do know that for us Navajos, the government's "livestock reduction" program ended in failure.

Historians name John Collier, the Commissioner of Indian Affairs from 1933 to 1945, as the instigator of the massacre. But I remember another man, E. Reeseman Fryer, who, during the New Deal, worked for the Bureau of Indian Affairs as the superintendant of the Navajo Reservation under John Collier. He served from 1936 until 1942, and was personally responsible for implementing much of the livestock reduction program. This man was especially resented. He was a white man, enjoying a position of power over the Navajo tribe.

The popular belief was that what Fryer fried was the Navajos.

The extermination went on for some six years, with different sections of Navajo land targeted at different intervals. By the time it stopped, the rain had stopped as well, and the grass continued to dry up.

The effect on the Navajo sense of community was devastating. In the time before the massacre, friends and neighbors helped one another. When someone fell sick, neighbors pitched in to care for their animals. Medicine men and women were summoned to cure both people and animals. Neighbors and family assisted by gathering together at night and praying for the sick to recover.

The livestock reduction challenged this sense of community by pitting Navajo against Navajo. Those who kept livestock resented the Navajo exterminators who worked for the Bureau of Indian Affairs. Neighbors put up fences to enclose their pastures, saving them for the sheep that they had left. The year-round migration from one community grazing area to another that had always been the norm as I grew up became impossible. As a result, ties between neighbors weakened.

The toll in self-respect was also huge. Families, unable to protect their own livestock, felt powerless. And nothing could have done more to erode the local work ethic. What was the point of working hard to build up wealth, a sizable herd, when the government just stepped in and destroyed it?

The massacre killed more than livestock. It changed the dynamic between neighbors; it changed the meaning of hard work; it changed everything.

After the Long Walk, the livestock massacre is considered the second great tragedy in Navajo history. A story now woven into oral tradition, the extermination is discussed wherever Navajos meet, so that like the Long Walk, it will never fade from memory.

Hot, dry summer days passed while I herded the remaining sheep, helped with repairs, chopped wood, and generally made myself useful at home. Occasionally adult relatives asked me to translate Navajo to English for them at the trading post. I always liked to help. Translating was interesting, and they paid me with a stick of licorice or peppermint candy. But just as good as the candy was the respect I got for my knowledge. School was paying off.

I hadn't talked during my summer days at home about the fighting at school or about how mean the matrons and teachers could be. I just wanted to enjoy being back in *Chichiltah* with my family. They looked at me with pride and treated me like someone special.

Even so, at the end of each summer I lay awake considering whether I should go back to Fort Defiance. It was so much nicer at home, despite the lack of amenities like hot running water and electricity. Those comforts were nothing compared to being treated well. And at home, I knew exactly what was expected of me, so life, though physically challenging, was stress-free. At school, it was difficult to know what the teachers and matrons wanted.

Still, in the end, I always returned. Even after some years, when Dora fell ill with tuberculosis and spent most of her time in the Fort Defiance sanitarium, I went to class. A couple of years after Dora got sick, my brother Coolidge finished school. Dora, though she recovered from the tuberculosis, was kept at home. So I returned to Fort Defiance alone. I forced myself to go, pushing the dread I felt to the back of my mind.

I wanted to make my family proud.

CHAPTER NINE

Marine Recruit

Late 1930s, Early 1940s

As the truck navigated rutted paths, heading home toward *Chichiltah*, a tremendous weight lifted from my shoulders. No more matrons. I was the last of the Nez children to graduate from Fort Defiance. While I was a student there, the school had expanded its program to include seventh and eighth grades. But I'd finally completed the two additional years.

Four years of school still loomed ahead. On my first day at public junior high school, in Gallup, New Mexico, I could hardly believe my ears. Navajo. Spoken in the hallways. Navajo!

The classes were conducted in English. But there were lots of fellow Navajos, and when I stepped from the classroom to the hall, I spoke to a few, sometimes in English, sometimes in Navajo. No one hit me across the shoulders with a ruler. I felt liberated!

From the first day, I noticed that the structure of this school differed drastically from Fort Defiance. At Fort Defiance there had been no letter grades. And English dominated the curriculum there, with the intent—I was now aware—of weakening our ties to Navajo culture, binding us to the white culture instead.

Here, at Gallup, there were many subjects. I had to study hard to catch up, but I liked the Gallup school. No matrons watched my every move. No tiny children cried in their beds at night, terrorized by the administration and the older students.

Chichiltah, although much closer to Gallup than to Fort Defiance, was still too far for a daily commute. So, while attending school in Gallup, I lived nearby at Fort Wingate. The fort boasted a football field and a complex of dormitories. The land, a soft blend of reds, tans, browns, and purples, felt like home. I shared an early-morning bus trip into Gallup each day with other Navajo students.

I finished ninth grade and was partway through tenth when the government again intervened. A Navajo boarding school in Tuba City, Arizona, was my next home. The school, founded by the Hopi Indians, was in desperate need of repair. The Hopis gave the deteriorating building to the Navajos.

Tuba City was a land of sandstone and wind. I spent a couple of years there, and I never grew to like it. In addition to the school building being in bad repair, the food was awful. And there wasn't much to do. We used to steal watermelons and peaches from local Hopi farmers.

I made many friends. But even with friends I found myself bored. News broadcasts told of fighting in Europe, but the United States had not yet joined in the conflict that would eventually be known as World War II.

In Window Rock, Arizona, however, the Navajo Tribal Council foresaw our country's involvement. Rather than waiting for the American government to jump into the fray, in late spring of 1940 they passed a unanimous resolution:

Whereas, the Navajo Tribal Council and the 50,000 people we represent, cannot fail to recognize the crisis now facing the world in the threat of foreign invasion and the destruction of the great liberties and benefits which we enjoy on the reservation, and

Whereas, there exists no purer concentration of Americanism than among the First Americans, and

Whereas, it has become common practice to attempt national destruction through the sowing of seeds of treachery among minority groups such as ours, and

Whereas, we hereby serve notice that any un-American movement among our people will be resented and dealt with severely, and

Now, Therefore, we resolve that the Navajo Indians stand ready as they did in 1918, to aid and defend our Government and its institutions against all subversive and armed conflict and pledge our loyalty to the system which recognizes minority rights and a way of life that has placed us among the great people of our race.

It might surprise non-Navajos to read this declaration of allegiance. No Navajo, however, would be surprised. We have always felt a deep allegiance to our motherland, our Navajo Nation, and our families. To this allegiance is linked a sincere desire to protect all three.

Even though I didn't like Tuba City, if I hadn't gone there, my whole life would have followed a different path. Something happened, something that would impact all of us, all across the country. Pearl Harbor transformed our boredom.

"The Japs bombed Pearl Harbor!" Word spread through the Tuba City dormitory like wildfire that Sunday morning, December 7, 1941. Soon, we all knew that Pearl Harbor was in Hawaii. Hawaii was thousands of miles away, and not yet a state, but it was also the home of a United States Naval base.

The Japanese had been allies of the United States and Britain in World War I. They had captured a German base in Tsingtao, China, and after the war, they had prospered through expanding trade, becoming a recognized political and economic force in eastern Asia. But their triumph had been followed by the great earthquake of 1923, which destroyed half of Tokyo. Economic disasters followed, in the form of an overabundance of rice, which drove prices down, and tariffs imposed on Japanese manufactured exports by Western nations. Exacerbating this was the burgeoning population. By 1937, the island nation of Japan held, in its limited space, more than eighty million people. Japan's resources were being depleted. The country needed to expand.

Planning to gain natural resources, a market for their manufactured goods, and cheap labor, Japan invaded China near Beijing. After a three-month battle, the Japanese won Shanghai in November 1937. With the capital, Nanking, then threatened, Chiang Kai-shek, leader of the Republic of China, relocated to Wuhan. Japan captured the demoralized city of Nanking in December. Japanese-led massacres in the aftermath of the Nanking defeat killed as many as two to three hundred thousand Chinese people.

America, shocked by the violence of the Japanese attack, refused to sell Japan items like scrap metal that could be used in waging war. In the summer of 1941, we nationalized all Japanese assets in the United States. Enraged, Japan signed a pact with Germany and Italy in September. The island nation, now aligned with the Axis powers against the United States, planned attacks on Pearl Harbor, Guadalcanal, Midway, and the Philippines.

After the Japanese attack on Pearl Harbor, the United States could not ignore their enemy's intent to take over the Pacific. We declared war against Japan the next day, December 8, 1941.

Our school principal called us all together. He wanted to be sure that we all understood what was going on. He had researched Pearl Harbor, and he shared what he had learned with us students, telling us about the Japanese, their aspirations to control an empire, and the damage they'd done to the United States Navy.

My roommate, Roy Begay, and I discussed the momentous events.

"What do you think this means?" asked Roy.

"Our country has joined the war. I think the military will want us," I told him. "We are warriors."

We, like other Native Americans, had been born to the warrior tradition. Like other Navajos, we saw ourselves as inseparable from the earth we lived upon. And as protectors of what is sacred, we were both eager to defend our land.

April to June 1942

After gaining permission from the Navajo Tribal Council, Marine recruiters arrived in Tuba City only months after the Pearl Harbor attack, in April 1942. Full of curiosity and excitement, Roy and I listened to their presentation. The Marines showed enthusiasm and pride. They looked strong and capable in their dress-blue Marine uniforms.

The recruiters announced that they wanted young Navajo men who spoke fluent English and fluent Navajo. The men were needed for a special project that would benefit their country. I glanced at Roy. He seemed riveted by the Marines' words. I, too, was intrigued. Joining the Marines would mean leaving school, leaving the reservation and the lives we had always known, and entering foreign territory—the home of the white man. That was scary . . . and intriguing. Joining the Marines would affect the path we traveled for the rest of our lives. It might end our lives, if we were sent into battle.

By that time the Japanese had conquered Hong Kong, Guam, and Wake Island. In a move reminiscent of their attack on Pearl Harbor, they had devastated the Australian port city of Darwin. And they had attacked the Philippines, causing President Franklin D. Roosevelt to remove General MacArthur from that archipelago.

Both Roy and I knew that a decision made in haste could lead to dire consequences. We talked it over. I wanted to see how people lived off the reservation. I was curious to learn about the possibilities and opportunities offered out there in the larger world. And, more than anything, I wanted to serve and defend my country. That was a man's responsibility. Roy felt the same way, so he and I agreed to take the test offered by the Marines. Three of our friends at school in Tuba City agreed to be tested as well.

We five young men accompanied Marine recruiters to Fort Defiance, Arizona, the place where I had attended boarding school. There, approximately two hundred more young Navajos, mostly from Window Rock, capital of the Navajo Nation, eagerly applied to become part of the Marines' special project.

Marines require first-time recruits to be between the ages of seventeen and thirty-two. We men had no birth certificates, and several added a year or two to their ages in order to be accepted. At least one man, Carl Gorman, said he was younger than his actual age. He was thirty-five.

The Marines talked to me, interviewing me in English about my family life and my education. I understood every word and responded accordingly, speaking carefully, using my best English. There were no interviews in Navajo. Apparently the Marines assumed we all spoke Navajo.

Silently, I thanked the teachers at Fort Defiance for forcing me to learn English. And I thanked my family for keeping me fluent in Navajo.

When all applicants had completed their interviews, Roy and I waited nervously. Would we make the cut? From the hundreds of applicants, only thirty were to be selected for the secret project.

I wondered what it would be like to be a Marine. Would I make it through the tough physical training I'd heard about? I had been away from home a good part of my life in boarding school, so I knew I'd handle the separation from my family. But I'd have to leave Navajo country entirely, not just my home. I thought about mixing with white and black Marines, not just with other Navajos. Would I be able to compete with those men who had grown up off the reservation, in a different world, a different culture? Would I make my family proud?

Word came. Roy and I made the cut. I congratulated Roy. His eyes glowed. Who could have guessed our schoolwork would pay off like this? At boarding school, we had grown accustomed to the constant tension and the need to avoid mistakes. Our ability to stay calm in the face of pressure, to think clearly under stress, had reaped rewards. We were Marines!

It was the luckiest day of my life. I felt like I was walking in a dream. But what now?

Two of the other three applicants from Tuba City were not selected for the project, but the third, Allen Dale June, joined Roy and me. Recruits from elsewhere in Arizona and New Mexico made up the rest of the group, which came to be called "the original twenty-nine." The project plan called for thirty men, and thirty were selected. However, one man dropped out. In all the excitement, I remember that incident only vaguely. I think it had something to do with the thirtieth man not being completely comfortable with the dialect of Navajo we used. In a combat situation, that could be deadly. Books on the code talkers have made other suppositions, one being that he was assigned special communications duty overseas while the rest of us attended basic training, and another that he was excused temporarily from attending basic training while he played high school football. At any rate, "the first (or original) thirty" became "the original twenty-nine," a label that would stay with us for the rest of our lives.

On May 4, 1942, we new recruits were taken by bus to Fort Wingate, New Mexico, the same place I had lived while attending junior high in Gallup. I had not yet told my family about enlisting in the Marines. They had no telephone, and there was no time to make the trip home to *Chichiltah*.

At Fort Wingate, we ate lunch and were sworn in as United States Marines. Then we climbed into a bus bound for the Marine Recruit Depot just outside of San Diego, California. Most of our families didn't know of their sons' new military status. My heart pounded. I looked around the bus at my fellow recruits. I was a man now. We all were, even baby-faced Wilsie Bitsie. We were men who would fight for our country.

"Make good use of your free time, men. Basic training starts tomorrow." It was Sunday, and our superior officer left us twenty-nine men to our own devices. We were assigned bunks at the Marine Corps Recruitment Center in San Diego, the city that would soon house Camp Pendleton, home of the 1st Marine Division.

We claimed beds, stowed our gear, and set off for downtown San Diego. A hodgepodge of new sights and sounds bombarded us. Most of us had never been outside the bounds of the four sacred mountains. The buildings in San Diego towered above us, their man-made peaks dwarfing nature. Trucks and cars roared along the endless network of streets. And the lights! It was like daylight, even at night. This was a far cry from Navajo land. We were seeing the world.

The nature of our mission remained a mystery. Several men guessed we'd be assigned desk work. After all, the selection process had involved our skills with English and Navajo. Some thought we'd join the actual fight overseas, a chance to prove our courage.

Civil engineer Philip Johnston, the son of a missionary couple, grew up on the Navajo Reservation. He is credited with proposing the idea for the secret Navajo mission. He convinced Marine brass that the Navajo language—unwritten, and spoken by only those who had lived with us Navajos—could become the basis for an unbreakable code.

Since the language was not written, it couldn't be learned from a book.[1] It was estimated that only thirty non-Navajos spoke our language. Even that estimate was contested by many *Diné*, who believed that the language was so complex it could be learned only if one began in infancy. Johnston himself was a fine testimonial to this belief. Although he'd moved to the Navajo Reservation at the age of four with his parents, and although his playmates were all Navajo, he had learned the language only well enough to be considered a speaker of "trader" Navajo. He never became truly conversant with the deeper complexities of the language.

Pronunciation of even one Navajo word is nearly impossible for someone not used to hearing the sounds that make up the language. During his first year of life, a baby grows accustomed to the auditory variations from which his native language is composed. As time goes on, children become less able to distinguish sounds from unfamiliar languages. Thus it is difficult for a non-Navajo speaker to hear Navajo words properly, and virtually impossible for him to reproduce those words.

Native American languages, notably Choctaw and Comanche, had been used in a very limited way during World War I. In Europe, Native American fighting men were asked to transmit messages in their complex languages in order to stymie the enemy. This effort involved no code, but was an on-the-fly idea utilized only by several innovative commanders. After the war, the Germans discovered which native languages had been employed, and they sent "tourists," "scholars," and "anthropologists" to many tribes in the United States to learn their languages. Navajos were not among those tribes. That, too, worked in favor of using our Navajo language in developing a code. And we had another advantage. We had resisted adopting English words and folding them into our language. We made up our own words for new inventions, things like

---

1 Father Berard Haile, OFM, wrote a Navajo grammar book published in 1926, the first edition of *A Manual of Navajo Grammar*, but it was known by very few people.

radios and telephones, keeping our language pure and free of outside influence.

Despite the skepticism of some Marine officers, communications officer Major James E. Jones agreed to get the necessary equipment and to arrange a trial for Johnston's idea. Major General Clayton B. Vogel, commander of the Amphibious Corps, Pacific Fleet, would observe the trial and rule on the potential of Philip Johnston's proposal. Knowing that his Marines would be heavily involved in the fighting in the Pacific, Vogel had already initiated discussions with Commandant Thomas Holcomb about the need for secure communications in that arena of the war. Vogel was eager for fresh ideas involving unbreakable codes.

In Los Angeles, a city where many *Diné* had moved seeking employment after the livestock massacre, Johnston found four men who spoke fluent English and Navajo. The men accompanied him to Camp Elliott, near San Diego.

In February 1942, at Camp Elliott, the Navajo men were given an hour to come up with Navajo words representing several military terms for which there was no direct translation in Navajo. Then, with Major General Vogel and Major Jones as witnesses, the Navajos and the Marine communications men both transmitted several identical messages resembling in style and content the military messages that would be needed in battle.

The standard "Shackle" code was written in English, encoded via a coding machine, and sent. Then the receiving end decoded the message, again via machine, and wrote it out in English. It took an hour to transmit and receive the test messages. When the same messages were transmitted and received in Navajo—with the men themselves acting as coding machines—it took only forty seconds for the information to be transmitted accurately. The Marines were convinced. Major General Vogel became a champion of the proposed code. He requested two hundred Navajo men for the pilot project. Due to some continuing doubts about the practicality of the project, he was granted only a trial number of men: thirty. The active recruitment of Navajos began.

The military asked the Bureau of Indian Affairs for advice on recruiting men for this special project. The BIA felt that we Navajo Marines should be reserve specialists who didn't have to go through basic training. The Marines didn't much care for that suggestion. As members of their attack forces, they wanted us to prepare rigorously for battle and survival, just as other recruits would prepare. Then the BIA offered to provide two men as instructors and interpreters for the new Navajo recruits. The Marines decided that this recommendation made no sense, since the corps would provide us with instruction and the selection process required that we must all speak excellent English.

After that, the Marines pretty much ignored the advice offered by the government's Bureau of Indian Affairs. They recruited the special-assignment Navajos as they recruited other men, except that they promised us a secret mission. Like other new Marines, we would go through the necessary physical and mental rigors of basic training. The other Navajo recruits and I were not to be tasked with simply transmitting and receiving messages in our native language. The Japanese had cracked every code the United States had used thus far, and the Marines in charge of communications were skittish. What they needed, they decided, was a new code, one that used the Navajo language as a base. Our group of twenty-nine Navajo men had some serious work ahead of us.

But we still had to complete basic training before we learned about our challenging mission.

The sound of our drill sergeant's voice—a 5 A.M. wake-up call—jolted me from a fitful sleep. *Monday. Basic training.* My feet hit the cold barracks floor, and I looked at my new Marine buddies. Their faces were solemn. Would basic be as tough as we had heard?

Yesterday, we men had lined up, and barbers shaved our heads nearly bald. We joked about how the Marines gave us the same haircut we'd had in boarding school. I relaxed a little. So far, I knew this routine. Then my twenty-eight fellow Marines and I were issued uniforms. The dress uniforms were dark blue, had a belted jacket with brass buttons over matching pants, and included a white hat with a visor, a raised band, and a flattened top. Very sharp looking. The working uniforms, the ones we would wear during basic training, were a very light brown jacket and pants of the same fabric and color. Our rifles were Springfield bolt-action '03s like the ones used in World War I.

We were also issued Ka-bars, fighting knives, about a foot long with a seven-inch blade. Those were excellent knives, sharp and strong. The grooved leather handle fit well into our hands, and it had a guard that kept fingers from slipping onto the sharp blade. Later, overseas, I was issued a .38 pistol that I hung on my belt and a .30-caliber Browning submachine gun that took ten-round and fifteen-round clips.

The recruits who'd finished with basic training at the depot always shook their heads and laughed when they saw us new guys. "You'll be sorrrrrrry," they'd say in a singsong voice. I don't know how they knew we were new recruits. We thought we looked just like them in our Marine-issue fatigues. But they knew just as surely as if GREEN RECRUIT had been stamped across our foreheads. I can still hear that "You'll be sorrrrrrry." And they were right. But today it makes me laugh.

At 5:30 A.M. sharp, training began. We ran along the beach, carrying pails of sand and salt water. We ran for a half hour. Not so bad.

Next we did a half-hour stint on the obstacle course. Rigorous, but still not any worse than the daily physical trials we'd endured at home. We performed various exercises in half-hour segments throughout the morning.

After lunch, the drill sergeant informed us that everyone must learn to swim. That raised a few eyebrows. Growing up in the desert, many of the men were uncomfortable in deep water. I was lucky. As a twelve-

year-old, I'd taught myself to swim in a reservoir my family had built for
the sheep on Grandmother's land.

Once everyone could swim, or at least stay afloat, we practiced abandoning ship. Jumping into the water from thirty feet up was not easy for
any of us. It required real resolve. But we did what we were instructed to
do without question.

Physical challenges were something all of us men were used to. The
early mornings, too, we took in stride. Doing laundry with a scrub brush
wasn't so bad either. The exhaustion that conquered many Marine recruits did not beat us Navajos.

Our training days lasted until around seven-thirty at night, with a
half-hour break for lunch and a break at the end of the day for dinner.
At meals, we were required to eat everything on our plates. A sergeant
stood by the trash can to keep us from throwing food away. Many
an Anglo Marine stood over that garbage can, finishing his leftovers.
Not us Navajos. The food was delicious and plentiful. We ate it all with
enthusiasm.

After dinner, we had one precious hour to ourselves. Bedtime was at
eight-thirty.

One afternoon, after we'd been in basic training for a few days, an
instructor, a corporal, told us Navajo recruits to line up. Then he walked
down the line, punching each of us in the gut.

"Let's see if you're getting tough,"[2] he said.

When the corporal reached Carl Gorman, Gorman hit him, knock-
ing him down. He and Carl put on boxing gloves. We Navajo men
cheered for Carl, who held his own with the Marine corporal.

Soon we learned that the real challenges in the military were cultural, not physical. Marine officers looked us in the eye and expected us

---

2 Some sources say that the corporal hit the recruits in the face, but I remember the incident as told
above. I felt it was all "in good fun," while other sources label the incident as evidence of prejudice
against us Navajo men.

to look back. To a Navajo, doing this was very bad manners. The drill instructor confronted us recruits, his face inches from ours, and yelled at the top of his lungs. We had always been taught to keep our voices modulated. The unaccustomed shouting rattled us, making it difficult to respond. There were times we men, accustomed to reservation life, felt like we'd arrived on a different planet.

The constant shouting and hassling took a toll on us. Several men feared they had made a mistake in joining the Marines. Some talked with me about how out of place they felt in this new "white man's" environment. And many had begun to wonder whether they'd make it out of the war alive. I listened to their fears, knowing that they were voicing the same doubts I felt. But we encouraged each other, together conquering any misgivings. We had not made a mistake.

Still, close-order drills proved to be a challenge for all of us. The drill instructor barked out marching commands. The shouted commands were confusing, and when one of us made a wrong move, he bumped into the rest of us, drawing attention. The drill sergeant's consequent yelling didn't help to clarify things.

But we were determined. When we got a break from training, we practiced close-order drill commands. The purpose of the drills was to get us to react quickly and to work well together, as one seamless entity, not many. Gradually we became comfortable with the routines.

The discipline at boot camp reminded me of those harsh days at boarding school. But I understood the reason for the strict Marine training. Soon our lives would be at stake. It wasn't like school, where the meanness had seemed arbitrary.

My buddies and I worked hard at learning everything we were supposed to learn. It paid off. The Marine Corps *Chevron,* the Marine newspaper in San Diego, carried an article about our platoon, number 382. It was kind of embarrassing, but at least it let us know that we were doing okay. An excerpt:

Magnificent specimens of "original American" manhood, they are already farther advanced than recruits usually are . . . Sgt. L. J. Stephenson, who has been handling new Marines as they passed through Recruit Depot for more than a year now, is unstinted in his praise of these men.[3]

Platoon 382 won over even the most crusty drill instructors. Every man in the platoon worked hard. The instructors bragged about our rapid progress. I'd always been pretty easygoing, and I began to feel confident about my place—and my buddies' places—in the Marines.

We recruits became good friends with our instructors. The drill sergeants got a huge kick out of commanding us to "count cadence in Navajo" as we marched. On the parade grounds, the heads of surrounding troops snapped around, everyone curious about what was going on. What was that strange cadence?

I especially liked the rifle range. It was like a game, with everyone competing. We men took turns setting up targets and recording the results of each recruit's practice volleys.

"Damn!" The instructor pored over our score sheets. "I've never seen anything like it." He shook his head. "Where'd you guys learn to shoot?"

We felt pretty comfortable on the rifle range and with our pistols, and Platoon 382 earned one of the highest scores in marksmanship of any Marine platoon in history. We graduated with one expert, fourteen sharpshooters, and twelve marksmen in our ranks. That got us another write-up in the Marine Corps *Chevron*. I was qualified as a pistol sharpshooter.

Eventually, my fellow recruits and I could handle handguns, 30-30 lever-action guns, and hand grenades without fear. The weapons still inspired a sense of awe and danger, but we knew how to use them safely.

---

3 *Chevron*, May 16, 1942.

Hand-to-hand combat practice with bayonets resulted in some bruises, but added to our self-assurance.

Grenades were especially heavy and cumbersome. We graduated from dud grenades to live ones, and I felt my throat tighten when I pulled the pin. Just as they'd taught us, I held the trigger in until I was ready to throw. Chest-high trenches protected us from the explosions. I threw from one deep trench into another—my arm muscles as taut as a stretched rubber band.

The supervising instructor nodded. "Good."

I scrambled from the trench, and the next recruit took his turn.

Survival training was also quite intense. We'd march for miles across the desert, with limited amounts of food and water. Often we spent the night out in the open, staying in improvised shelters. It was like herding sheep all over again.

The fieldwork was pretty demanding, but there was classroom work, too. We learned about the various weapons in detail. By the end of training, each of us could disassemble and reassemble his rifle while blindfolded, meeting or beating a specified time limit.

We all attended communications school, learning Morse code and semaphore, which utilized flags. We also learned to fix radios and to take them apart. At the time this seemed to be just one more required skill. We were not told what a large part these radios would play in our future in the Pacific war.

There were plenty of women in the Marines. They didn't go into combat back then, but we often saw women in the motor pool, women who trained as nurses, women who handled the food service. Although I never met any of them, they were a constant reminder of why we men were preparing to fight.

When we completed our seven weeks of basic, Platoon 382 stood final inspection. It was June 27, 1942. Colonel James L. Underhill, base commanding officer, addressed the troops. He gave us Navajo men high praise, and was quoted in the Marine Corps *Chevron* the following week:

This platoon is the first truly All-American platoon to pass through this Recruit Depot. It is, in fact, the first All-American platoon to enter the United States Marine Corps. We have had individual members of the Indian nations in the Corps, but never before a group like this one . . .

Yours has been one of the outstanding platoons in the history of this Recruit Depot and a letter has gone to Washington telling of your excellence. You obey orders like seasoned and disciplined soldiers. You have maintained rugged health. You have been anxiouus [sic] to learn your new duties, and you have learned quickly. As a group you have made one of the highest scores on the Rifle Range.

The Marine Corps is proud to have you in its ranks, and I am proud to have been the Commanding Officer of the Base while you were here.

You are now to be transferred to a combat organization where you will receive further training. When the time comes that you go to battle with the enemy, I know that you will fight like true Navajos, Americans and Marines.[4]

The article also carried pictures of Platoon 382. And one headline tried to give all of us swelled heads:

FAMED PLATOON OF NAVAJO INDIANS
FINISH RECRUIT TRAINING.

The intense training had built up our confidence. By the end of basic training, I felt satisfied that I had learned everything I needed to know to stay alive in combat.

---

4 *Chevron,* July 4, 1942.

CHAPTER TEN

Unbreakable Code

July to September 1942

Platoon 382, all twenty-nine of us, eagerly anticipated a ten-day leave. After they completed basic training, our white Marine buddies took off to see their families. But an officer pulled us Navajos aside, explaining that our mission was very critical. The men of Platoon 382 could not be spared for ten days.

While those other Marine recruits sat around dining tables with sisters, brothers, and parents, I sat in the barracks trying to compose a letter. I pictured Grandmother, Father, and Grandfather at home on the Checkerboard, enjoying the sunny, warm days of summer. My family thought I was still living at the school in Tuba City. I wasn't sure how to tell them that I had joined the Marines or that I was going to war. Finally I just wrote the facts flat out and sealed the envelope.

It was our second day at Camp Elliott, near San Diego, our home for the next thirteen weeks. Riding out there on the bus, we had speculated about our "critical mission."

A Marine officer strode with a no-nonsense gait to a classroom building, and we followed. He opened the locked door and marched to the front of the room as we piled in behind him. Standing tall, his uniform spotless, his expression unsmiling, he waited for us to sit. Then he spoke. I felt a small knot tighten in my stomach.

The officer wasted no time. He looked around the room at each of us, the twenty-nine carefully selected Marine recruits, and told us we were to use our native language to devise an unbreakable code. I read expressions of shock on every face. A code based on the Navajo language? After we'd been so severely punished in boarding school for speaking it?

For starters, you'll need a word for each letter of the alphabet, the officer told us.

The officer locked the door as he left, telling us we'd be released at the end of the day to get dinner. Someone would bring lunch to the room. Other than that, we were on our own, forbidden to speak to anyone outside that room about our task. And if we needed to go anywhere, we had to go in pairs. We were to practice the buddy system at all times. Anyone caught alone would be punished.

Hearing that door lock click closed, I again felt my stomach tense. The windows of our classroom were protected by security bars. Now what?

After some discussion, we began to see the wisdom in our assignment. Navajo was a very complex language. And, since it was not written,[1] the Japanese could learn it only from a Navajo or from one of the rare non-Navajos who had lived on the reservation and learned to speak the language. To be honest, I don't think they could have learned the language even then. It was just too complicated.

Still, apprehension set in. How could we, twenty-eight of whom had never worked with the military, develop a code robust enough to be used in battle? One that could be responsible for sending life-or-death mes-

---

1 A couple of missionaries (among them Father Berard Haile) had devised methods of recording Navajo. But in general the language was unwritten.

sages? The task loomed ahead like a black unmapped cavern. Where to begin?

We stared at the locked door of the room in which we sat. One of our men, Gene Crawford, had been in the reserves. He had worked with codes before, and he offered to share his knowledge with all of us. There were certain things that were important. The code words chosen must be clear when spoken on the radio. Each word must be distinct from other words chosen, in order to avoid confusion. The officer who'd locked the room was correct: a good way to begin was to select a word to represent each letter of the alphabet.

Gene Crawford and two other men from among the twenty-nine, John Benally and John Manuelito, played a strong part in setting the direction for our group as we developed the new code.

On that first day, we decided to use an English word—generally an animal, a plant, or an object that was part of our everyday world—to represent each letter of the English alphabet. Those words would then be translated into Navajo, and the Navajo word would represent the English letter. As Gene had suggested, we chose Navajo words that could be easily distinguished on the radio, words differing clearly in sound from other selected words. *A* became "red ant," not the English word for ant, but the Navajo word, pronounced *wol-la-chee*. *B* became "bear," pronounced *shush* in Navajo. *C* was "cat" or *moasi*. *D* was "deer" or *be*. Thus a double encryption was used. Each letter became an English word beginning with that letter, and the English word was translated into a Navajo word.

We tried to make the letter equivalents easy to remember. And we discussed pronunciation—since emphasis on the wrong syllable, a slight change in tone, or a glottal stop could totally change a word's meaning in the complicated Navajo language. Any differences in dialects between us men had to be resolved into one firm code. In the heat of battle we could afford no ambiguities.

Although Navajo is spoken less and less frequently today, the boarding schools in the 1920s and '30s had—happily—failed in their efforts to erase the language from the minds of their students. We men in that locked room were articulate in both Navajo and English.

Navajo bears little resemblance to English. When a Navajo asks whether you speak his language, he uses these words: "Do you *hear* Navajo?" Words must be heard before they can be spoken. Many of the sounds in Navajo are impossible for the unpracticed ear to distinguish. The inability of most people to hear Navajo was a solid plus when it came to devising our code.

The Navajo language is very exact, with fine shades of meaning that are missing in English. Our language illustrates the *Diné*'s relationship to nature. Everything that happens in our lives happens in relationship to the world that surrounds us. The language reflects the importance of how we and various objects interact. For example, the form of the verb "to dump something" that is used depends upon the object that is being dumped and the container that is being utilized. If one dumps coal from a bucket, for instance, the verb is different from the verb used to describe dumping water from a pail. And the verb again differs when one dumps something from a sack. Again, in Navajo you do not simply "pick up" an object. Depending on what the object is—its consistency and its shape—the verb used for "to pick up" will differ. Thus the verb for picking up a handful of squishy mud differs from the verb used for picking up a stick.

Pronunciation, too, is complex. Navajo is a tonal language with four tones: high, low, rising, and falling. The tone used can completely change the meaning of a word. The words for "medicine" and "mouth" are pronounced in the same way, but they are differentiated by tone.[2] Glottal and aspirated stops are also employed. Given these complexities, native

---

2 Nathan Aaseng, *Navajo Code Talkers*, p. 18.

speakers of any other language are generally unable to properly pronounce most Navajo words.

But the complexities of the Navajo language provide a wonderful tool for spinning tales. Our speech does not simply state facts; it paints pictures. Spoken in Navajo, the phrase "I am hungry" becomes "Hunger is hurting me."[3]

The conjugation of verbs in Navajo is also complex. There is a verb form for one person performing an action, a different form of the verb for two people, and a third form for more than two people.

English can be spoken sloppily and still be understood. Not so with the Navajo language. So, even though our assigned task—developing a code—made us nervous, we realized that we brought the right skills to the job.

Several white Marines who'd grown up on the Navajo Reservation and knew quite a bit of Navajo later applied to code talker school. But there were always words or syllables they could not pronounce correctly, so they didn't make it as code talkers.

There was no dissension among us in that locked room. We focused. We worked as one. This was a talent long employed in Navajo culture—many working together to herd the sheep, plant the corn, bring in a harvest. When we were children, distant relatives visited for weeks at a time, strengthening the bond of family. Neighbors cared for one another's livestock when someone was sick or had to travel, knowing their friend would someday do the same for them. The ability to live in unity, learned on the reservation and the Checkerboard, proved invaluable to our current assignment.

Day one ended, and the fledgling new code had already begun to

---

3 Thinkquest.org.

take shape. We twenty-nine Marines had come up with a workable structure. When I looked around, relief showed on every face. We slapped each other on the back, and joked to let off steam, feeling good about our work. The impossible-seeming task suddenly looked possible. We would not let our country or our fellow Marines down.

An officer arrived to unlock the room. He collected the working papers we'd generated that day and locked them in a safe. Hearing that safe slam shut, I was again impressed by the seriousness of our mission.

It was Saturday, three-thirty in the afternoon, after a long week of code work. Roy Begay sat on his bunk in the barracks, his blanket pulled tight like a drum, military style. He grinned at me as I sprawled on the adjacent bunk.

"Spell 'beer,'" Roy said.

I chuckled, *"Shush dzeh dzeh gah."*

"Good," said Roy. A smile lit up his face. "Let's find the other guys and get some *shush dzeh dzeh gah*. Now."

I swung my legs over the side of the cot. *"Ouu,"* I said.

I liked how things were "wide open." The other code talkers and I were generally released from our work in late afternoon, around four or five o'clock. And on weekends we were free. Not tied to duties like sheepherding, we spent our leisure time exploring San Diego. I was happy about being in the Marines, being in San Diego, and having a secret mission. I felt as though I'd stepped up out of my old life into a new, exciting world.

Everyone in San Diego asked us questions. About being Indian. About being Marines. After a few beers, it was easy to converse with people who were so different from us, and visiting bars became a popular pastime. Many of my Navajo Marine buddies had never tried beer, or any alcohol, before. I had, and I didn't much like the taste, but did like the way it warmed my insides, relaxing me.

We often wound up at a favorite watering hole, a sort of enlisted men's club on base we called "The Slop Chute." There they served food in addition to alcohol, so we could have a meal and a drink or two without getting sloppy.

When we left base and ventured into San Diego, we arrived at bars wearing our Marine uniforms and were served with no questions asked. But many Navajos worked in San Diego's factories. When Native Americans arrived out of uniform, they were told that Indians would not be served alcohol. The popular idea was that a drunk Indian was a bad Indian. That was just the way it was. We all accepted it.

Tijuana, Mexico, just across the border from San Diego, was another popular destination. One bar at the border had a white line drawn on the floor. On one side of the line was the USA, on the other Mexico.

Mexico was wilder, and behavior there was less restrained than in the United States. Military men returning from Mexico were assumed to have gotten into trouble. Often medical checkups, performed by the military, were required at the border.

Military Police watched over us Marines in San Diego as we drank, and anyone who appeared inebriated was sent to the barracks. On weekends, my group had to be back at barracks by early evening, around seven-thirty. We took our new job seriously and always returned on time. We never got so drunk that we had to be brought to the base by other Marines.

Even though we were watched by our fellow military men, the sense of freedom, of having days off, was like a rebirth for me. On the Checkerboard there was always work to be done, never a day off. Now we were unencumbered by the duties and obligations to family that had filled our hours at home. In San Diego, we discovered thousands of lights, noisy crowds of people, endless blocks of buildings, thousands of vehicles, and the ocean.

Most of the men had never seen the ocean before. Normally an event as big as seeing the ocean for the first time required a blessing. An even more serious blessing was needed before swimming in the ocean. The blessings helped us to maintain a balance with nature. But things in the military were different, and we just came upon the ocean all of a sudden during basic training. We all practiced jumping into the water and running on the beach. Landing on the Pacific islands, in combat, would mean swimming and wading through the water. We had to be ready.

Every night we quizzed each other on the code. As part of our task, we devised phonetic English spellings for the previously unwritten Navajo words. This was all top secret, as was the rest of the code. The new phonetic spellings allowed us to review and study the Navajo words that became part of the new code, words that needed to flow like water in the midst of battle. It was impossible to study too much.

We practiced writing. We decided that everything should be printed, no script. Each word had to be legible, and most of us wrote in upper case, each man's letters the same as all the others. I still print today, out of long-ingrained habit.

It took about five days for us to devise Navajo word equivalents for the full alphabet. The code pleased all of us with its unique words and the ease with which it could be memorized. The most difficult letters were *J* and *Z*. We finally settled on "jackass," code word *tkele-cho-gi*, and "zinc," code word *besh-do-tliz*.

We quizzed each other, spelling messages until we knew the Navajo-word equivalents for the English alphabet without a flaw. If someone had trouble with the memorizing, we all quizzed him until he got it. We knew that the strength of the group made us all sharp. And in combat, the code would only be as strong as both men using it—the one on the sending end and the one on the receiving end.

Despite the efforts of boarding schools to repress it, Navajo oral tradition remained strong. Stories were still told around the campfires at home, memorized, and told again . . . and again. Memorization, for each of us, was second nature.

And, again despite the efforts of boarding schools, from the time of their birth, Navajo children in a traditional environment were exposed to the exacting and complex thought processes required by the Navajo language. This helped contribute to their ability to deal with decisions and complexities in their lives. Certainly it contributed to the abilities required to be a code talker: learning quickly, memorizing, and working under extreme pressure. I am thankful that my father and grandparents taught me my Navajo language well.

We knew that the Navajo code words would be spoken, but never written, when utilized in battle. English messages were to be encrypted *orally* into Navajo and sent by radio. When a message was received, it would be orally decrypted from Navajo back into written English. In the heat of battle, not one of us could afford to be rattled. We studied till we were exhausted, then studied some more.

Certain military terms would be used frequently—so frequently that we didn't want to waste time spelling them. Those words needed direct translations. We men, barely off the reservation, were not familiar with military terms, the names and capabilities of various ships and planes, types of artillery, and other equipment. Words like "echelon" or "battalion" stymied us. We also had to figure out a way to indicate various officers—"captain," "major," "brigadier general," "colonel," "first lieutenant," "second lieutenant," "major general." How were we supposed to find equivalents for all of those? We asked for three Navajo-speaking military men to help us. Felix Yazzie, Ross Haskie, and Wilson Price were pulled from their Marine duties and assigned to help us with the code. These three men fit in, becoming one with the rest of us, indistinguishable in my mind from the original twenty-nine. After we developed the code together, they went into battle with us. I don't know why historians insist on separating them from the original twenty-nine. For me, it was the original thirty-two. They deserved credit for the code just as much as any of us did.

Of course, even after we compiled a comprehensive list of military terms, there was still a problem. In Navajo, no equivalent for words like "fighter plane" existed. We chose animals and other items from our everyday world that resembled the military equipment. So "fighter plane" was represented by the quick and maneuverable hummingbird, code word *da-he-tih-hi*. The huge transport planes were represented as an eagle who carried prey, *atsah*. A battleship was a whale, code word *lo-tso*, and a destroyer was a shark, code word *ca-lo*. A cruiser was a small whale, code word *lo-tso-yazzie*. In choosing each code word, we talked about how the animal chosen lived and hunted, and we did our best to link it up logically with a piece of military equipment. Sometimes we used non-animal items to represent certain things. A hand grenade was a potato, or *nimasi*. Bombs were eggs or *a-ye-shi*. Japan was slant-eye or *beh-na-ali-tsosie*.

There is no Navajo equivalent for months of the year, since we did not divide our calendar into twelve chunks. Instead, we used concepts to describe each month. January, a cold month, was "crusted snow" or *yas-nil-tes*. The month of April, when spring sprouts begin to grow, was "small plant" or *tah-chill*. June, when much planting is done, became "big planting" or *be-ne-eh-eh-jah-tso*.

In addition to the alphabet, we devised nearly 220 terms for various concepts and diverse types of military equipment. A code name, *Ne-he-mah*, was chosen to represent the United States of America. *Ne-he-mah* translates to "our mother."

Living the Right Way, we men knew that things must be in harmony. We didn't compete with each other. We continued to help any of our buddies who needed help. As traditional Navajos, we had a bond of understanding. In our new roles as Marines, we continued to work together.

We thirty-two were an interesting blend of personalities. Eugene Crawford was husky and real smart. He had a good sense of humor. Wilsie Bitsie was short and chubby. He, too, made us laugh. Felix Yazzie, one of the three men assigned to help us original twenty-nine develop military code terms, was tall and lean, another joker. Charlie Begay, a tall, skinny man kept us laughing, too. He was good to be around. Those four joined

Carlson's Raiders at some point. I think we were on Guadalcanal when that happened. Their officer, Lieutenant Colonel Evans Carlson, was a strong leader. He appreciated the code talkers and was good to us. And the raiders were real brave. They'd go behind enemy lines under cover of dark—or even sometimes during the day—to raid Japanese camps or airfields and to clean up hot spots. Dangerous work.

Then there was Samuel Begay, who had a good sense of humor like Charlie Begay. Cosey Brown was quiet, another tall, thin man. John Chee, again tall and skinny, was intelligent. He knew a lot about all kinds of subjects. David Curley was well educated. He often talked about school. Ross Haskie, another of the three men assigned to help the first twenty-nine, was a big guy who looked kind of like a white man. Alfred Leonard was just the opposite—short and skinny and, like so many of the others, very funny. William McCabe was another well-educated member of the team. Lloyd Oliver was very serious, tuned in. I liked to hang out with him. No matter where we were, he always knew what was going on. John Benally was a little guy, very sharp, with a complexion so light he looked like a white man, not a Navajo. He learned the code perfectly, later staying on at Camp Elliott as an instructor who trained the new code talkers. Oscar Ilthma was one of the older guys, also light-complexioned like a white man. John Brown was a very good guy, smart, with a dry sense of humor, kind of like Jack Benny. Wilson Price, the third of the men who came into the classroom at Camp Elliott to help with military terms, was quiet and very serious.

Lowell Damon was a real nice guy, my best buddy. He was fairly tall and skinny, serious about our assignment. I always wished he could have accompanied Roy Begay and me when we went overseas together. George Dennison was funny, kind of tall also. James Dixon was funny, too, one of the older guys. Jack Nez was also a good buddy, not related to me, although his name was Nez, like mine. Frank Pete was a small guy, and quiet. Balmer Slowtalker, who changed his name to Joe Palmer after the war, was a joker, with a fun sense of humor. Nelson Thompson kept to himself. Harry Tsosie was tall and quiet, and he didn't socialize much. John Willie, a small guy, was quiet, too. Johnny Manuelito kept to himself. He also ended up being a code instructor. Benjamin Cleveland was funny and short. Carl Gorman, at thirty-five, was the oldest of the original code talkers. He liked to talk and to joke. He was a very good guy. William Yazzie, who later changed his name to William Dean Wilson, was about my size, quiet and gentle. Allen Dale June was a good guy, about my height, and husky.

Then there were Roy and me. We were both serious guys, and we paid close attention to our assignments. Roy was close to six feet tall, and I was much shorter, five feet six inches. We both had wiry builds, and we depended on each other. Although neither of us made many jokes, we laughed a lot with the other guys. They were all good men, and it makes me feel nostalgic, thinking about those guys, my buddies. We Navajos have long been known for our sense of humor, and looking back, I am struck by how many of the men were born entertainers. It was good for morale.

We finished the development phase. We felt sure we had a code that even a native Navajo speaker would not be able to crack. Our classroom was unlocked, and we code talkers went out on maneuvers to test the code and to practice, practice, practice. When we saw the letter *C* we had to think *moasi*. In battle, there would be no time to think: C, *cat. That's* moasi. It had to be automatic, without a conscious thought process. We were to be living code machines.

Several Marine generals came to the room to listen as the code was refined. As part of the training, those men arranged to put some of us on shipboard—both submarines and surface ships—and some on land. We often spread out like this for field maneuvers aimed at practicing the code.

Someone not involved with our group heard the messages, and all along the California coast troops suddenly went to "condition black" (a state of readiness where weapons were prepared for immediate use) thinking that the Japanese had invaded the United States mainland at San Diego. A couple of the code talkers were taken to North Island Headquarters, where they quelled the panic. They listened to the tapes of "Japanese" made by the officers and identified the language as Navajo. One of the colonels involved with the program told his superiors that the strange language was their own Navajo Marines speaking a code that they had developed. He promised to give headquarters advance warning of future field maneuvers involving the code so that the Navajo words wouldn't be mistaken for Japanese and wouldn't cause panic.

The new code was leagues more efficient than the "Shackle" code used previously by combatants. Once they stopped being troubled by the foreign-sounding words, the generals were impressed.

Still, some had doubts. Over and over we demonstrated the speed and accuracy of our code for various high-ranking officers. Some observers even thought the code was so accurate—word for word and punctuation mark for punctuation mark—that we must be cheating somehow.

That bothered us. What point would there be in cheating? That wouldn't cut it in battle. We wanted our code to work as much as anyone else did. Maybe more. But we didn't let on how much that accusation insulted us.

To see whether we were scamming, some officers separated the men transmitting from those receiving so we couldn't see each other, then posted guards by each so we couldn't cheat in any way. Our messages were still fast and accurate. Eventually the observers had no choice but to admit that our code worked.

As a further test, expert code breakers from the United States military were assigned the task of breaking our code. They tried for weeks, but not one man met with any success in breaking the Navajo code.

Finally, the Marine brass threw their considerable weight behind the code. We had earned staunch allies.

Later, new code talker recruits expanded this code, adding two more Navajo words to represent most letters and more than four hundred additional words for other military terms, bringing the code to around seven hundred words. When a code talker transmitted the letter *A*, he could then use the Navajo word for "ant" or "apple" or "axe." The code talkers might spell a word containing three *As* using each of the three words for *A*. This broke the pattern of one-letter-one-word, a pattern in which a code cracker might discover the symbol for *E*, the most common letter in English, and other letters based upon how frequently they were used. The extra letter symbols made the code even more complex and more impossible to crack, and the added words for military maneuvers and equipment made transmission even faster.

In late September 1942, our thirteen weeks in Camp Elliott came to an end. We graduated as Navajo code talkers, Marine Corps MOS (Military Occupational Specialty) number 642 and were promoted to private first class.

We hoped to get some leave, but again our officers talked to us. They explained that we were badly needed in the Pacific theater of the war, where the Japanese had already taken Guam, the Philippines, and Burma on the Malay Peninsula. They had attacked New Guinea and prevailed in the Battle of the Java Sea. The Bataan Death March in the Philippines, in which more than five thousand Americans perished, had been well publicized back in April, around the time we had been recruited.

The U.S. victories at the Battle of the Coral Sea and the Hawaiian island of Midway were also known to us. Midway had been the first major Japanese Naval defeat in 350 years. And, of course, we were familiar with the valiant ongoing struggle by the United States to take Guadalcanal.

So, again, we were not allowed to visit our families. We immediately prepared to board ships bound for the French islands of New Caledonia. It was autumn, before the middle of October.

Our Japanese enemies, we were informed, had always managed to crack American communications codes. Past experience gave them a well-earned confidence that they could decipher any code devised by the United States. But they were unaware that a new era of wartime communications had begun.

CHAPTER ELEVEN

New Caledonia

October to early November 1942

The ocean swelled and subsided, wave after wave, motion without end. I half stood, half leaned against the ship rail. One of my buddies leaned beside me. Our hands and faces clammy, neither of us spoke. That morning, most of the men had thrown up the antiseasick pills that were routinely handed out on board ship.

Another code talker joined us and groaned. "Are we there yet?"

En route to the French islands of New Caledonia, a group of islands off the east coast of Australia in the South Pacific, we traveled light. Our dress blues stayed back in San Diego, as did anything else we wouldn't need in battle. Some of the guys sent stuff home, but I just loaded a seabag and left it at the base in San Diego. I never got any of its contents back, except for my dress blues.

Our ship, the luxury ocean liner USS *Lurline,* had been converted for military use. The vessel, once ringing with the clink of crystal glasses, faint memories of haunting melodies drifting just beyond earshot, was now a military transport vessel. I could almost see the former passengers—

moneyed men, like movie stars, resplendent in tuxedos, bejeweled women hanging on their arms. But now, in the fall of 1942, one big barracks area replaced the private rooms, and the separate dining areas had become a single mess hall. So we troops slept and ate together.

The elegant vessel, armed with hastily mounted artillery on deck, moved toward a destination that had never graced its peacetime itinerary: the Pacific islands of World War II.

When our transport ship docked in Hawaii the next day, only officers were granted shore leave. There were ten of us code talkers on board, and most were too sick to care about carousing onshore. We went below, where hammocklike beds were strung from a metal framework, four high, with racks for our rifles bolted onto the wall next to them. We climbed into our beds in the stuffy, hot hold of the ship. My bunk was on the third tier, and when the man above me climbed into his hammock, it hung down burdened with his weight, nearly touching my nose. The smell in there—of sweating bodies and vomit—was terrible, but we could forget it for a while if only we could sleep. After a while I gave up and climbed out of my bunk. I went up on deck and slept in the fresh air, with a breeze rustling the leaves onshore and my blanket wrapped around me.

We code talkers remained on board with the other enlisted Marines, wondering whether we'd ever stop feeling seasick. We stayed in Hawaii a few days, always aboard ship. At this time a new contingent of Marine recruits boarded.

The ship departed for New Caledonia, and the newly boarded recruits soon began to turn green. Like us, they had to develop their sea legs. The seasoned sailors assured us that we would all be fine by the time we reached our destination.

I woke at 5 A.M. for breakfast, managing to eat a few bites. We practiced the new code all morning. At lunch, most of us were able to eat at least something. After a week, our bodies had begun to adjust to the constant rolling of the ship. After lunch, I did calisthenics with the other code talkers—the sick ones joining in with the well. Then we cleaned our rifles and practiced close-order drills.

Finally, in late afternoon, we had some free time. Some of the men read, taking books from the ship library. I was never too much of a reader, although occasionally I'd pick up a book. That afternoon, I joined a few of the others to play blackjack. Poker and blackjack were very popular. I didn't have much money, and had no money to waste, so I didn't play cards all that often.

It was a long trip to the South Pacific—a couple of weeks—and it was hot. The weather was one of the most difficult things we had to adapt to. Coming from the desert, we were used to heat, but we couldn't seem to get used to the constant humidity that transformed the ship into a sweat bath like the ones in our sweat huts back home. Those, though, we only stayed in for an hour or so. This muggy heat we couldn't escape.

Often the men got together and sang. I always liked that. Someone grabbed a guitar, and a couple of others played harmonicas. Sometimes we sang religious songs like "Rock of Ages." Other times we sang popular songs. "Don't Sit Under the Apple Tree" and "I've Got Sixpence" were two of the favorites. Those songs always made me think of home. They reminded me of the beautiful land and the people I loved—everything I was fighting for.

We'd play rough-and-tumble, stealing one another's food and spraying each other with hoses on deck. Pretty frequently we'd get to watch a movie. Everyone looked forward to this. It was a great diversion from thinking about war. We needed that kind of thing.

In addition to reminding us about the secrecy of the code, Marine trainers had warned us to concentrate on our purpose—communications—and not to think about whether we'd live or die in the Pacific war. But those thoughts just came into my mind. I couldn't help it. It was impossible not to think.

In general, we ten code talkers on the ship stayed close, talking Navajo and practicing—always practicing—the new code. Sometimes other Marines in our battalion overheard our practice. "What are you doing?" they'd ask.

We shrugged. "Speaking Navajo," we'd answer. We were not allowed to reveal the details of our secret assignment even to our fellow Marines.

Cards, reading, and the constant practicing of the code provided our most frequent distractions from the ordeal ahead. Unlike the meals during basic training, where food was a hearty and a welcome diversion, the food on board ship was not as plentiful as we would have liked. We did get two small bottles of sage beer every day, one at about eleven o'clock in the morning and one in the evening. And there was lots of coffee. But to augment our allotments of food, we code talkers volunteered for kitchen duty. We had to wake at four in the morning, but figured it was worth it.

Some of the kettles in the galley were so big we'd walk right into them in order to scrub them! And we'd scrub the smaller pots and pans, too. It wasn't bad work. While on kitchen duty, when not suffering from seasickness, we ate as much as we could hold—our own meals plus leftovers.

Grande Terre, the largest of the New Caledonia islands, loomed as we approached. We gathered along the railing for a view of our next home. The ship slowed as the water grew more shallow, and a small pilot boat came out to guide us in. The captain of the pilot boat came aboard the *Lurline* to help our ship captain navigate the unfamiliar harbor waters of Noumea Bay. As the ship drew into the American base there at Noumea, I imagined the feel of solid earth under my feet.

Mountains ran the length of the island, dominating the scene before me, and conifer trees, a rare sight on a tropical island, lined the beach. They reminded me of the piñon and juniper back home. I quickly squashed that thought. The challenging job at hand required my entire focus. I didn't need to be homesick for New Mexico.

Onshore, we ten code talkers from the USS *Lurline* reunited with others who had come on different vessels. It felt good to be together

again. Through Marine boot camp, followed by the serious job of designing and memorizing the code, we men had forged a real bond.

Of the original thirty-two men who had worked together at Camp
Elliott (including the three—Ross Haskie, Felix Yazzie, and Wilson
Price—who'd been added to our ranks during the development of the
code), thirty were sent to war in the fall and winter of 1942. We all
served in the Pacific. Only John Benally and John Manuelito were missing from the ranks of the fighting men. Those two had stayed in California to train new Navajo recruits in the secret code. It wasn't until later
that they entered the war as combatants.

On Grande Terre, we code talkers continued our combat training.
We were warned early on not to stray from the base. Some of the French
occupants of New Caledonia didn't like Marines, and there had been
several instances of unfriendly confrontations with the inhabitants of the
island. The French were our allies in Europe. Germany and Italy had
declared war on the United States just a few days after the Japanese attack on Pearl Harbor. I never quite understood the unfriendliness of the
inhabitants of New Caledonia, but they definitely did not want us there.

We Marines stuck together, working hard at our training, swimming,
roughhousing, and occasionally sitting around a bonfire and telling stories or singing songs. We provided our own entertainment.

Roy Begay and I, soaking wet, lay on the beach. We'd just practiced
abandoning ship, a drill that we had to complete several times while on
New Caledonia, just in case we'd forgotten all our practice back in San
Diego. Our uniforms dried quickly, but later that night, again drip-
ping wet, we crouched and slithered along the beach in the dark. It was
our third night-landing practice since our arrival on Grande Terre. We
moved with stealth, avoiding the spotlights trained on the beach—lights
simulating enemy surveillance.

Next morning, I woke early, unfastened my mosquito net, and nudged Roy.

"Wake up, lazybones."

Roy groaned and turned toward me in the foxhole. "Is that you, Grandmother?"

We grabbed our mess kits—two sectioned plates that fit together with utensils inside—and crawled out of the foxhole. All of us code talkers walked together to breakfast. The mess hall was located some distance from camp, down the beach.

I nodded at the man lined up ahead of me for food.

He wrinkled his nose and pressed his mouth closed. "Jeez, eggs from a can, again."

Another Marine chuckled. "Don't forget Spam."

Roy craned his neck to see the food. "Those little hot dogs, too."

I'll admit it was a limited menu. But the food, big barrels of it, was—for me—one of the best parts of being in the Marines. It was good and it was plentiful, a real treat after boarding school. I know most enlisted men complained about Marine food, but I liked all of it. Spam was my favorite, and Vienna sausages were great, too. So was the canned corned beef. I even liked the crackers.

After eating, we dipped our mess kits in boiling water and returned to the beach encampment.

In a half hour, the instructor arrived with that day's orders. Each day was similar to the one preceding, but the anticipation of battle hung heavy in the air, and we knew that this training was important. I concentrated. I intended to survive.

That day we practiced hand-to-hand combat. The steamy island—populated with tropical birds, snakes, fist-sized spiders, lizards, monkeys, mosquitoes, and flies as big as my thumbnail—was a different world from any I had ever experienced.

After lunch, we attended classes, learning in depth about our waterproof radios. I, like most of the other Navajo men, had always lived in a home without electricity. But I memorized everything the instructor said about the electric crank radios, adding it to the store of knowledge I'd already gathered in basic training. I focused all of my energy, knowing that even though I was tired from last night's maneuvers, this knowledge could save my life. And the lives of other Marines.

Physical and mental challenges were constant. Drill sergeants advised us that we'd face the same kind of challenges in battle, only then our lives would be on the line.

I slapped at a mosquito on my arm, then scratched a bite on my neck that had swollen to the size of a quarter. Whooping, I ran into the ocean fully clothed. Roy, Wilsie, and Eugene followed. No mosquito would follow us there. We desert-bred men dunked and splashed each other, finding some relief from the heat. The water was warm, though, too warm to be really refreshing. It held that warmth even at night. When we staggered out onto the beach, our fatigues dried almost instantly in the mind-numbing heat.

That night, crammed with Roy into a foxhole maybe three feet deep and four feet wide, I actually managed to sleep. I liked knowing Roy was there. Partnering with my roommate from Tuba City was good, when everything else was so foreign. It was tough sleeping in a semisitting position. But both of us had grown up sleeping on desert ground, ground baked harder than the sands of New Caledonia.

We woke up to a pleasant morning. The temperature was less wilting than it would be later in the day. Here on Grande Terre, no sounds of bombing or guns disturbed our sleep. We knew we'd better enjoy the silence while we could.

By late October 1942, we felt ready. The code was indelible, engraved into our brains. We had practiced night landings and hand-to-hand combat. Thirteen of us code talkers from the New Caledonia training camp, me and Roy among them, received our orders. We would join the other members of the 1st Marine Division who were already invading Guadalcanal. I looked around at my buddies, noticed the sudden stiffness in their posture. Everyone was scared.

The Japanese who held Guadalcanal were trained not to surrender. Their war strategy revolved around the Bushido code, an ancient "way of the warrior" first developed by the samurai. This code of conduct extolled loyalty and obedience. Soldiers were required to fight to the death and to take as many of their enemies with them as they could. Even facing impossible odds, Japanese soldiers chose to blow themselves up—hoping to kill American soldiers in the process—rather than surrender. They would die for the emperor. Their Shinto religion taught that this behavior was both expected and honorable.

The Japanese believed that they, by divine right, should rule the world. Their societal structure was perfect, and all other nations should be subjugated to the Empire of the Rising Sun. Their belief in *Hakkō ichiu,* Japan's manifest destiny, taught them that all eight corners of the world would one day be under one roof—that is, the control of Japan's imperial and divine emperor.

The Yamato race, the dominant race in Japan, had taken its name from the Yamato Court in fourth-century Japan. Sixteen centuries of history and culture had given the Yamatos a feeling of solidarity and entitlement. Their bloodline was pure, while according to their propaganda, that of many Americans had been mongrelized by crossbreeding. In the minds of the Japanese, Americans were weak, materialistic, and unwilling to die for their country. The people of the Land of the Rising Sun convinced themselves that the Americans were subhuman. For a soldier of this pure race to return from war alive when his peers had been killed in battle was a disgrace. To drive this point home, it was not unusual for a Japanese commander to beat one of his own soldiers senseless.

Soon the barbaric behavior of the Japanese, whose wounded soldiers would try to kill Allied corpsmen who came to their aid, made *them* seem less than human to the Americans.

Americans did not share the Japanese desire to die. U.S. soldiers fought valiantly, but when the odds became impossible, they knew that capture was no dishonor. Some thought of it as preferable to death, while others, having observed the cruelty of our enemy, feared capture more than death. At any rate, there was no judgment rendered by United States troops against a man who was captured. Facing an enemy who thought so differently from the way we did was scary.

CHAPTER TWELVE

The Secret Code Passes Muster

Early November to December 1942: Guadalcanal

Roy and I had made it to the beach alive, wading among floating bodies. We'd dug our first battle-time foxhole and now sat, soggy and scared, in that hole.

The Japanese preferred to attack at night. We had been told that almost every night, at midnight, a single bomber flew over. "Midnight Charlie," the island veterans called him, although there were undoubtedly many "Charlies," each taking his turn at keeping U.S. troops awake. Midnight Charlie flew slowly, his siren wailing and navigational lights blinking, making sure everyone knew he was there. Men on the islands would fire artillery at him, but he generally flew too high to be in range. Then he'd drop his bombs.

If the enemy attacked that night, Roy and I had our equipment ready. Each of us had been issued three hand grenades, a small packet of bullets, dextrose and salt tablets, some sulfa pills and sulfa powder in case we got shot, a field dressing, and K rations. We'd been instructed to take a sulfa pill and sprinkle sulfa powder over any open wounds if we got hit.

The powder was supposed to keep the wound from getting infected. Popular word was that the powder felt cold on the skin, and it helped to alleviate pain. We all hoped that was true. Sulfa drugs were the precursors of penicillin.

Ironically enough, one of our staples was a bar of Fels-Naptha, the same brown soap we'd had our teeth brushed with in boarding school. We were expected to do our own laundry whenever we got a chance, using that lye soap. A waist-belted pouch held some of the necessities, specifically ammunition, and we wore a cartridge belt as well. We placed our mess kits in a top-opening haversack that we carried on our backs, and our canteens hung from a loop on the back of our belt. Our folding shovel was attached in an upright position to one side of the haversack. A bedroll coiled in an upside-down *U* around the top of the haversack, and a poncho was either slung around the bedroll or stuffed inside.

In the wet foxhole, each of us had his ammunition pouch belted on and his haversack within easy reach. We could put our hands on anything we needed in the dark. In addition, we each had two mosquito nets, one for our head and another to cover our body.

"You awake?" I whispered.

Roy whispered back, *"Ouu."*

"What are you doing?"

"About to check on my grenades," Roy said, thrusting one hand into his ammunition pouch.

"Yeah. I got mine." I felt for my hand grenades, encountering three spheres, furrowed like pineapples. For a moment I could almost feel I was back in boot camp, where I'd first hefted a grenade. Heavy and deadly. "I'm all squared away," I said, using the lingo we'd learned in boot camp.

Roy tapped his rifle. "I hope this thing fires okay wet. No way to keep it dry. I might have got some sand in it, too."

"It'll fire," I said. "No sand. You just cleaned it. Don't worry."

"You think I should zip it into that sack?" Roy referred to the long leather sack that zipped open to accept a rifle. Although the sacks were designed to keep water and sand out of the rifles, we hadn't used them on Guadalcanal because we wanted our weapons to be easily accessible. None of us wanted to fumble with a zippered case when we needed our rifle *now*.

"What if the Banzai come?" I asked him.

Both of us had heard horror stories about the Japanese suicide attackers whose name, Banzai, was shorthand for the phrase *Tennō heika banzai,* meaning "May the emperor live one thousand years." They struck on foot, at night. When we heard them yelling, *"Banzai! Banzai!"* we knew we would witness a suicide, unless they killed us first. The anticipation of either possibility was awful, demoralizing.

"If they come, and your rifle is all zippered into that case . . ."

"You're right," said Roy. "I'll keep it out."

I felt inside my ammo pouch. The packet of bullets was soaking wet. But they, too, would fire. Everything had to work, even underwater. Uncle Sam had planned for that.

"You think they gave us enough bullets?" asked Roy.

I shrugged. "They must know how many."

"You think we'll use them all?"

My jaw tensed. "I hope not." Shooting a man wouldn't be like shooting a coyote. Or a porcupine.

The next morning before sunrise, Roy, still crouched in the foxhole on Guadalcanal, pulled out his medicine bag. I reached into my pants pocket and did the same. The soft thumb-sized object, buckskin stitched into a cylindrical shape, gave me comfort. Designed to protect me, it had been made by my family and blessed by a medicine man. That medicine bag connected me to home, to the prayers of my relatives. It protected me, and gave me confidence that I would survive. I rubbed the tiny black arrowhead attached by a wrap of rawhide to the outside of the bag. A white rock and several other small objects tucked inside had special meaning for me. The bag also held corn pollen, taken from the tassels of corn plants back home.

Roy's medicine bag was different from mine, but they both had the same purpose: protection. No two medicine bags were identical, because their contents were personal, but one ingredient was always the same— bright yellow corn pollen. The other elements were specific to the person who owned the bag. Perhaps a small piece of turquoise, or other small mementos. No one talked about the contents of his medicine bag. Someone who disliked you could use their knowledge of the bag's components to cause you harm. Only people real close to you, like your children, should know about the contents of your medicine bag. There's a lot of power in those things. It's something you don't play with.

Inside the medicine bag, my finger touched the pollen, a velvety-smooth powder. It hadn't stayed dry—nothing had during the landing— but it was safe. *Good.* Keeping it in the heavy pocket of my pants had been the right move. I pinched some pollen, touching it to my tongue and the top of my head. Like the other Navajo men, I always knew which direction was east—where the sun rises, where life begins. I gestured to the east, the south, the west, and the north, completing my first morning blessing sitting in a wet hole in the South Pacific war.

A white T-shirt hung on a branch, maybe twelve feet away from Roy's and my foxhole. Someone had tossed it there the night before. Other arriving Marines had dug in farther down the tree line—some ten or twenty, others thirty, forty, and fifty feet away from Roy and me. During the night, the men all seemed to notice the shirt at different times. Was it a Jap? Shots, aimed at that shirt, rang out all night long. They zipped just over our heads.

I tapped Roy's shoulder and gestured toward the shirt with a movement of my lips. "Look."

"*Ouu!*" Roy shook his head.

The shirt flapped, a torn rag in the breeze. As dawn broke, someone pulled it from the branch, counting the twenty-one "friendly fire" bullet holes. Roy and I had made it safely through a night riddled with bullets. We'd slept very little, if at all, but the blessing helped to refresh us. We needed to be sharp. Today was the day we were going to start using the new code in battle.

Some communications officers on Guadalcanal greeted us Navajos with skepticism. Yes, they'd been given notice about the arriving code talkers. And yes, the old Shackle coding system was slow. Yet the notion of changing to something new during the heat of conflict filled battle-weary minds with doubt.

My group of code talkers was assigned to just such a doubter, Lieutenant Hunt, signal officer under General Alexander Vandergrift. When we Navajos assigned to him had arrived, Hunt just shook his head. He knew of our mission, but he had never worked with a group of Indians, and he had faith in the old code. Also, he was one of the officers who hated the idea of switching tactics in the middle of a major military operation.

He had decided to test the new code immediately and had given us a message to send out on our first night. Directly after the transmission began, panicked calls came in. Hunt's other radio operators jammed our Navajo speech, thinking the Japanese had broken into their frequency. By then it was dark, and the annoyed Hunt postponed the test.

That next morning Lieutenant Hunt continued with the trial of the code. He ordered his radiomen not to jam the transmissions, then told us code talkers to do our best. The test would determine whether or not he could use us! Both the code talkers and the standard communications men were given the same message, one Hunt estimated would take four hours to transmit and receive using the old Shackle protocol.

With the Shackle method, a mechanical coding machine was used to encode a written message. The encoded message was then sent via voice. These encoded messages were a jumble of numbers and letters, and unlike the Navajo code, were meaningless to the person transmitting them. At the receiving end, a cipher was used to decode the message. The entire process was cumbersome and prone to error.

While the men utilizing the Shackle code waited for the encoding machine to accomplish its work, one of our men, I think it was William McCabe, transmitted the message to another code talker. I can't remember who. The message that Hunt had estimated would take four hours by Shackle took only two and a half minutes by Navajo code—an impossible feat by current standards. And the message was transmitted accurately, word for word. Lieutenant Hunt was impressed.

But we Navajo code talkers already knew our code was good. None of us wanted it to go unused. With a code that could keep military plans and movements secret, our country would outmaneuver the Japanese. We were sure of it.

Even after Hunt's test, American fighting men who overheard the Navajo messages continued to be alarmed, thinking the Japanese had broken into the U.S. frequency. Communications men tried to jam the strange sounds. To identify ourselves as U.S. troops, and to keep our transmissions from being jammed, we code talkers needed a clear tag. We initiated our messages with the words "New Mexico" or "Arizona." That was followed by the time and date, spoken in Navajo. We finished off with the time and date again, then with either *gah, ne-ahs-jah,* the letters *R* and *O,* standing for "roger and out" or with simply *ne-ahs-jah* for "out."

None of us liked to think about it, but we had also planned a strategy in case we got captured. If the Japanese ever forced a code talker to send a message, he would alert the person on the receiving end by embedding the words "do or die," in Navajo of course, somewhere inside the message.

When I looked around me at the other men, I could easily pick out the members of the 1st Marine Division who'd been fighting on the island for three months. They moved like zombies, their eyes focused straight ahead. None smiled or changed expression. They seemed not to notice us new guys—or anything else.

That first full day on Guadalcanal, after we passed Lieutenant Hunt's test, runners began arriving with messages. The runners, also called spotters, performed the dangerous assignment of scouting ahead of U.S. lines into enemy territory and reporting back on the locations of Japanese troops and armaments. They delivered messages involving combat details to communication personnel, to the front lines, and to the rear echelon. It was a dangerous job, especially at night, when they could be mistaken for Banzai. It was a job originally assigned to us code talkers, one we had trained for, and occasionally we went out on a run. But generally we were too busy sending messages.

Roy and I grabbed the radio. We both wore headsets. We moved to a position close to a Japanese nest of eighty-millimeter machine guns. A continuous barrage of shells from those Japanese guns wrought heavy damage on our U.S. fighting men.

A runner approached, handing me a message written in English. It was my first battlefield transmission in Navajo code. I'll never forget it. Roy pressed the transmit button on the radio, and I positioned my microphone to repeat the information in our code. I talked while Roy cranked. Later, we would change positions.

"Beh-na-ali-tsosie a-knah-as-donih ah-toh nish-na-jih-goh dah-di-kad ah-deel-tahi." Enemy machine-gun nest on your right flank. Destroy.

Suddenly, just after my message was received, the Japanese guns exploded, destroyed by U.S. artillery.

I shouted, "You see that?"

"Sure did." Roy grinned, but didn't stop cranking the TBX radio he held. The radio, the size of a shoe box, weighed thirty pounds. It stored up electricity generated when the crank was turned. Both of us wore headphones so we could hear each other. Thin red and yellow cords attached the microphone and headsets to the radio. There was a button for transmitting and one for receiving.

"U.S. artillery nailed them," I said.

As I viewed this small victory—a direct result of my transmission—the wet, the fear, the danger . . . all receded for a few seconds.

Roy and I ran and crawled to a new position, knowing the Japanese were experts at targeting the locations from which messages had been sent. The enemy picked up U.S. radio signals and delivered mortar shells to those locations. We never stayed on the radio a second longer than we had to. And the frequencies we used changed every day. Each day we were careful to dial in the new frequency on the TBX box.

Immediately we focused on sending the next message, moving, then sending the next. Bullets zipping around us kept the level of noise high but that didn't keep us from hearing incoming messages. Luckily both the headsets and our ears were good, and we heard the Navajo words in spite of the war exploding around us.

Occasionally, I looked over at Roy, who tirelessly carried and cranked the radio. He nodded, still cranking.

After a couple of hours, we switched positions. I cranked and Roy spoke. My head reeled with Navajo and English words, with coordinates, with messages sent. It was good just to crank for a while, good not to worry about slipping, making a mistake that could cost lives.

Artillery shells whistled past us. I dived, the radio under me. Roy lay flat out on the ground. We never stopped transmitting.

More than twenty-four hours passed before we were able to grab a few hours of sleep.

We woke, still exhausted, in the hole we'd dug two days before.

"I'm starving," said Roy.

Snaking our way to the mess tent on all fours, we ducked bullets and artillery shells. At the mess we grabbed some cold food for fuel, waved the omnipresent flies away as best we could, and ate ravenously.

"Not like the hot food in boot camp," I said.

"Heck, no. That food was *good*," said Roy around a mouthful of cold Spam.

"Yeah, well, I'm eating everything I can hold," I told him. "You better do the same. No extra meat on those bones." I pointed at Roy's lanky frame with my thumb.

Roy grinned. "I weigh more than you do, I bet."

I shoveled a forkful of cold eggs into my mouth and swallowed. "Not too bad."

We returned to relaying messages. My throat grew raw with talk. Never before had I spoken so many words without a break. I gestured to Roy. He handed me a half-full metal canteen that looked like an over-blown whiskey flask. I drank, grabbed the TBX radio, and started crank-ing. We tried to ignore cramped muscles, gnawing stomachs, and the ordnance exploding around us.

Warships crammed the once-tranquil ocean along Guadalcanal's north shore. Bodies covered the beach. Then darkness moved in, thick with smoke, masking the grisly products of war.

Our messages relayed calls for ammunition, food, and medical equip-ment back to the supply ships waiting offshore. Messages transmitted the locations of enemy troops to U.S. artillerymen. Messages told of something unexpected that had happened in battle. Messages reported on our own troop movements. Messages forwarded casualty numbers, the Navajo code keeping the Japanese from learning of American losses in each foray. Throughout the days of battle to come, we sent those num-bers back to our commanders on the ships each night.

After being in operation for just forty-eight hours, our secret lan-guage was becoming indispensable.

The hilly terrain on Guadalcanal posed real problems for the men oper-ating mortars and artillery. Muzzle-loaded mortars were low-velocity, short-range weapons with a high trajectory, particularly well suited to uneven terrain. A mortar could drop into an enemy trench that artillery fire flew right over. Shells fired by field artillery reached a higher velocity and followed a flatter trajectory. Howitzers were similar to mortars in function, but larger.

The men firing all of these weapons dealt with a serious issue.

Artillery, howitzers, and mortars targeted an enemy who was frequently nose to nose with the American soldiers at the front. Marksmen had to clear the hills and the heads of our own troops, causing them no injury, while drawing an accurate bead on the enemy. This became especially ticklish when we were "walking fire in." That meant that our weapons were shooting behind the enemy and drawing them closer to the American troops at the front line. As they drew closer, we continued to fire behind them, moving both our fire and the Japanese troops closer and closer to our own troops. There was no room for error in a maneuver like that. The old Shackle communications system took so long to encode and decode, and it was so frequently inaccurate, that using it for the transmission of on-the-fly target coordinates was a perilous proposition. Frequently, in the midst of battle, instead of using the Shackle code, the Marines had transmitted in English. They knew the transmissions were probably being monitored by the Japanese, so they salted the messages liberally with profanity, hoping to confuse the enemy.

We code talkers changed all that.

Roy and I traveled close to the mortars. And the mortars, due to their short range, placed us well within the enemy's line of fire. Not as close as the riflemen, who were always out front leading the attack, but still close.

Sweat streamed down my back. I transmitted coordinates detailing the locations of Japanese and American troops. I knew men's lives depended upon the accuracy of each word. I wiped my brow with a sleeve, but never stopped talking. Out of the corner of one eye, I saw a flash of fire. Sand and shrapnel kicked up into the heavy gray sky. I kept talking.

Just then, a spotter, sent out to locate a pocket of Japanese soldiers and artillery, returned. Someone handed a slip of paper to me, bearing the exact Japanese location. The same paper also reported the location of forward U.S. troops.

I squinted, rubbed my eyes, read the paper again. Any error could cause the death of my fellow fighting men. I'd sent hundreds of messages. Messages swam in my brain, jamming and tumbling over one another. I shook my head to clear it.

I translated the data into Navajo code and spoke into the microphone that fit neatly into my fist like a baseball. I glanced in the direction my transmission would travel. Roy and I crouched so close to the American artillery and mortars that I could almost have shouted the information.

I spoke clearly, carefully. I pictured the code talker who received my message translating it back into English for the gunnery men. I imagined those men planning a trajectory, one that would fire over the heads of the Americans and hit the Japanese.

If a soldier was shot right beside us, we had been warned not to stop and help. Our transmissions could not be interrupted.

That day, as the afternoon waned, communications slowed. Roy and I whispered in Navajo, joking with each other, trying to stay awake. Messages generally started coming in around 5 A.M., so we woke up and plunged right into work. When things were busy, nothing else entered our minds, just the delivery of information. Lulls were more difficult than a steady stream of messages. Periods of quiet allowed exhaustion to creep into our brains like a work-worn dog, turn around three times, and settle down, demanding sleep.

We lay on our stomachs, on a relatively level stretch of land. Normally we tried to stay away from flat places, because they afforded poor protection. But we had a clump of bushes for cover, and the enemy had been lobbing constant fire, hitting the ground only a dozen yards away, so we didn't dare run to a more protected place.

I rested my Springfield bolt-action '03 rifle next to my torso. I knew the hardware well, the smooth metal and wooden parts fitting together like the work of a fine craftsman. I had taken that rifle apart and put it back together blindfolded, in complete darkness. But the well-made weapon—of World War I vintage—was less important than my communications gear. I knew I would have to use that rifle, especially at night when the Banzai came. Yet even though we code talkers had proven ourselves to be excellent marksmen in basic training, our responsibilities differed from those of other combat Marines. Our primary job was to talk, not to shoot.

The red light on the TBX radio blinked on. A small beep sounded, loud enough for Roy and me to hear, but not loud enough to alert the Japanese. A message. I pushed the receive button, and we both listened. It was Roy's turn to talk, mine to crank. An explosion flared, not three hundred feet away. It was a daisy cutter, the kind of bomb that threw shrapnel out sideways, exploding outward rather than up. A jagged piece of shrapnel dug a hole in the beach nearby, but Roy didn't seem to notice.

I whispered to myself, "Damn Japs."

Roy pressed the earphones to his head, obviously straining to hear the Navajo message. He nodded, translating the message in his head to English and writing it down.

"Artillery lieutenant," Roy said, turning to me.

I signaled a runner, who grabbed the message. "The lieutenant," I said, raising my chin in the direction of a U.S. tank bearing ninety-millimeter guns. The runner took off.

A few minutes later, he was back with a response. Roy read the English note, and—as all of us did—simultaneously translated it in his head to the Navajo code. He transmitted it.

The Navajo code words were never written when we transmitted messages. That made us men living, walking code machines. And even if the enemy somehow managed to link our Navajo language to the new code, there was nothing written to help them learn the unfamiliar words.

If the Navajo oral tradition had not been as strong as it was, human error could have rendered this method of communication impractical. But we code talkers called upon powers of concentration that had been developed by the constant exchange of unwritten information. As far as I know, we generally transmitted our messages flawlessly. If someone did make an error, someone else in the Navajo network would catch it and send an alert. And we never relaxed, never let up.

I looked around and realized it was growing dark. Roy and I had been transmitting all day and would continue through the night and the next day with—if we were lucky—an hour or two to decompress before starting in again. I pulled a roll of tape from my cargo belt and bit a piece off with my teeth. I stuck the tape over the message light of the radio, masking the red light from Japanese eyes in the dark.

"You think we'd get more sleep on board ship?" Roy asked.

"What?" I chuckled. "And miss all this fun."

We men worked in pairs. Officially, two pairs of men who partnered together were coupled into a group of four, and two groups of four worked together with two rotators, bringing the total number in each band to ten. Generally, we ten sailed together on the same ship. When we reached an island, four of the code talkers in our band remained on board ship and the other six disembarked. Our positions—land versus ship—changed with different campaigns. Once onshore, the land-based men stayed in touch with those on the ship and with each other so everyone knew what was happening.

I spent most of my time onshore, actively sending messages. And I, like the other code talkers, stayed in communication with all the talkers as much as possible, regardless of assigned groups. We'd report what was happening in battle around us. We'd let the rear echelon know when we needed reinforcements and give them the hot dope on whether a particular strategy was working. If someone screwed up and our men were targeted by friendly fire, we'd send a message through requesting a halt. That type of message was always heeded when sent by Navajo code, because the Navajo men receiving our messages knew the Japanese could not fake them.

Our staying in touch had another advantage: if a man heard an error being made in a transmitted message, he'd click the transmit and receive buttons on his TBX radio several times. That click acted as a signal, telling the transmitter to recheck and retransmit his message. When messages were flying, it was difficult to tell where the click came from and to determine which message might contain an error. But we were fierce about deciphering any problems and correcting any misunderstandings. People make too much of how difficult the code was. We knew it like we knew our own names, so it wasn't difficult for us. But every man worried about making some sort of error. The strain of having to be perfect ate at us. It weighed upon us every minute of every day and every hour of every night. Every bit of information had to be accurate: where the Japanese were, which way they were going to move, how many men they had. No one wanted any mistakes to get through and to endanger our own men.

In addition, we had a battle liaison, a communications man, to whom we reported the day's events, especially during periods of fighting. Each morning, he attended strategy sessions and tried to prepare us for what to expect of the day ahead. The Marines cared well for us men and attempted to fully utilize our skills in gaining an advantage over the enemy.

Despite my exhaustion and the danger on Guadalcanal, I was glad to work the land position rather than the sea. When there was a communications lull aboard ship, I knew the code talkers there were assigned other duties. They might be ordered to unload cargo or inventory the supplies. Their attention was diverted from the battle at hand. On the island, there was rarely a lull, and we concentrated on one crucial thing only: relaying the needs of troops in the midst of combat.

A spotter arrived. He ducked down next to me to hand me a message. I now manned the microphone.

"Fighter pilots," he said.

American planes were scheduled to drop bombs ahead of the American line. The message I held gave the coordinates of forward U.S. troop locations on the island. Before we code talkers arrived, some of the pilots had dropped their bombs as soon as they reached the island, hitting U.S. troops with "friendly" fire, then reversing course and flying back to their aircraft carrier. I'd heard how the brass got all over the pilots' butts when they almost bombed my 1st Marine Division. Now we code talkers were utilized, relaying coordinates that would be forwarded to the pilots, making sure that the pilots knew the locations of their own troops.

The runner took off, crouching low to avoid enemy fire. Exhausted, I took a sip of water from my canteen and translated the information into code. I relayed it to an aircraft carrier sitting offshore. As I finished, another runner arrived with another message to be sent.

Roy reached into his shirt pocket and handed me a crushed packet of crackers. "Here. Eat something. You look like hell."

As it grew darker, we moved in closer to a couple of Marines who wielded a machine gun. Around nine at night, we heard footsteps. We made out a Japanese soldier running towards our position, waving a sword. He began screaming, *"Banzai!"* He ran straight up, his full height, not even crouching to try to protect himself. When he was maybe a hundred feet away, one of our guys opened fire. Several bullets hit the Banzai warrior, but he didn't drop. He took his sword with both hands and plunged it into his stomach. Then he dropped. A sacred death. It made me feel sick, seeing that, seeing how a Japanese would gut himself rather than be captured by the Americans. I thought about American men I had seen butchered by the Japanese, trying to feel like it was okay that the guy had stabbed himself. But it never felt okay. Seeing death come, on either side, was something I never forgot.

Total madmen, the Banzai terrified U.S. troops all through the war. Each Banzai was a one-man suicide mission, intent on getting himself killed while taking out as many enemy combatants as possible. The Banzai adhered to the Japanese doctrine of blind obedience to authority, even when it meant their own death. The suicidal Japanese always attacked the foxholes after dark and before dawn. The random nature of the attacks kept us Marines awake in our foxholes. And if we managed to sleep, we knew we could wake with a Japanese sword slicing our throat.

After a few minutes, when the Banzai didn't move, one of the non-

Navajo Marines dashed toward the body. He bent down and took the Japanese sword. "Souvenir," he said, turning back toward us and scrambling back under cover in his foxhole. If the brass found him with that sword, they would confiscate it. It was against rules to take anything from an enemy's body.

That particular prohibition wasn't needed for most Navajos. Our religion taught us that you didn't touch property belonging to the dead. However, there were some Navajos willing to risk touching the dead in order to acquire pieces of clothing or hair to be used back home in ceremonies. I wasn't one of them. Those dead Japanese were in no danger from me. I would have avoided the dead altogether if I could have.

Things were quiet. I found it eerie how some days could feel almost normal, how men walked around almost as though we weren't engaged in war. It was morning, and I had managed a few hours of sleep the night before. Roy and I and a couple of the other code talkers sat among the endless thickets of palm trees and vines, eating military rations—Spam, and corned beef out of a can, and crackers.

"Just like Grandma makes," joked one of the men.

"At least there's plenty of it," I said, forking a large bite of Spam.

"Yeah," Roy said, "When we have time to eat." He stuffed a packet of crackers into his shirt pocket.

A man held his nose as he chewed.

"Tough to eat with the smell of rotting bodies, enit?" someone said.

I said, "What's tough is knowing what that smell is."

Roy glanced back toward the beach, although we could only smell it, not see it, from where we ate. He had that faraway, combat-veteran look in his eyes. "All those men. Theirs and ours."

The stifling smell of decaying bodies permeated the moist, hot air. Soldiers driving bulldozers tried to cover the bodies with sand when they could, but often they were thinly covered or totally exposed.

A Marine picked his way through the underbrush with his dog, a German shepherd, close by his side. Heads turned and we watched the pair pass by. Those dogs were impressive. They sneaked up on the Japanese, hunting them as a soldier would. When we came upon an enemy bunker, the dogs could tell by the smell whether it was empty or occupied. They also located snipers, high up in the trees. And even at night they could sniff out hostiles. Their handlers would turn them loose, and they'd range back and forth across the area. Their tails stood up when they had found an enemy combatant, and their ears stood up at attention, their nose pointing. The dogs never attacked the Japanese, though. They were too valuable to be put at risk, which is kind of ironic, when you think about all the men who were lost. The dogs were really smart, and it made me feel good knowing that one was on patrol while we ate.

My feet were covered with blisters, huge things that were always growing larger, so full of fluid that they felt like they could explode. I took out my knife—my Ka-bar—and popped the blisters to relieve the pressure, then spread a butterlike substance provided by the corpsmen over them. I stood and pulled my socks from the branch of a bush where I'd hung them to dry, then brushed sand from my bare feet. I tossed a second pair of socks to Roy.

"Here. Dry."

He sat down to pull on his boots, raising each and shaking it first to make sure a scorpion hadn't crawled inside. We'd been warned to dry our feet and socks whenever we could in order to avoid foot problems, like toenail fungus. Any scratch could become an open sore, and sores festered in the tropical climate. Some of the men developed fungal infections and ringworm. Almost everyone got sores that ulcerated, festering like chicken pox. We called them "jungle rot." They itched so much that you couldn't help scratching, and that made them worse. The corpsmen gave us a salve to heal the sores, but we seemed to keep getting them. Dysentery, with extreme dehydration, was also a common complaint. So was typhus, which was caused by jungle insects. Corpsmen handed out various pills to all of us. Used to these daily doses of medicine, Roy and I swallowed them dry. Malaria-carrying mosquitoes arrived like fleets of fighter planes, attacking in swarms, especially virulent at night. For that, we were given small, bitter yellow pills—atabrine—and were administered various shots at least once every week or two.

"Hear that?" I asked.

"What?" said Roy.

"The bells. Like the sheep."

"No sheep here," said one of the men.

Another said, "It's prayers. Someone back home is praying for us."

I had noticed the bells before, usually around noon. Even thousands of miles from home, in conditions I could never have imagined, it was comforting, the sound of the sheep and goats coming in. Even though I had not been able to attend, my family had performed a protection ceremony for me, a Blessing Way, after basic training. I felt sure they continued to pray for me and burned sage or chips of cedar, fanning the smoke over their bodies. Their prayers were carried across the miles as the pure, bright chime of the bells. The clear tones told me that I was still in good faith.

In this place, with its constant fog, heat, and more than one hundred inches of annual rain, I pictured the dry sunny days, the crystalline clarity, of New Mexico. Guadalcanal's mountains, their highest peaks as tall as eight thousand feet, reared up as a natural barrier between the northern and southern coasts of the ninety-mile-long island. So there were no sweeping views like the ones at Grandma's place, unless you looked out at the ocean. And vegetation, much more dense than that of New Mexico, covered most of the flat areas of the South Pacific island. Clumps of kunai grass, taller than a man, with edges that cut like hacksaws, grew like lethal weapons in the high meadows. When we tramped through that grass, we crossed our arms over our chests, under our jacket or T-shirt.

Still, I saw in my memory the oak trees and piñons of home.

Sitting in a soggy foxhole, wondering always where the Japanese were and whether they'd attack that day—or worse, that night—my fellow code talkers and I endured. During our first weeks entrenched on Guadalcanal, the war news was mixed. The Japanese and American navies traded victories. And after that, the battles shifted in favor of the United States.

The Slot shipping lane between Guadalcanal and the neighboring Florida Islands had become a supply corridor controlled by the Japanese. The task of resupplying their soldiers could only be accomplished by ship, since the United States controlled the single airfield on the island. And the Japanese were masters of Naval battle. Soon, however, the Americans developed their own skill at sea.

In mid-November 1942, the United States made up for the heavy losses they'd suffered in August, early in the Guadalcanal campaign, before we code talkers arrived. The three-day Battle of Guadalcanal, fought off Tassafaronga Point and Cape Esperance, resulted in the American Navy sinking thirteen Japanese ships: two battleships, a heavy cruiser, three destroyers, and seven transports. That battle was fought in a portion of the Slot that came to be nicknamed "Ironbottom Sound" because of all the sunken ships that lined the ocean floor there. The United States damaged nine other enemy ships. Aircraft from Henderson Field destroyed another four Japanese transports. American losses came in at two light cruisers and seven destroyers, with nine other ships damaged. The United States was making a dent in the Japanese Naval mastery of the Pacific.

On November 30, Americans sank another Japanese destroyer near Tassafaronga while losing a cruiser and taking on heavy damage to three other cruisers. Despite the major damages that the U.S. fleet had sustained, the Japanese Navy withdrew from Guadalcanal, taking with them troops and supplies that they had been unable to land. After that, the Allies gained confidence in their ability to rout the Japanese seagoing forces. Our enemies, who preferred transporting supplies in the dark of night, were unable to adequately resupply their troops on Guadalcanal.

Meantime, the Marines on the island, and with them we code talkers, fought the more than twenty thousand Japanese troops. After three weeks or so, even with the bombs and bullets flying, I began to feel at ease. I felt sure of myself. I knew what I was doing out there, just behind the front lines. Most of the Marines I was with knew we had a special job, using our own language. They treated us well. I never experienced any bad treatment. We all got along, and it was important, knowing that our buddies were there at all times, looking after us and us after them. In the throes of combat, especially, everybody looked out for one another. We did our best to see that everyone was safe.

Many Japanese soldiers fled to the chain of mountains that bisected Guadalcanal from west to east. These mountains dominated the land, leaving only a narrow coastal region on the east, south, and west, with a wider strip of sea-level land to the north where the American troops had landed. Heavily forested Mount Austen, actually the summit of a group of steep ridges, provided shelter for many of the enemy, becoming a key Japanese stronghold. From Gifu Ridge, abutting Mount Austen to the southwest, the enemy could look out over Henderson Field.

We Marines had to take Mount Austen.

CHAPTER THIRTEEN

We Must Take Mount Austen

December 1942 to February 1943: Guadalcanal

The entire 1st Marine Division fought two enemies: exhaustion and the Japanese. Battle-weary guys shuffled along like they'd lost everything. In heavy, prolonged combat, we all felt like we were losing our minds, our memories. We moved with our eyes about to pop out, looking straight ahead, not really focusing on anything, dragging ourselves around like scarecrows. After a while, we didn't even look up when fighter planes flew overhead—even though they might be dropping the bomb that had our name on it.

During a lull, we could look around and see the guys who weren't going to last. They began talking to themselves in a steady stream, and their eyes focused where there was nothing to see. It was sad and really scary. I prayed to the Navajo Gods and to the Anglo God when I saw those guys. Prayed for them, and prayed that I wouldn't end up like them.

By the time Mount Austen became the hot spot on Guadalcanal, hiding thousands of Japanese troops in caves that pockmarked its rough terrain, days and nights followed each other in a sleep-deprived blur. It was lucky we worked in pairs, helping each other with the translations into and out of code. Exhausted as we were, I think any man working alone would have collapsed under the pressure. We listened to each other's transmissions to be sure that no mistakes were made, helping our partners through the long days. Muggy heat brought near-continuous rain. Men, many weakened by malaria, fought on the sword edge of exhaustion. Too many died. Tractors assigned to bury the mangled bodies couldn't keep up with the number of corpses piling up on the beach.

In a rare few hours of quiet, Roy and I sat with several other Marines in a multiple-man foxhole. Stout protective coconut logs spanned the roof of the shelter. We men ate cold K-rations. We each held a small bottle of beer, and most nursed it slowly. The Marine brass had okayed the beer because it helped us relax. Some Marines from the deep south had even set up a still, producing homemade liquor. They shared with everyone, but right then their supplies were depleted, and beer was the only alcoholic drink available.

"You think we'll ever get off this island?" I asked.

"Soon," said Roy. "We're almost done here, don't you think?"

Another Marine, not a Navajo, dropped a Vienna sausage, brushed the sand off it, and took a bite. "I heard we're going to be relieved. Another regiment of the Second Marine Division is coming."

"You sure?" I asked him.

The man shrugged. "That's what I heard."

Speaking Navajo, I turned to another code talker, asking him what he thought. Face hollow and eyes exhausted, my buddy answered in Navajo, "I hope it's soon."

"Hey, talk American, Chief." The Marine wiped fat flies from a miniature hot dog, took another bite, and grinned. "No offense."

I switched to English. "I hope those reinforcements come soon." Then I smiled, not minding the Marine's request for English. "English. Just like boarding school. English all the time."

The other Navajos groaned. "*Ouu,* boarding school," several said at once.

I leaned forward, feeling that sinking feeling that thoughts of boarding school always brought, even there at war. Then I looked up at the others. "Without boarding school, we wouldn't be code talkers."

It was a good thing, serving our country. I couldn't argue with that. Elbows propped on knees, I looked around at my buddies. I just hoped the war would end soon. Before my life and their lives ended.

It was December of 1942. We men of the 1st Marine Division looked at one another in disbelief. *Finally,* our tired eyes all seemed to say. Then someone cheered, and bedlam erupted.

Official word had come. Relief. Major General Alexander Patch was ordered to take command of the Guadalcanal effort. The 2d Marine Division, soon to be joined by their Sixth Regiment, would stay on Guadalcanal. General Vandegrift's battle-weary 1st Marine Division, most of whom had been fighting on Guadalcanal since August 7, would go for R&R (rest and relaxation). I couldn't wait.

I celebrated with the other men of the 1st Marine Division. I looked around at the torn, pockmarked landscape we would soon be leaving. Worn out mentally and physically, I said a prayer of thanks for the coming relief:

In beauty I will rest my heart.
In beauty all will be in balance.
In beauty all will be restored.

"You ever been to Australia?" Roy asked me.

I laughed and shook my head.

"Me either. Never left the reservation until I joined the Marines."

"*Ouu.*" I grinned. "But Australia is exactly the place I want to go."

Australia was a country few of us Marines had ever visited. But when R&R was scheduled there, spirits soared. A Marine slapped me on the back. Aping an Australian accent, he said, "We'll get a side of Aussie beef, mate. Grill it up and eat it all in one sitting. Yeah."

With relief from battle imminent, I let myself relax a little. The sights and sounds of war had become familiar, and although they would never feel normal, at least I was able to cope. I knew there were still other islands to be taken, but pushed that thought to a back compartment of my mind, telling myself to think about R&R, to forget the battles waiting just beyond the horizon. At least, now, I felt reasonably sure that I would not let my country or the Marines down.

The corporal in charge of communications gathered us men. "Good job," he said. He singled out us Navajos. "Far as we can tell, the Japs haven't decoded one of your transmissions. Not one."

One of the Navajo men laughed. We others, even though we didn't know what was so funny, couldn't keep from joining in. Finally, holding his sides, the man gasped out, "What would the matrons back at boarding school think?"

"Yeah," said Roy. "Bars of brown soap for everyone."

Rain poured over the island in thick sheets. Nothing new for soggy Guadalcanal.

Roy and I sat in our shared foxhole. He wrung a pair of socks between his hands. "Darn things won't dry. Seems like I haven't had dry socks for weeks." He looked down at his feet, raising one from the water in the hole. "Look at these feet. They're going to rot."

I nodded. My feet were soaked, too. "Better put your socks and boots on. Wet is better than nothing."

Roy tugged the wet socks onto his feet, then pushed his feet into soaking boots. "When we get out of here, I'm going to hang socks outside the hogan every afternoon. Put them on when they're all hot. Hot and dry."

"*Ouu.*"

Roy and I prepared to leave Guadalcanal along with the rest of the 1st Marine Division. But at the last minute, a lieutenant pulled ten of us code talkers aside, Roy and me among them.

"Men, you've done an excellent job." He stopped, cleared his throat. "I'm afraid we can't afford to let you go. You are vital to the success of this campaign. The Second Marine Division still needs you men here."

Heavy silence settled over us. This was war. Any argument was useless, and we knew it. I looked across the beach, littered with the broken and worn-out equipment of war. I felt just as worn out as those useless vehicles and broken-up gun emplacements. But a used code talker couldn't be replaced by a new model off the factory floor. And there were too few of us to expect replacements the way other infantrymen could expect them. It was a crushing disappointment, not to be leaving with the rest of our division. We'd made good friends on the battlefield, where everyone depends on his buddies. It would be hard to see them leave while we stayed with the 2d Marine Division.

But we had no choice. We got ourselves squared away. We resolved to keep fighting.

On December 9, we watched as the other Marines from the 1st Division boarded transports for Australia. Many of the embarking men suffered from dysentery and malaria. They were emaciated, too weak to climb the rope nets on the sides of the transports. Sailors swarmed down the nets to help, and lines were dropped. The sick men were lifted bodily aboard the ships.

We code talkers waved good-bye to the friends we had made in the 1st Marine Division—some of whom were best buddies—and tried to prepare ourselves mentally to forge new bonds as the war continued.

Part of what was so hard on Guadalcanal was thinking that no one back home even knew what we Marines were doing. Or where we were fighting. And men were dying there. Thousands of men. We were all so tired and wrung out that we couldn't think straight and could barely speak—except when we had no choice, sending the code.

In actuality, we 1st Division Marines had been on the front pages of all the papers back home. And everyone had heard of Guadalcanal, an island none of us even knew of before the war. And when the rest of the 1st Marines reached Melbourne, Australia, they were met with cheering and ticker-tape parades. The Australians, whose port city, Darwin, had been attacked by the Japanese just as Pearl Harbor had been, loved the Yanks.

We were heroes back in the United States. But I don't think any of us, struggling as we were to keep going and to do our jobs, could have felt less like a hero.

As promised, General Alexander Patch arrived on Guadalcanal the same day the 1st Marine Division left us, December 9. We ten code talkers worked alongside the 2d Marine Division men who remained on the island. More than twenty thousand Japanese still infested the island, most of them in the ridges and mountains. Until the Sixth Marine Regiment arrived to round out the 2d Marine Division and the Army infantry troops who still remained, Patch assigned us to clean up hot spots around the jungle perimeter near Point Cruz and in the series of hills just west of Point Cruz.

General Patch assigned an assault on Gifu Ridge, southwest of Mount Austen, to the 132nd Infantry, an Army regiment. On January 1, 1943, the 1st, 2nd and 3rd Battalions from the 132nd Regiment approached Gifu from the east, southeast, and north respectively. The 2nd Battalion, approaching from the southeast, reached Mount Austen's summit, but was driven back. Five more times the men attempting the summit were forced back down by Japanese troops led by Colonel Oka.

Roy and I relayed messages as rain poured over us and our weather-safe equipment. Fire from the Americans battered the Japanese on the ridge. Each shot was painstakingly positioned using information transmitted by us code talkers. Those artillery bombardments on the Mount Austen ridges eventually saved the infantry's 2nd Battalion from being overtaken by Oka's Japanese troops.

Now our Allied troops threatened the Japanese who were holed up in the ridges of Gifu and Mount Austen from every direction except the west. We dug in, awaiting reinforcements.

Finally relieved for a few hours, I leaned against my backpack, tried to get comfortable in the foxhole. Rain trickled down the neck of my uniform, snaking its way across my chest and back. I pulled out my Ka-bar and opened a can from my box of field rations. That knife was issued as a fighting knife, but it worked great as a can opener and a food chopper, too. I even cut bushes and small limbs with my Ka-bar and used it to loosen rocks and dirt when digging a foxhole.

"Don't forget to save that," Roy said.

I grunted, knowing what he meant. We'd been told to save the cans from our food. We'd put a few pebbles or pieces of other cans in them and string them up around our camp at night on wires so they'd make noise if an enemy came near.

In the sporadic light generated by munitions fire and enemy flares, I glanced at Roy. Out of traditional Navajo politeness, our eyes did not meet. "Remember all the grass?" I whispered. "How it grew up to your knees?"

Roy, sitting so close in the cramped foxhole that I heard his every breath, caught right on. "And no fences," he said. "The sheep could graze anywhere."

"*Ouu,*" I said. Yes.

I bent my knees so they stuck up above the water level in the foxhole. Even soaking wet, I felt enervated by the terrific heat and the humidity. Our body heat, coupled with the tropical weather, kept the water warm, too warm.

Somewhere nearby I heard a stage-whispered curse. "Damn crab, I'm gonna rip your guts out!"

Then, from farther away, several shots rang out. The guards must have been shooting crocodiles again.

Japanese were not the only scary inhabitants of Guadalcanal. We'd been warned about the crocodiles, which were plentiful and mostly active at night. They made several strange sounds, one that was a dry, trilling rasp, another that sounded like a cross between an inboard motor and the roar of a juvenile lion, and a third that was almost a purr, but very deep and ominous, punctuated with a higher rattle resembling a maraca. All those sounds were chilling at night, when you couldn't see where the animal was. And they were even more chilling when the animal tried to crawl into your foxhole. That happened to a couple of the men. They had to shoot the crocs.

Then there were huge crabs—blue-black or red-orange in color, some with bodies a foot in diameter—that ate the bodies of dead soldiers and attacked the live combatants at night. The crabs were ugly with long strong legs and viselike claws that could clip a finger off. They were more aggressive than the crocs. They dug into the sand during the day and came up to the surface at night. You'd hear a cracking noise as the crabs dug up through the sand. When we sent up flares to see whether there were any enemy troops near our foxholes, the red light of the flares would reveal a beach alive with thousands of dark crabs scuttling around looking for food. Crab bites were painful and prone to infection. Once they latched onto a leg or an arm, the crabs refused to release it.

The engineers built fences, from poles, that were designed to keep the crocs away from where we men bathed and swam. Sometimes that worked okay, but often the guards who were posted ended up shooting the crocodiles. The big animals swam so quietly that we couldn't hear them coming. But nothing kept those crabs away.

My thigh bumped against a lump in the water. I flinched. Carefully I prodded with my rifle butt. *Whew!* Just my canteen. The primal screech of a parrot raised the hair on the back of my neck. Seconds later, another bird responded from a palm tree behind the foxhole.

The stench of bodies filled my nostrils, so strong it became a taste in my mouth. I'd smelled the bodies of sheep killed by a coyote and left to rot after the predator had eaten his fill. I'd smelled burned animal carcasses after the livestock massacre. But these were the decaying bodies of men. I tried, but could not block that fact from conscious thought.

"I miss the smell of piñon," I said.

Roy grunted. "*Ouu*. Me, too."

I gazed out over the ocean. Maybe ten miles away there were lights. Ships. I gestured with my thumb. "Theirs or ours?"

Roy looked at me, his brows pulled together. "What?"

"Out there." I raised my chin toward the lights. Roy and I still practiced the Navajo custom of never pointing with our index finger, only with our chin, thumb, or lips. Using an index finger was disrespectful, almost as though the person pointing was going to poke someone.

"Let's hope they are ours," said Roy.

It was nerve-racking, not being able to tell about those ships. From ten miles out, shells from a ship's artillery could hit the island. A bullet whined. Then another. Bullets, not artillery. *Probably just the croc hunters,* I told myself. Still, the sound brought goose bumps to my arms, reminding me that the next rotting body could be mine. Or Roy's. I hunkered down, drawing my head into my shoulders. This Marine gig had looked so appealing from the warm, dry land of home.

Concentrate. Pray. I prayed to both the white and the Indian Gods. In boarding school, the Catholic priests had taught us to ask God for what we needed. And at home, my father had taught me to ask to walk in beauty. Those prayers pulled my thoughts away from death and back home to New Mexico. Immersed in thoughts of home, I tried to pass the last few hours of night in this waterlogged place.

Damn rain. Would it ever let up?

"Japanese sniper at your twelve o'clock! Japanese sniper at—"

"Chester! Wake up. You're dreaming."

I groaned and slit one eye open. Roy leaned over me. "The Sixth Regiment is here," he said. It was January 4, 1943. The Sixth Marine Regiment, part of the 2d Marine Division, was needed to augment the number of troops on the island now that the 1st Marine Division had left Guadalcanal for Australia.

I pulled myself up to a sitting position in the foxhole. Sure enough, a new flotilla of United States Naval vessels sat just offshore.

We watched as the regiment landed. Their approach to the island was peaceful, with most of the enemy holed up in the mountains. I waded out to help a couple of the men with their equipment. Even though they were facing no real fire, the new Marines looked just as scared as Roy and I had been back in November.

We ten code talkers left on Guadalcanal would provide secure communications for the fresh troops. Drained as we were, we mustered the strength to stay alert.

New code talker recruits arrived with the Marines, joining us veterans. Roy and I, partners since we'd first landed in the South Pacific, were each assigned rookies. It wasn't easy to take on new partners when we had worked so well together, but the new men needed to work with experienced code talkers, men who could help them get acclimated.

I met my new foxhole partner, Francis Tsinajnnie,[1] a man whose surname meant "shadow" in Navajo. I wondered whether Francis would be battle-ready. He and the other new men had been trained as code

---

1 Francis must have changed his name after the war, as William Yazzie and Balmer Slowtalker did. He is not listed as Francis Tsinajnnie in any of the books about code talkers. It is also possible that he was one of the code talkers whose documentation was lost.

talkers back in Camp Elliott, where John Benally and John Manuelito were still working as teachers.

Meeting Francis, I noted that his eyes continually darted around, never resting for long. *Nerves.* He moved quickly and jumped at any chance to please.

I showed him the ropes. I filled him in on how, prior to the code talkers' arrival in the South Pacific, the Japanese broke every code used by the United States. And they broke those codes quickly. Sometimes, the enemy would be lying in wait at a specified U.S. bivouac point before the American troops arrived. Losing the element of surprise drained the strength from Allied attacks, and the United States couldn't gain a firm foothold anywhere. The Allies stood in imminent danger of losing the war.

But months after we code talkers had arrived, the Japanese still had no clue about how to break the strange new code. Transmissions, previously intercepted and interpreted at will, flew back and forth with no danger of the enemy learning strategic plans. In an arena as huge as the South Pacific islands, with thousands of miles separating one military installation from another and the safe movement of troops, weapons, and provisions over these miles depending upon secure communications, this was crucial.

"Nothing to it," I told rookie Francis. I knew he was worried about whether he'd do a good job as a code talker. I nodded at the TBX radio clutched in my new partner's arms. "Just try to relax."

We sent a few practice messages back and forth with my former partner Roy Begay and his assigned rookie, Roy Notah.

"Perfect," I said, grinning at Francis. "Benally and Manuelito are good teachers. You know the code as well as I do."

The 2d Marine Division, bolstered by the arrival of its Sixth Regiment, was immediately assigned to take Galloping Horse, a ridge to the west of Mount Austen. Three units of the Army's 25th Division joined the Marines. These troops, positioned on the west, provided the fourth side of the box already outlined on three sides by the 1st, 2nd and 3rd Infantry Divisions entrenched in the east, south, and north. The series of ridges composing and surrounding Gifu Ridge and Mount Austen were finally completely enclosed. Gifu Ridge was taken by the Americans. The Japanese troops on Mount Austen were cut off and rendered ineffective.

U.S. troops moved westward along the northern coast of Guadalcanal and then inland, planning to intercept Japanese troops fighting under General Hyakutake. Hyakutake and some of his senior commanders had already left Guadalcanal, but their fighting men remained. As the American troops approached Hyakutake's men, Japanese ships again maneuvered the Slot. In late January, they managed to quietly evacuate somewhere between seven thousand and thirteen thousand Japanese troops before the Americans arrived to engage them in battle.

The Japanese had had enough. General Alexander Patch reported that on February 9, 1943, we officially secured Guadalcanal.

March 1943 through October 1943: Guadalcanal

We four men—Francis and I working in tandem, and Roy Begay and Roy Notah doing the same—became a team. I watched as my new partner finished reassembling his rifle.

"There," he said. "No sand. Good as new."

Francis reached into his ammunition pouch and inventoried its contents. He had finally begun to relax, to take things more in stride. He and I had been able to attend to small tasks these last few days, things we'd had no time for during the battle for Mount Austen.

Word had come down from high command that the 2d Marine Division would take R&R. I wiped sand from the butt of my rifle. "Just in time. I'm beat." I looked down the beach, twitching my mouth in the direction of a couple Marines who lay with their shirts off, dog tags glinting in the sun. "We all are."

We joined the sunbathing Marines and someone, sitting there on the sand, started to sing. *"Don't sit under the apple tree with anyone else but me. Anyone else but me. Anyone else but me . . ."* I sang along, feeling proud of my buddies, proud of how they'd all kept up their spirits, even in the worst of times. We were really happy as a troop. And we managed to keep that spirit of brotherhood and camaraderie alive even when some of us were dying.

But once again, even though the island was secured, we got word that we would not be leaving for R&R. The 3d Marine Division had been assigned to Guadalcanal for training, in preparation for an attack on Bougainville. They would need the code talkers. This time, both my new partner, Francis, and I would stay. Roy Begay and Roy Notah were also staying.

We code talkers, battle weary, joined the incoming 3d Marine Division, units of which began arriving on Guadalcanal in June 1943. It took quite a while before we were able to feel at home with our new cohorts. Not that there was anything wrong with the men. They were scared, just like everyone in war, and hoped to do a good job. It's just difficult to feel the same closeness you felt with men who risked their lives alongside you. The new officers were different from our old officers. Again, not bad, but it took time to get used to new idiosyncrasies and preferences. You depend on your officers in war. They tell you what to expect each day, what they need you to do. There are many times when your life, literally, depends on them. We missed the closeness we'd had with the officers and men of the 1st Marine Division. I wasn't wise enough, then, in the ways of war to know that the next campaign would bring us close to our new fighting partners.

We fought with the 3d Division for the rest of the war.

Now 3d Division Marines, we had survived the battle for Guadalcanal, the longest of the Pacific war. The entire battle lasted more than six months, and we code talkers had been involved for more than three. The U.S. invading forces numbered around 60,000. Between 1,200 and 1,600 American troops died on the island and in the surrounding waters. Many others were wounded in action. Estimates run from 3,000 to 4,400. Although estimates of Japanese losses vary drastically, their dead were thought to number between 24,000 and 30,000 out of a total force of close to 38,000.

Now that the Japanese were mostly gone, we had more time for things like fortifying our foxholes with sandbags. During the fighting, we'd been too busy to spare any time for filling bags with sand. Ironically, when things got safer, we had time for additional precautions, precautions that were no longer terribly necessary.

A screen was erected, and we got to watch movies—cartoons like Tom and Jerry and other stuff that made us laugh. Nothing heavy. I especially liked one Gary Cooper picture, *The Westerner*. Betty Grable was a big morale booster, too. Her musicals were always good. Much of our entertainment came courtesy of the Army. They tended to arrange that type of thing, while the Marines, for some reason, didn't. We'd sneak out and join the Army troops for the fun. They didn't mind. Nobody ever kicked us out. Occasionally, when there was no danger of additional hostilities, there was even live entertainment, kind of like vaudeville or burlesque, with good-looking women dancing and singing. I can't remember whether we had any of that on Guadalcanal, or whether it happened later. After a while, when you've been fighting, everything tends to run together.

We were able to eat hot food and bathe on a somewhat regular schedule. Showering felt especially good, and let us think about things going back to normal. Francis and I stood in line for the portable showers. Several rows of showers, made from thirty-two-gallon barrels with a hose attached, stretched for thirty or forty feet down the beach.

"Guess we'll be shipped off to another island soon," said Francis, a towel looped around his neck.

"We've secured Guadalcanal," I said. "Enough for now."

A couple of weeks after the Americans took Guadalcanal, we communications men were lounging around. Most of the non-Navajos were smoking. A man offered a cigarette to Francis and me. We both shook our heads. My father had told me stories about smoking, that it was a health hazard. Apparently the other Navajos had been raised the same way. Only occasionally would any of us indulge in a cigarette. We donated our rations of cigarettes to the other men. But I smoked any cigars I could get.

Now that things had quieted, we had daily mail call. That was a morale booster, although you felt kind of sad when you didn't get mail. That was me, most days. I knew my family followed a strenuous regime of praying for me, but Dora was the only one at home who wrote and read English, and they weren't too big on letters. Most everyone who got mail shared it with us, though, reading out loud.

We spotted a small group of people, six of them children, approaching our Marine encampment. The children—a couple of them less than five or so—walked slowly, dragging their bare feet. An adult woman carried a baby in a sling made from woven tree bark. The baby had been hit by shrapnel. Several Marines directed the family to the medical tent, where we knew corpsmen would treat the injury.

More and more of the island's native Melanesian population had begun to trickle into camp. They'd hidden in the mountains during the fighting. Many brought children and babies injured by the war in which they'd taken no part. American corpsmen cared for them and gave them medicine. American troops gave them food.

"They seem peaceful," said Francis, watching the little group of Melanesians trudge toward the tent holding our medical personnel.

"That didn't save them from war, though." The native people gathered around the medical tent.

I ran a hand through my hair, which hung down over my ears. When I looked into a mirror, I resembled a bogeyman, with all of that heavy growth. But my beliefs wouldn't let me get a haircut on land during battle. It was dangerous enough getting your hair cut during peacetime, when you could be sure that the hair was properly disposed of. During battle, I sure didn't want to take a chance. But a shipboard haircut, after the battle was done, was okay. There, the cut hair would be burned, disposed of properly, along with the garbage. I told myself I needed to get out to the ship for a serious trim. Some of the men were okay with getting their hair shaved during hostilities on land, even though the hair was often not disposed of properly. It all depended on what your family taught you. And my family had taught me to let it grow until I could get away from the battle site. That went for your beard and mustache as well. No shaving. Of course, I had no beard. Many of the Marines were too young to grow beards. We Native Americans had very little facial hair, regardless of age.

I nodded toward the group of island natives. "They're lucky we Americans secured this island. The Japanese would have got rid of them all."

Huge tractors lumbered along the beach at Guadalcanal, burying bodies. Dog tags collected from the American dead contained each man's name and serial number. The tags would be sent home to their next of kin. Sometimes we were able to erect wooden crosses over the graves of our men, but often sheer numbers made individual graves impractical. Then, dead American troops were buried in mass graves, the enemy dead alongside them.

A group of us Navajo communications men sunned on the "cleared" part of the beach after a dip in the ocean.

"You know, they're trying to recruit more talkers. A hundred per division, I heard," said Roy Notah.

"And guess where the First and Second Division Marines are right now?" asked Roy Begay. He pointed across the ocean with his chin and answered his own question. "Hawaii. Training."

A Navajo Marine shook water from his hair and ran a towel across his chest. "And here we are, the Third Division, still no R and R." He grinned. "Wonder what island is next?"

CHAPTER FOURTEEN

Bougainville

November 1943 to May 1944: Bougainville

Black beach canted up at a sharp angle from the ocean. Waves crashed against shore, turning Higgins boats sideways. Roiling ocean swamped several nearby boats, driving them into the land, like beached whales. That was bad. The boats were supposed to drop their men, return to the ships offshore for supplies, then bring those supplies back to the troops who were in the process of invading the island.

Francis and I advanced toward the beach at Cape Torokina, Empress Augusta Bay, in our Higgins craft. Wind whipped the inhospitable west-central coast of Bougainville. It was November 3, 1943.

Our assault had begun on November 1. Landing on the treacherous, steep coast had proved a painstaking job, and when darkness fell, we stopped loading into the shore-bound craft and waited for first light, next day. That day, November 2, the Japanese Navy stationed in Rabaul, New Britain, dispatched four cruisers and six destroyers to Torokina, attempting to intercept the American troops while we were still in the process of landing. The enemy ships made it to within forty-five miles of Torokina before being intercepted and driven off by Admiral Merrill's four cruisers and eight destroyers in the three-hour Battle of Empress Augusta Bay.

Now, on November 3, we were finally nearing shore.

Our assault on Bougainville was one prong of Operation Cartwheel, a two-pronged attack aimed at rendering the mighty Japanese base on Rabaul, New Britain, useless.

Admiral Chester W. Nimitz controlled Allied forces from the Pacific Ocean Areas command. His forces, with me among them, advanced through the Solomon Islands to take Bougainville. In the Southwest Pacific Area, Supreme Allied Commander General Douglas MacArthur was in command of the other prong of the attack. His forces proceeded along the northeast coast of New Guinea to take nearby islands. The Allied forces involved in both prongs included troops from the United States, New Zealand, and Australia, as well as from the Netherlands.

We code talkers were always part of the offensive, even though I can't remember ever attacking the beaches with the first wave. After we stormed the beach in the second or third wave, other assault waves followed. At the end came the regimental reserve. Troops waiting to land watched what was happening with us men who went ahead of them. Each wave offered feedback on the previous assault, letting commanders know about any snafu,[1] so that corrections could be made.

The unforeseen challenges of landing men on Bougainville threw all schedules off. Supplies and stores of ammunition sat in the holds of ships, waiting to be off-loaded and delivered to shore. Those ships sailed

---

1 A slang word indicating confusion or mistakes: situation normal, all fucked up.

from Empress Augusta Bay at noon on November 3, as scheduled, with many of our supplies still stashed in their cargo bays.

U.S. strategy had been designed to mislead. On the northern tip of the island, at Buka and Bonis, sat two Japanese airfields. Four Japanese airfields and a seaplane base had been constructed at Buin, on the island's southern end. The airfields were heavily garrisoned with enemy troops. Eight Allied destroyers and four light cruisers had bombarded the northern and southern ends of the island prior to the U.S. landing, leading the enemy to assume that American troops would land in either the north or the south.

However, we Marines were counting on the element of surprise. Those men from the Land of the Rising Sun had not expected us to invade at Cape Torokina, approximately halfway up Bougainville's western coast, an area which boasted no airfield and was scantily defended.

Despite the meager Japanese defenses, enemy bullets strafed the beach sporadically. The expanse of sand provided poor cover, and the footing was hazardous. Strange black sand flexed underfoot like a bog. Water squeezed out of that black sand with each imprint of our boondockers. There were scattered patches of quicksand. Picking our way across quicksand and bogs, we hit areas where the sand was tan-colored and firm. That gave us a false sense of security, when we really needed to use caution with every step.

Francis and I, crouching low, made our way to the tree line—maybe 250 yards away. Roots and more swampland greeted us. The soggy terrain of Bougainville made Guadalcanal look almost dry. There was nowhere to dig a decent foxhole.

Still, with most of the Japanese soldiers stationed at the distant airfields on the northern and southern ends of the island, the U.S. military took Cape Torokina that same day.

That evening, we dug in as best we could in the saturated, root-filled soil. Wind blew and the night actually grew cold. We'd been warned to stay in our foxholes, with smoking lamps out—which meant no smoking and no striking of matches—because of the possibility of Japanese soldiers arriving from elsewhere on the island, seeing the burning tips of our cigarettes, and attacking.

I tried to get comfortable, but didn't dare stand. My jacket was soaked and clammy, but at least it offered some protection from the wind. We wore our helmets, even when sleeping, over the mosquito nets that covered our heads. You can get used to almost anything when you're tired enough. I stretched one leg out as far as I could. When the other began to cramp, I switched legs. I rubbed my arms and crossed them over my chest for warmth. Francis seemed to be asleep.

A shot sounded nearby.

Francis jerked. "What was that?"

"I thought you were sleeping."

"Not a chance."

The next morning we discovered that one of the code talkers, Harry Tsosie, had crawled out of his foxhole and stood to take a leak, or maybe to say a prayer. A tall man, he was spotted by an American corpsman, who aimed his .45 revolver, shot, and killed him. Not till morning did the medic and the rest of us Marines realize that the man who was killed had been one of our own. Harry, mistaken for a Japanese suicide warrior, or Banzai, had been a buddy—one of the first code talkers. His death made us all sad. And we felt nervous, too, knowing we could be next.

Not too many nights later, we had trouble sending an important message. For some reason, our message couldn't be received by radio. So Francis and I acted as runners, leaving our foxhole and our buddies and venturing out into hostile territory. We only had to go four or five hundred yards, but it seemed like miles. The moon was really bright that night, and the trees cast dark shadows. We dashed from shadow to shadow. We heard mortars and gunfire everywhere, and of course we thought about Harry Tsosie and his death by friendly fire. Man, we were scared. But we made it.

Our U.S.-held beachhead surrounding Cape Torokina expanded

slowly. Since most of their forces were concentrated in the northern and southern airfields, the Japanese lacked the numbers they needed to attack us en masse on the ground. Instead they snaked through the island, set traps, climbed trees, and sniped at any American soldier they saw. Nowhere could we feel safe. Of course, we Americans had snipers, too, the telescopic sights on their rifles almost as long as the barrels. But we held the beach, not the high ground, and the series of high ridges and volcanic mountains forming the backbone of Bougainville gave the entrenched enemy an advantage we needed to eliminate.

U.S. troops nicknamed an especially dangerous ridge "Hellzapoppin." An unknown number of Japanese had fortified the ridge, which overlooked the Cape Torokina area. From their vantage point, enemy snipers were picking off too many Americans. Several Marine assaults on the ridge failed when we were forced back down the steep slopes.

One morning around six o'clock, Francis, myself, and a few others ran along the beach, heading toward the forward line. Artillery fire and the explosions of hand grenades pursued us.

I manned the microphone and nodded toward a large tree. "There," I said.

Francis, attached to me by the umbilical cord of the radio, ducked behind the tree with me. When I'd caught my breath, I peered to the left of the thick trunk. Was it safe to resume our dash? As I turned back to the right, a sniper's bullet whined by my head. *Shit!* I reached to touch the medicine bag in my pocket. It was there, safe, protecting me.

Francis's eyes rounded out like marbles. "That was close."

We continued running toward the front, hearts beating like drums. We zigzagged as we ran, keeping close to one another. The sniper who had targeted me was shot by one of my fellow Marines.

Finally in heavy foliage, Francis and I cut our way through with machetes. The foliage was tough to plow through, but it provided good cover. The long, thin cord connecting the headset to the radio became tangled in the vegetation. I unhooked my headset. Almost immediately a beep and a flashing red light warned of an incoming message. I plugged back in.

Considerably larger than Guadalcanal, Bougainville held thirty-five thousand Japanese troops and was well fortified, especially in the north and the south. The island was 125 miles long, dwarfing Guadalcanal's 90-mile length. Two active volcanoes pushed up from Bougainville's interior. A narrow strip of beach ran around the border of the island, and huge areas of swamp connected the beaches to the overgrown interior.

Despite the inhospitable conditions on Bougainville, the 3d Marine Division and 37th Infantry Divisions, under Admiral "Bull" Halsey, proved indomitable. We drained swamps and slashed roads through the jungle. The American Seabees, Navy construction personnel, somehow built three airfields at Torokina while suffering intermittent air attacks from Rabaul and artillery fire from ridges like Hellzapoppin that overlooked Torokina and Empress Augusta Bay.

Christmas approached and the men were called together. We sang songs and devoured cookies and coffee. It sure didn't feel like home, but it was a nice change from being involved in battle.

Then, on Christmas Day 1943, the Marines, aided by air cover, managed to scale the steep slopes of Hellzapoppin and take the ridge.

As long as we had good cover, Francis and I felt fairly secure. Now that we had taken Hellzapoppin Ridge, the fighting on Bougainville had pretty much stopped—temporarily. Everyone worried about air attacks, but even those had abated. Star shells occasionally floated down at night on small parachutes. The light attached to them lit the landscape in eerie white and cast shadows that moved with the movement of the parachutes. Our riflemen would try to shoot them, causing them to burst above us and preventing them from hitting the ground near the troops and exploding.

The island—like most of the tropical islands we fought on—was covered with beautiful flowers, with red and white blossoms as big as the tops of barrels. These bloomed at sunrise, and they smelled wonderful. We occasionally used petals plucked from them for underarm deodorant!

The way we smelled after a prolonged battle was in sharp contrast to those fabulous flowers. We could smell ourselves and everyone else. I remember dirty sweat rolling down my back, arms, and legs, collecting wherever my uniform made contact with my body. During heavy fighting, when we had no access to showers, I looked forward to rain so I could rinse off a bit.

Still, our smell couldn't begin to compete with the stench of dead bodies. In the heat, bodies began to decompose within a couple of hours, and despite liberal sprayings of DDT, the flies and maggots had a field day. Of course, the flies and maggots didn't limit themselves to dead bodies. They'd attack the dead skin around a wound, too.

The tropical birds were noisy and brilliantly colored, with dazzling yellow and red feathers. The palm trees were lovely, like a travel poster, and the whole tree—trunk and fronds—swayed in the breezes. Unfortunately, many trees were bomb-blasted, and we had to slash our way into the jungles with machetes, cutting vines and flowers. I always hated the feeling that we were destroying something really beautiful. Sometimes, when I was resting, I'd see monkeys come down from the trees. We men would feed them. During quiet periods, I often thought about those wonderful animals and flowers and wondered how they were going to survive the war. As a Navajo, I'd been taught to respect the earth, and the devastation made me feel sick.

We found we couldn't really trust this period of relative quiet. That was one of the toughest things about war; you could never really relax, not even for a few moments. Even after an island was secured, there was always the possibility of the Japanese trying to win it back. And Bougainville wasn't yet secured.

One morning, Francis and I had just loaded our breakfast trays when someone yelled, "Incoming!" Japanese Zeros whined and their sirens sounded. That familiar ominous clicking made our pulses race. We grabbed our trays and ran for cover in a roofed foxhole, not losing any of the food. Bombs exploded as we downed our breakfast.

Enemy ground troops had received very little in the way of reinforcements. General Hyakutake, the Japanese commander on the island, made no attempt to attack the Torokina area. The Japanese general was, at first, convinced that the Torokina landing was a mere diversion. After we Americans began airfield construction and took Hellzapoppin Ridge, he finally realized that he had to pull troops from the northern and southern coasts of the island and attack Torokina.

It was slow going for the Japanese troops, slashing their way through dense jungle to Torokina, dragging heavy weapons. We military men took advantage of this time, creating a U-shaped defense line manned by heavy artillery, mortars, and antitank guns. American troops mined the swampy approaches to our fortifications.

Hyakutake and his men arrived in March 1944. Suddenly the quiet island erupted. Ferocious attacks tore up the beach and the surrounding swamplands. In constant demand, we code talkers manned our radios.

For seventeen days, the battle raged. When men ran out of ammunition, many of them fought hand-to-hand using the bayonets affixed to their rifles. Combatants dodged from one tree to another. Japanese troops emitted terrifying screams. Everyone refused to give up. It was—if such a thing were possible—worse than being fired upon by artillery.

But the Japanese, who had traveled overland, abandoning their heaviest weapons along the way, were definitely outgunned. We Allies prevailed, maintaining control of the three new airfields we'd constructed at Torokina.

That long, bloody battle decimated Japanese troops. By the end of April 1944, the Americans secured Bougainville, although skirmishes continued throughout May.

More than one thousand Americans and over seven thousand Japanese died on Bougainville.

With Bougainville secured, we code talkers with the 3d Marine Division figured we would finally get some R&R somewhere, far from the sights and sounds of battle. We joked and talked, went out to the ship to have our hair trimmed to a Marine brush by military barbers, changed into clean fatigues, and read mail from home. We washed our clothing, especially socks and underwear, knowing it would have ample time to dry without attracting enemy bullets. Dry underwear was a luxury. Dry socks were, too. Several Navajo men packed up their well-worn combat uniforms and sent them home, where families would use the clothing as personal items in ceremonies designed to keep the men safe.

A couple of us discovered that the Naval Construction Battalions (Seabees) had great food. None of the rice spiced with worms that we sometimes ate as Marines. Instead they had things like ice cream, excellent steaks, and delicious bread. Word spread quickly, and frequently we code talkers lined up with the Seabees for rations. Seabees built airfields, bathrooms, and anything else that needed building. They set up the tents that housed hospitals and cafeterias. Their facilities were superior, and they were happy to share with other fighting men. They'd fill our canteens with fresh, sweet water and fill our plates till they couldn't hold any more, then invite us to come back for seconds.

In addition to sharing their good food, we often used the Seabees' showers. A shower was a luxury after bathing in the streams and pools that dotted the island—streams and pools shared by crabs and crocodiles.

When not joining the Seabees, we often used small camp stoves as cook fires. We'd remove the cloth cover from our helmets, rinse them out, and cook our dinner in them. Large cook fires were prohibited, because Japanese soldiers were still hiding on the island. The resolute Japanese took any opportunity to skulk in and take potshots at us Americans.

I pulled a couple of sardines from a can. The Marine sitting next to me had sunken blue eyes, blond hair, and bony shoulders. I handed him a sardine, keeping one for myself, then took a pull on a bottle of military-issue beer.

"What was it like at home for you guys?" the sunken-eyed Marine asked.

"It was good. Peaceful," I said. "Mostly we herded sheep."

"Did you have houses like ours?" The Marine stirred something that had been warmed in his mess kit, probably spaghetti with meatballs.

"Just summerhouses, branches and twigs, at first. Pretty rough. But then, when I was ten or twelve, we built a hogan from tree trunks and mud."

"Tree trunks and mud? That still sounds rough."

"Nah," I said. "It was home."

We Marines all enjoyed a special camaraderie. I had trusted my life—over and over—to this Marine and to others. They, in turn, had entrusted their lives to us and our critical transmissions. After fighting alongside the men of the 3d Marine Division, I felt at home with them, just as I had with the 1st Marine Division. War makes buddies of strangers pretty darn fast, and we had become buddies.

We were generally tight with the officers, too. I never saw a Marine, Navajo or otherwise, question the orders of an officer, although I know there were times when we weren't happy about what we'd been commanded to do. Generally, the officers were good, and they treated the code talkers with respect, as though we were also officers. Our skin color didn't work against us in the military. Our leaders took care of us. We men counted on them just like they counted on us.

Bougainville had been secured for a few days when suddenly the signal lights on the TBX radios lit up. We code talkers relayed an unwanted and unexpected message to our fellow Marines: the Japanese were returning to the island by ship, in an attempt to wrest it back from the United States.

Immediately, a code black was issued. A code black (or condition black) differed from a code red, which was issued in the thick of battle. During a code black, all weapons were readied for use, but we weren't actively engaged.

Francis and I sat in our foxhole on the beach near the tree line and waited, armed with grenades and extra ammunition for our rifles. Radio equipment at the ready, we were poised to resume vital communications in the heat of battle. The other Marines maintained a state of readiness as well, with weapons poised and night-vision binoculars within easy reach in case our wait extended into the dark hours.

It was noon. Seconds ticked by.

"What I don't get," whispered Francis, "is why these Japs are so eager to die."

I shook my head. "Makes no sense to me either."

"I mean, when they're surrounded, with no hope, why can't they just surrender? Any sane person would." Francis shifted in the foxhole, tried to stretch one leg. "Why do they have to fight till we kill them?"

"It's all about honor," I said. "If they surrender, they're shamed for life."

Francis shrugged his thin shoulders. "I'm glad we're Americans, not Japs."

"*Ouu.* Those Japanese are scary."

For a while we both remained silent. Tense minutes passed slowly. Then I spoke, again in a whisper. "You think we'll get off this island soon?"

Francis looked out at the ocean. "Sure as hell can't swim out."

"Where would you go, if you could?" I asked him.

"Guadalcanal, I guess. It's safe there, now." He chuckled. "And from there, home."

I saw a movement from the corner of my eye. I reached down and grabbed a black, eighteen-inch lizard, flinging it out of the foxhole. I turned back to Francis. "Remember how it used to take us days walking back from boarding school?"

"You walked?" asked a Marine in the next foxhole.

"*Ouu.* The school truck dropped us off near Gallup, at Manuelito."

"How old were you?" he asked.

"Eight the first time. My sister was five." I stopped for a minute, thinking. "There was no way to contact our families. No phone."

"Damn! What did you eat?" the Marine asked.

"The truck driver handed us each a stack of sandwiches."

"And water?"

I shook my head, although, from his foxhole, the man I spoke with couldn't see me. "The walk took, maybe, three days. We had to find water along the way."

"But I thought you lived in the desert?" said the unseen Marine.

"Yeah," I said, "but some years weren't so dry."

The Marine let out a low whistle. "Jesus! Eight years old. You Indians are tough."

I liked thinking about home in that hellhole of a place. The school truck driver dropped me, Dora, and a handful of others west of Gallup. He handed us peanut-butter-and-jam sandwiches, or sometimes hot dogs, and told us to walk the rest of the way. We drank from snowmelt and rainfall that, if we were lucky, created puddles in the arroyos. Confident from our years herding sheep, we followed horse trails across arroyos and mesas. Sometimes people we encountered along the way invited us to spend the night inside a shelter. Otherwise, we slept out in the open. It was usually not too cold in May.

I pulled my thoughts back to the present. Everyone was growing more and more quiet, waiting for the Japanese Navy to attack. Three o'clock in the afternoon came and went. Four. No Japanese fleet. Every sound of men in nearby foxholes—shifting their weight or adjusting a weapon—made the hair stand up on the back of my neck. You could almost hear nerves pinging in the air.

My radio beeped and the red light blinked on.

"Message." I pressed the headset to my ears. I felt a huge grin break across my face. "Our Navy beat the Japs. We're condition yellow." Condition yellow meant "all clear."

The United States Navy, the branch of service to which the Marines belonged, had intercepted the Japanese fleet as they approached Bougainville. A sea battle had ensued, with the Americans emerging victorious.

We Marines cheered our Naval brothers in arms. On shipboard, Navy men and Marines often harassed each other. Fistfights broke out on the battleships and destroyers when a sailor called a Marine a "jarhead" or a Marine referred to a sailor as a "swab jockey." That day, though, all of the rivalries were forgotten. We thanked God for our sailors.

Francis, the other code talkers, and I sent the message out to the rest of the troops on Bougainville. Men cheered, and relief poured over us all, palpable as a bucket of cool water. Everyone's biggest fear had been that the enemy would wait for the cover of darkness, then attack the island the Americans had fought so diligently to secure.

CHAPTER FIFTEEN

Onward to Guam

June to July 1944: Training, Guadalcanal

The terrain of Guadalcanal was familiar, but the island seemed eerily quiet. Scattered foxholes, splintered trees, and the occasional broken-down tank testified to the battles we had fought there. It felt strange to be on an island that wasn't in the midst of combat. After taking Bougainville, my 3d Marine Division had returned to the site of the code talkers' first campaign. The island had become a jungle training base and a staging area for war equipment and supplies.

This wasn't R&R. Generals had gathered on the island, where, huddled over maps of the Pacific, they discussed which islands should be invaded next and wrangled over the details of the United States' war strategy. How many men should be sent? How long should we bomb the island prior to invading? The generals may have planned the war, but we men on the ground lived it.

A special liaison kept the code talkers informed of plans, and we were asked to forward strategic information to military leaders who weren't at the meetings.

Guadalcanal had been a beautiful tropical island before the war hit. Now broken heavy equipment was buried in the sand or hauled out into the ocean and sunk. Vegetation was trampled and shattered. Dead and broken palm trees had gone from green to brown. The brush was cut and dying. Bomb craters disfigured the once-pristine sweep of beach. It was awful, seeing all the things that had been destroyed.

But it was safe, a good place for training. We learned additional words as they were added to our Navajo code. It was a flexible secret language, sensitive to the dictates of battle, and always growing. Our vocabulary expanded throughout the war to accommodate new equipment or practices, anything that was needed by our troops and officers.

One I remember was the bazooka, a terrible gun, rocket-propelled, recoilless, and very effective as an antitank weapon. It delivered HE (high explosive) warheads and wasn't used by American forces until 1943, after we had already developed the original code. The gun was operated by two-man teams, aimer and loader, and its accurate range was limited, maybe three hundred feet, but it could take out any tank and was also used with great success to attack fortified positions. Bazookas were so effective that the Germans, back in Europe, copied the design and used our own innovation against us. The code talkers had to come up with a word for the new weapon. Someone chose *ah-zhol,* which means "stovepipe" in Navajo. That made perfect sense, since, in the field, the bazooka was nicknamed the "stovepipe." All the code talkers learned the new word, as well as other words required by similar innovations. Upgrade code training was always stressed, since the original and the newer code talkers had to be in sync, and everyone had to be familiar with new vocabulary. Drilling on the code never ended.

Occasionally we were assigned to work detail. When there was no real work to accomplish, we dug holes, six feet deep, only to turn around and fill them. It was a strange assignment. I guess the Marines figured digging was a good way to get exercise.

I relaxed. Even strenuous Marine training was less exhausting and stressful than the fierce fighting we had endured on Guadalcanal and Bougainville. The bulk of the Pacific islands still remained in the hands of the Japanese. Our victories at Bougainville and at Guadalcanal provided United States troops with jump-off points for future conquests.

When night arrived on the Guadalcanal training base, everything was quiet, almost surreal. With no ear tuned for the sound of enemy troops, I slept soundly there for the first time in months. I woke early, to the sounds of men swimming and roughhousing, the smells of food cooking. What a life!

We prepared for our assault on Guam, an island much smaller than Bougainville and Guadalcanal. But at only 212 square miles, it was the largest and most southern island in the Mariana Islands chain. The Mariana Islands lay due east of the Philippines, and the United States' command saw them as stepping stones to an eventual attack on Japan.

Operation Forager pursued the objective of capturing several of the Mariana Islands, foremost among them Saipan, Tinian, and Guam.

July to August 1944: Guam

Guam had been a territory of the United States from 1900 until the Japanese captured it in late 1941, immediately after their invasion of Pearl Harbor. The Japanese perpetrated many atrocities against the island natives, the Chamorro people. They were tortured, beheaded, and treated as slaves. The Chamorros, who had been well treated during the American occupation, naturally favored the Americans. And the United States military knew that for strategic reasons, they needed to wrest the island back from the Japanese.

Prior to our land invasion of Guam, American bombers and ships strafed the beach near Apra Harbor. The bombing lasted for thirteen days.

On July 21, 1944, Marines and infantry invaded Guam. We Marines in the 3d Division landed north of Apra Harbor, an important deep-water

harbor on Guam's western coast. Our goal was to capture the Japanese
Naval yard located there. A regiment from the Army's 77th Division,
along with the 1st Provisional Marine Brigade, landed south of Apra.
Their assignment was to capture the Orote Peninsula and its airfield.

Bullets fell like deadly sleet. Francis and I waded ashore from our landing craft. Ahead, I could see much of the island. The vegetation was close
to the ground, and the terrain was more hilly than mountainous. At least
the Japanese wouldn't have a mountain stronghold that overlooked the
entire island.

But the enemy did have several vantage points atop a series of ridges
and cliffs that overlooked the beach. Bombs and bullets flew everywhere.
A daisy cutter hit the beach near me. Shrapnel exploded outward. Something slammed into my foot. I looked down at my left boot. A piece of
shrapnel had lodged there.

"Corpsman!" someone yelled.

I said nothing, just gritted my teeth. We Navajo men never screamed
when we were hit, and we waited for someone else to call the medic.
We'd been raised to suffer silently.

A medic fought his way through the assault. The shrapnel had sliced
my left foot between my big toe and the toe adjacent. The corpsman
wrapped the injured foot. "You can keep going, Chief," he said.

"Okay, Doc. Thanks."

Business as usual, I told myself, diving behind a bush with Francis.
The radio beeped and blinked. An American cargo plane flew overhead,
dropping crates full of supplies onto an empty portion of the beach. We
listened to the message, then ran behind a three-by-five-foot crate and
hunkered down.

Francis and I survived days one through four on Guam. Our 3d
Marine Division captured the beachhead north of Apra Harbor while

the American troops five miles to the south fought to isolate the Orote Peninsula.

During the night of day five, stuck in our foxhole, I tried to ignore the throbbing of my foot. I concentrated on my bladder, which felt as though it would burst. I nudged Francis. "Gotta take a leak."

"Me, too," he said.

"Don't try to crawl out." I shuddered, thinking about what had happened to Harry Tsosie on Bougainville.

We Marines had been warned numerous times about relieving ourselves at night. We should never stand up. Some men would leave their trenches on all fours, flying in the face of our superior officers' warnings. But we were always told to simply stay and do our business in the foxhole. Our helmets did double duty as chamber pots.

"Crawl out? Not me," said Francis.

I crouched lower in the foxhole. No one could forget the Japanese Banzai who lurked out there or their war cry, "*Banzai! Banzai! Banzai! Marines, you die!*"

"Better not leave this hole," I said.

I could hear the smile in my partner's voice. "Right!"

We had plenty of things to worry about, and being delicate about biological functions wasn't one of them. Besides, we'd learned that we stayed drier in the tropical climate if we didn't wear underwear, which served only to hold the wet against our bodies. So we went "commando," which made things easier when we had to pee. We pissed in the foxhole, feeling better after responding to nature's call. Then, careful to keep our heads low, we tried to get comfortable in the cramped trench. I closed my eyes, hoping for sleep.

But before dawn our radio came to life. Shouted messages told of a Banzai attack. No time to even think about an injured foot. Thanks to Lieutenant General Takeshi Takashina's leadership, the Japanese attackers were better organized than previous Banzai had been. They'd slipped between two regiments of our Marine 3d Division, actually attacking U.S. positions just before dawn.

When we Americans responded, the walking wounded from the division hospital joined the fray, and the nonwalking wounded shot at the enemy from their hospital cots. The Japanese drive broke up, with groups of the enemy losing both their leaders and contact with one another. The battle dissolved into a series of isolated skirmishes.

The Navajo radio net was busy all night. Everyone needed ammunition. Everyone needed grenades. Everyone needed night flares. Messages zipped back and forth as fast as we could send them. Exhausted, Francis and I, both with headsets, wrote the incoming messages down and quickly compared them to make sure we had made no mistakes.

In the full light of morning, dead Japanese lay everywhere, 3,500 of them. There were many fewer dead Marines. Thanks to our Navajo code, our U.S. troops had been warned. When the smoke of battle cleared, we Americans still owned the beachhead.

That same night, as the Japanese approached our beach north of Apra Harbor on foot, U.S. troops just south of the harbor completed their assignment to take the Orote Peninsula. We Americans owned both the airfield at Orote and Apra Harbor with its Naval yard.

A group of Seabees had built several large foxholes on the island, huge holes covered with palm logs and camouflaged with dirt and leaves. Sometimes they dug the holes into a hill, making something like a cave, and covered the door with branches. The "super" foxholes measured maybe twelve by fifteen feet, with one side open, and were so deep you could almost stand in them. Officers and enlisted men all dove for those shelters when we thought an attack was coming. The officers mixed with us men and often removed signs of rank so the Japanese wouldn't target them. We all huddled together, feeling safer than in a standard foxhole. Although the officers sometimes had a tent to sleep in at night—not like us enlisted men, who slept in foxholes—they were just regular guys, seeming every bit as scared as the rest of us.

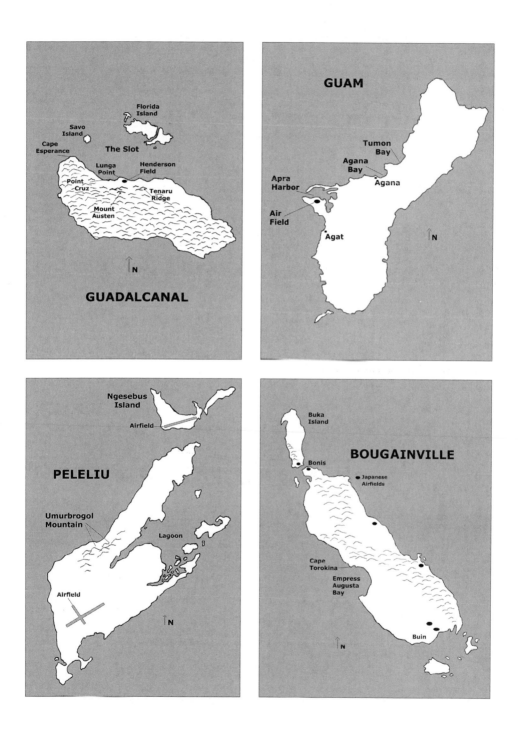

ABOVE:
My dad, D'ent Nez, a very tall man
Courtesy of Chester Nez

RIGHT:
My sister, Dora, dressed for a pow wow
Courtesy of Chester Nez

View from Grandmother's hogan, Chichiltah
Courtesy of Michael Nez

TOP:
Red rocks with sheep corral
on Grandmother's land
Courtesy of Judith Avila

LEFT:
Grandmother's summer-
house
Courtesy of Judith Avila

A hogan with its dome caved in, still standing on Grandmother's land where I grew up
Courtesy of Michael Nez

The original 29. Five are missing.
(Front row): William Yazzie, Frank Pete, me (Chester Nez), Benjamin Cleveland, Allen Dale June (Second row): John Benally, John Brown, Jr., Roy Begay, Charlie Begay, Nelson Thompson (Third row): Eugene Crawford, Wilsie Bitsie, Cosey Brown, John Chee, Lloyd Oliver, Jack Nez, Carl Gorman (Fourth Row): Alfred Leonard, Oscar Ilthma, George Dennison, James Dixon, Harry Tsosie, Johnny Manuelito, Samuel Begay
An unknown relative of one of the recruits took this photo

Me in California, a Marine recruit
Courtesy of Chester Nez

Navajo Marine Platoon 382—First 29
(Front row): Frank Pete, Corp. L .P. Kohl, Sgt. L. J. Stephenson, Corp. R. J. Hays, Wilsie Bitsie (Second row): Chester Nez, Eugene Crawford, John Brown, Jr., Cosey S. Brown, John Benally, William D. Yazzie (later changed name to William Dean Wilson), Benjamin Cleveland, Nelson Thompson (Third row): Lloyd Oliver, Charlie Y. Begay, William McCabe, Oscar Ilthma, David Curley, Lowell Damon, Balmer Slowtalker (later changed name to Joe Palmer), Alfred Leonard, Allen Dale June (Fourth row): James Dixon, Roy Begay, John Manuelito, Harry Tsosie, George Dennison, Carl N. Gorman, Samuel Begay, John Chee, Jack Nez, John Willie
Official Marine Corps Photo

Lloyd Oliver, a good man. Other than myself, the only of the original 29 code talkers still living as of February, 2011.
Official Marine Corps Photo #57876

Code Talkers Wilsie Bitsie and Eugene Crawford at ease
Official Marine Corps Photo #61431

Code Talker William Yazzie
Official Marine Corps Photo #146005

Code Talkers Oscar Ilthma, Jack Nez, and Carl Gorman taking a photo break.
Official Marine Corps Photo #82619

Code Talkers Carl Gorman and Jack Nez keep watch.
Official Marine Corps Photo #83714

Guadalcanal, flooded Marine camp
Official Marine Corps Photo #74085

Bougainville, knee-high in mud
Official Marine Corps Photo #67151

Guam, another beach landing
Official Marine Corps Photo #88089

Peleliu, U.S. planes bomb Japanese forces hidden in the hills
Official Marine Corps Photo #97977

Peleliu, an island made desolate by war
Official Marine Corps Photo #96764

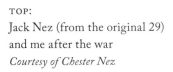

LEFT:
Relaxed in Tuba City
Courtesy of Chester Nez

RIGHT:
Philip Johnston, the man who suggested a code based on the Navajo language
Official Marine Corps Photo

A posed shot taken in the service
Courtesy of Chester Nez

TOP LEFT:
My wife, Ethel Catron, before we met
Courtesy of Chester Nez

TOP RIGHT:
Back from Korea, spending some time
with Ethel
Courtesy of Chester Nez

Here we are on the steps of Saint
Michael's Catholic Church.
Courtesy of Chester Nez

TOP:
Proud dad with my two oldest boys, Michael and Stanley
Courtesy of Chester Nez

BOTTOM:
My sons, Michael, Stanley, and Ray
Courtesy of Chester Nez

One of the Ye'ii figures I painted in the VA Chapel, Albuquerque
Courtesy of Latham Nez

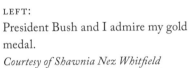

LEFT:
President Bush and I admire my gold medal.
Courtesy of Shawnia Nez Whitfield

RIGHT:
I salute President George W. Bush when he gives me the Congressional Gold Medal.
White House Photo, Courtesy of Chester Nez

Here I am with Allen Dale June, Lloyd Oliver, John Brown, Jr., and New Mexico senator Jeff Bingaman.
Courtesy of Michael Nez

TOP RIGHT:
Imagine that! Blessing the Red Sox and tossing out the game ball.
Courtesy of the Boston Red Sox

BOTTOM LEFT:
I really liked actor Roger Willie, who starred in *Windtalkers*.
Courtesy of Michael Nez

My son Mike and me at sister Dora's place
Courtesy of Judith Avila

(Front row): grandaughter Shawnia Nez Whitfield, me, and Rita Nez (Michael's wife). (Back row): grandson Michael Nez, great-grandson Emery Whitfield, grandson Latham Nez, and son Michael Nez
Courtesy of Michael Nez

When bombs dropped, generally we code talkers couldn't just curl up in a shelter. We were almost always needed to transmit information, to ask for supplies and ammunition, and to communicate strategies. And after each transmission, to avoid Japanese fire, we had to move.

One morning, my squad huddled in a bomb crater large enough to hold eight men. Francis and I stayed close, connected by our communications gear. Our leader, a tall, skinny second lieutenant from New York, was not popular with the men. He had a mean streak and a desire for personal glory that made him especially dangerous to the men under his command. He ran back and forth on the crater's lip, yelling at us to "move the fuck" out. A shot rang out. I saw the lieutenant fall. He was hit either in the ass or the nuts. Corpsmen arrived immediately and patched him up.

"He'll get evacuated." I said to Francis. "Lucky guy." I didn't say it, but I felt relieved that he would no longer be commanding us.

The lieutenant's injury would send him home. A "million-dollar wound" was the general term for a non-life-threatening injury that got you out of the war. Of course, if he had really been wounded in the nuts, as scuttlebutt suggested, it was a wound none of us men envied.

His retirement brought another man to duty. A sergeant major from Philadelphia took over for the New Yorker. We breathed a sigh of relief. The Philadelphia man was well liked, and he knew what he was doing. He was extremely careful about us men when giving orders. He tried to be sure we knew everything we needed to know to avoid being killed. And he was a take-charge guy, always able to get supplies, whatever we needed, with unusual speed. A man like that, with the ability to get what his troops needed, was invaluable in war.

After my wound, the wounding of our squadron leader, our victory over the Japanese Banzai offensive, and the seizure of the Orote Peninsula airfield, the Marines assaulted Sugar Ridge. It was July 30, 1944. The five-hundred-foot-tall, perpendicular ridge offered a clear view of the portion of beach midway down the western shore of Guam, right where we Marines had landed. It also housed multiple Japanese caves, pillboxes, and other fortifications.

Marines made their way up that ridge, scrabbling with boots and fingernails to gain an inch at a time. By midday on the thirtieth, an Allied command post was established, about halfway up. The next day, July 31, 1944, Sugar Ridge fell to the Americans.

After taking the ridge, the Marines were able to move in close to Agana, Guam's largest city. We bombarded Agana with artillery and mortar fire, destroying many of the buildings there. When we moved in for the final conquest, we discovered that it had been abandoned.

After Sugar Ridge and Agana were taken, Chamorro natives began to come out of hiding. Hungry, they climbed the coconut palms for food. Slinging a rope around the segmented trunk and holding it with both hands, they leaned back to pull the rope taut, then worked their way up by sliding the rope up first and following with their feet. It was something to watch. Whenever possible, the Chamorros gave the Americans information about hidden Japanese troops and munitions.

Then, on August 7, we learned that the Japanese had abandoned their fortifications at Tumon Bay, just northeast of Agana Bay. This gave the Marines an opening, and we immediately secured the Tiyan airfield, to the east of Agana Bay and south of Tumon Bay. Code talker Charlie Begay's unit was badly shot up during the assault on the airfield, and Charlie, not breathing and with his throat sliced from one side to the other, was left for dead. We code talkers all felt sick about it. But Charlie somehow woke up and was taken to a hospital ship. He later rejoined us at Guadalcanal. I saw him there, and he was doing all right.

A couple of heavy Japanese tanks tried to ambush the Marines as they moved farther north and east, but we Allies were not taking any more guff from those boys and their Land of the Rising Sun. We repelled the tanks and fighting pretty much came to a halt for us.

I think it was during that quiet time that a couple of us crawled into an empty Japanese bunker to take a look around. The hair on the backs of my arms prickled, and the smell of human feces soon drove us out. I thought about the Japanese who had lived for weeks—and maybe months—in that bunker. Man, the things people will go through in order to wage war.

By August 10, 1944, Japanese resistance on Guam officially ended, just in time for the arrival of four top brass: Admirals Nimitz and Spruance and Marine Generals Holland Smith and Vandergrift. We were done with Guam, except for the occasional enemy soldier left behind, who continued to come down from the island's ridges even months after our U.S. victory.

We took the island just three weeks after our July 21 landing. No one wanted any more long sieges. The Navajo code, still unbroken, had allowed United States troops to move and attack, secure in the secrecy of their plans.

In a time when black and white soldiers, and even blood supplies, were segregated, the Marines put absolute trust in us Navajo men.

Signal Corps commanding officer G. R. Lockard wrote, "As general duty Marines the Navajos are without peers . . . these people are scrupulously clean, neat, and orderly . . . They are . . . uncomplaining . . . Navajos make good Marines, and I should be very proud to command a unit composed entirely of these people."[1]

Marine Henry Hisey Jr. remembers, "The Navajos were extremely dependable. They were the kind of guys you wanted in your foxhole, so I always tried to choose them when something had to be done." Hisey asked for help from two Navajos from his unit when he had to do night repairs of some communication wires on Iwo Jima. Moving from the foxholes at night was extremely dangerous. Always on the lookout for Banzai, men fired from their foxholes at anything that moved. Soldiers

---

1 Deanne Durrett, *Unsung Heroes of World War II*, p. 65.

mistaken for Banzai, like the unlucky code talker Harry Tsosie on Bougainville, ended up just as dead from friendly fire as they would have been from the enemy's guns. But the critical wiring job couldn't wait till morning. The Navajo men agreed to help, and the wires were successfully repaired.[2]

I'm not saying we were heroes, but we Navajo men always tried to do our best, just like we'd been taught by our families back home.

My foot was healing well. I stood by the tree line and wolfed a can of spaghetti and meatballs. Man, that was good. Then I decided to take a short walk. The U.S. military on Guam had built a heavily guarded stockade for our Japanese prisoners, and I walked down a small hill to take a look. I was standing by the fence when a prisoner, young looking, just a boy really, walked up to me. He looked me up and down. He appeared to study my arms and then looked down at his own arm. His skin looked about the same color as mine. We stared into each other's eyes from opposite sides of the stockade fence, saying nothing.

I knew the Japanese behind that fence ate well—U.S. rations. They had plenty of water to drink. Medical care was provided for any who needed it. Many of the U.S. troops resented the fact that the enemy prisoners were so well treated. They knew these men had tortured and killed American military troops. And rumors were circulating that one hundred percent of captured Americans had been killed by the Japanese.

It was growing dark, and I turned away from the fence. A wonderful smell, straight from home, reached my nostrils. My stomach growled. *Fry bread.* Several Navajo men had worked it out with the supply depot. Every so often they got deliveries of flour and lard, or butter if no lard was available.

---

2 Sally McClain, *Navajo Weapon*, p. 176.

A couple of my buddies approached. "D'you smell that?"

Francis, who was with them, tilted his head back. His eyes closed. "Fry bread. Let's go."

Lard, ladled into a helmet, was already melted and boiling when we stepped up to the butane stove. Dough, crisp and golden, sizzled in the fat.

All of us Navajo men knew how to make fry bread. First we'd dump two or three heaping tablespoons of lard into a helmet. We'd heat that up while making the dough: a couple cups of flour, some salt, and baking powder if it was available. We added warm water to the flour mixture and made a ball of dough. We flattened the dough and dropped it into the hot lard. As the dough fried, the "cook" turned it with a stick.

We men swore we could smell that fry bread turning golden in its oil from two or three miles away.

More than medical services were provided to the native Chamorros on Guam. My code talker buddy Wilsie Bitsie got the Red Cross to promise they'd find a good home for a seven-year-old Chamorro boy whose entire family had been killed. When Wilsie met him, the boy had been alone for a while, and he was scared. He attached himself to Wilsie. We Marines made sure he had enough to eat, and that he felt safe. He seemed like a really good kid. Brave.

I watched as a Red Cross representative talked to the boy, who spoke perfect English. It sounded as though the Red Cross would take good care of him. I know Wilsie hated to leave him, but what else could he do? We were at war.

The good treatment of the prisoners and natives on Guam made me glad to be an American. I knew that captured Japanese were not *always* well treated, but I feel sure that any Americans who mistreated the enemy were ashamed. There was no boasting, and no one wanted to talk about that kind of thing. The two cultures—Japanese and American—differed drastically in the way they valued human life.

I readied my equipment in preparation for leaving Guam. This time we didn't leave by ship. As I boarded the ponderous transport plane, a

C-47, I wiped sweaty palms on my pants. It was my first time flying. It was probably the first time for most of us code talkers, who were climbing on board. I settled myself and my gear. The craft began to taxi. We left the ground in an amazingly short time, this heavy craft loaded with men and cargo. Noise from two large engines, driving the dual propellers, roared in my ears. Turbulence jostled my equilibrium. Still, the effect wasn't nearly as bad as the rolling of a ship had been before I'd developed my sea legs.

Among the other passengers on the plane was a general. The officer knew about our secret mission, knew we were code talkers. He engaged us in conversation. We told him about being recruited, and he told us what a difference we were making on the islands. He talked about how the code had allowed the United States to make headway against the Japanese in the Pacific. Everyone felt real good about that.

The general's uniform, I noticed, was free of the stars worn by most generals, although it sported four discreet black bars. He talked easily, treating me and the other men as equals, pulling no rank.

I looked across the fuselage at one of the other code talkers. The man glanced at the general and back at me, raising his brows. Everyone seemed to appreciate that the general didn't try to be a big shot.

The Marine brass was like that; none of them that I met pulled rank. I met then-Colonel (later General) "Chesty" Puller on a ship off Guadalcanal, and he was the same, personable and concerned. He became one of the most decorated Marines in history, earning five Navy Crosses and numerous other citations, and had already earned his share of awards, but in battle we fighting men all became equals.

A bout of turbulence shook the aircraft. I noticed the tense expression on Francis's face and on the faces of the other code talkers. But the turbulence paled compared to the fear we all had of being shot down by the Japanese.

Luckily, the trip back to Guadalcanal was much quicker than it would have been by ship—and safe.

CHAPTER SIXTEEN

Peleliu and Angaur

September 1944: Peleliu

We slept stacked four or five high in the belly of the transport ship. I woke every time the man above me turned in his hammock. The odor of bodies, strong in the poorly ventilated hold of the ship, filled my nose. I pulled my blanket over my head, concentrating on the comforting aroma of the wool.

When I woke up, the anticipation of battle hung like something oppressive and palpable in the air. There was only so much time we could kill by loading bullets into cartridge belts and playing cards. The rest of the time it was difficult not to worry. On this, my fourth campaign, I was an old hand at sea travel. I barely noted the movement of the ship and never felt sick—which was lucky, because our trip to Peleliu would take a good two weeks.

I ran a series of new code words through my mind. Command had declared that the unbreakable and widely acclaimed Navajo code would be the only means of communication during the landing on Peleliu. The 1st Marine Division, not our 3d, was assigned the assault, but they didn't have enough code talkers to support the battle plan. Several of us 3d Division code talkers were asked to go along. Francis and I, along with Roy Begay and Roy Notah, had embarked from Guadalcanal around September 1, 1944.

Operation Stalemate had begun without a lot of fanfare. Peleliu was an island shaped like a lobster claw and located 470 miles east of the Philippines and about 500 miles north of New Guinea, in the Palau Island chain. It was a tiny island, only six miles long and approximately two miles wide. Nothing hinted that it would be, in many analysts' opinion, the worst battle of the war.

More than thirty thousand Japanese soldiers, strategically placed across the various Palau Islands, lay in wait for American troops. Approximately one-third of those enemy soldiers waited on Peleliu.

The Japanese defenders on the small island had constructed an impressive network of heavy-duty tunnels and fortified caves, some with sliding steel doors. There were approximately five hundred caves. Often the entrance shaft to a cave dropped straight down, maybe four or five feet, and horizontal tunnels branched off at the bottom, but some of the tunnels and caves were buried as many as six stories deep. These were designed to withstand American bombs. It took a direct artillery hit into the entryway, with a large-gauge ninety-millimeter shell that exploded once inside, to have even a minor effect on those subterranean fortifications. They were wired with electricity and lighted, somewhat dimly, with bare bulbs. In addition, Peleliu was so heavily covered with vegetation that U.S. reconnaissance had trouble spotting any enemy fortifications. As a result of these two factors—the strength of the cave/tunnel system and the invisibility of the enemy—we would soon land on an island whose 10,700 defenders had not been substantially weakened by U.S. artillery and air strikes. Although the island was battered mercilessly before our invasion, most of the enemy fortifications and troops had survived. And U.S. brass, believing the island had been largely subdued from the air, was unaware of their survival.

The general formula for numbers of invading troops needed to overcome entrenched troops was three to one. Thus we needed thirty thousand Marines to vanquish the ten-thousand-plus Japanese hidden in caves and tunnels on the island. The First Marine Division, the primary invading division on Peleliu, had only about nine thousand infantrymen, plus their 11th Regiment, Division Artillery. These numbers were reinforced with "support" personnel, many of whom would not do the real fighting or get anywhere near the front lines. We 3d Marine Division code talkers were among the reinforcements who would join the 1st Marine Division infantrymen in the thick of combat. I later found out that Colonel "Chesty" Puller had warned that this was not enough combat personnel. Still, Field Commander General William H. Rupertus bragged that his Marines would take Peleliu in three or four days.

After two weeks at sea, I was relieved to arrive at Peleliu, and I think pretty much everyone else was, too. Soon, we hoped, the fight would be history.

On the morning of September 15, 1944, the first wave of Marines landed across from the airfield on Peleliu's southern tip. The Japanese held their fire, making it seem as if there were no defenders waiting as American troops approached the island. But when those first invading men reached the beach, the enemy unleashed their firepower. The beach exploded. Projectiles of all types kicked up sprays of sand, water, and coral. The deadly shelling came from all directions.

Francis and I were dropped onto the volcanic coral reef that surrounded Peleliu, maybe five hundred yards from shore. The LVTs (landing vehicles, tracked) that delivered some of the Marines lumbered in over the coral on their huge caterpillar tracks, but our Higgins boat, with its four-foot draft, couldn't get in over the reef. The bow dropped open, and we clambered down the ramp, trying to protect our heads by hunching them into our shoulders like turtles. We stepped into ankle-deep water.

Ahead we could see the airfield, but getting to shore proved nearly impossible. We waded, battered by crashing waves and threatened by a constant hail of artillery shells. An undertow pulled our feet out from under us, dropping us onto sharp coral that sliced into our hands and knees. Each time the waves receded, we were pulled backward, losing several hard-gained yards. Bomb craters pockmarked the shallows, and we dropped unexpectedly from ankle-deep water into chest-deep water. Hot machine-gun bullets hissed as they hit the ocean.

Soggy American currency washed back and forth in the waves, poker and blackjack winnings from the pockets of dead Marines. With the world exploding around me, and a sick feeling in my gut, I never thought about reaching for the bills. I saw no one else who did, either.

Just to the north side of the beach, jutting twenty-five yards into the sea, were a series of steep pinnacles and crevasses, collectively called "The Point." From the Point, Japanese hidden in five concrete pillbox bunkers targeted struggling troops as we tried to reach land. Countless geysers sprang up where mortar shells hit the ocean. Bodies sloshed in the shallow water. The forty-five minutes I stumbled and swam against the force of the waves and the undertow felt like three hours. The Japanese picked men off almost at will as we pulled ourselves toward the beach. Finally, Francis and I reached shore.

Water ran in streams from our drenched uniforms. Everything was in chaos. The bodies of American military dotted the sand, despite General Rupertus's announcement that Peleliu would be a quick conquer. Panic tried to rise as I recognized a buddy lying dead on the beach. But I'd become an expert at numbing my thoughts and concentrating on the task at hand. I gritted my teeth and pressed my lips closed against the bile rising in my throat. I pushed down the scream of anger that wanted to burst from my chest. I was a Navajo, a Marine, a code talker. I would not dwell on death. I would not lose my concentration.

The noise deafened us, and bullets slashed across the sand at waist height. I could see no cover, so I dropped and rolled, trying to get beneath the sheet of bullets. Somehow, I managed to clutch my gun and the radio. Luckily, Francis and I had not yet plugged in, so we were free of each other.

After a few seconds, I noticed that the terrain seemed to slope a little. I stopped rolling, realizing I had reached a shallow depression. It was full of rocklike shards that pressed sharp and warm against my back. Probably a bomb crater. Recent. I turned my head without raising it, scanning for Francis. He was only a couple of feet away, behind a sizable chunk of loose coral.

A runner, no doubt noting my TBX radio, dove flat out beside me and handed me a message. I inched over toward Francis till I was close enough to plug in and started cranking. He reached for the message and sent it.

"Over there," Francis yelled above the din. We had finished sending the message and needed to move. He pointed with a twitch of his lips. Before the Japanese could pinpoint the location from which our message had been sent, we dashed toward an even smaller depression in the sand. We were, of course, still connected by our radio equipment. We kept our heads down, legs pumping, and dove into the shallow shelter.

BAM! A group of American guns—nine-millimeter artillery—exploded, the percussion pounding against our eardrums like a jackhammer breaking up rock. Someone cussed, yelling something about a failed firing mechanism. The defective American gun and the munitions surrounding it had exploded.

Shit!

I glanced around for better cover. There were many loose rocks, and Francis and I piled some up to create a makeshift blockade. Like every other day on the islands, you had to do for yourself or die.

At five o'clock in the afternoon, Japanese Colonel Kunio Nakagawa ordered his crack 14th Division troops to cross the airfield and attack us Americans. Tanks and troops advanced toward the beach. But this time we were ready. The thinly armored enemy tanks were vulnerable to our Marine artillery and to just about every other Marine weapon. When heavy Marine Sherman tanks bombarded them, the lighter Japanese tanks crumpled as though made from tin. Then a Naval bomber targeted the enemy, sending them back to the far side of the field in retreat.

Around midnight, Colonel Nakagawa bombarded us with mortar fire. And the next morning he again attacked, with mortars and grenades. We Marines suffered heavy losses, but kept fighting. The Japanese retreated. Whether their retreat had already been planned, or whether something in the fracas caused them to panic, I don't know. But those men from the Land of the Rising Sun suddenly drew back toward the caves and pillboxes of Umurbrogol Mountain. The so-called mountain was actually a series of coral ridges, riddled with caves, that ran north of the airfield in a northeasterly direction.

Although we Americans had chased the Japanese from the airfield, we couldn't make use of it. From their fortifications in Umurbrogol Mountain, the Japanese targeted anyone who dared enter the open area surrounding the intersecting runways. But there was no other way to get to them. So, on day two, we were ordered to cross that airfield.

I remember approaching the field. It was wide open with no cover, the kind of place any fighting man wanted to avoid at all costs. The terrain was pockmarked and alien looking, like a gray moonscape devoid of life. The splintered trunks of dead trees poked out of the rock at wide intervals. Not a blade of grass, nothing green, was visible. It was difficult to believe that this island had once been so densely forested that our American intelligence people hadn't been able to penetrate the trees with their surveillance cameras.

As we drew close to the field, shots whipped out of a Japanese bunker. We hit the ground. Our riflemen, who were ahead of us, targeted the bunker, but the deadly Japanese artillery continued to pepper us. Someone ran up to the side of the concrete bunker with a flamethrower. We held our fire as he inched his way along the front of the blind bunker, then ran to the narrow front opening and thrust the nozzle of the flamethrower in. Flames bloomed, and within seconds Japanese soldiers ran from the bunker, babbling, their uniforms on fire.

My stomach twisted and I felt like throwing up. The men's screams echoed above the sound of bombs exploding. Marines raised their rifles and picked them off. The screams stopped.

After that we rushed toward the bunker. Someone made sure there were no more enemy troops inside. Artillery fire swept nonstop over the airfield. We couldn't move forward under the heavy fire, so we took shelter there for a few minutes.

When we left the bunker and started to move forward again, we were totally unprotected. Many men got shot, killed or mutilated, crossing that airfield. The corpsmen were flooded with medical emergencies— too many to handle with their thin-stretched resources. The corpsmen who served with the United States Marines were Navy personnel, but they wore uniforms just like ours except for a red cross on the sleeve. We all called them "Doc," and we admired their bravery and selfless behavior under fire, when they'd endanger their own lives to help a wounded man. I saw many of my brave corpsmen friends get cut down, on every island. There were never enough "docs."

Injured men struggled to their feet and kept moving. Men dragged and carried their dying buddies across the field.

By the end of day two, Francis and I were still alive, no thanks to the 110-degree heat. Sweat blinded us, leaking from under our metal helmets like a tropical downpour.

The Marines field-tested a new grid system during our attack on Peleliu, blocking maps of the island off into squares. Both air and artillery strikes were coordinated by means of those squares. The new mapping method helped us direct strikes toward the Japanese while keeping friendly fire away from our own men.

U.S. troops managed to hold our narrow strip of beach, as well as the unusable airfield, through the second day of fighting. But we couldn't get supplies. The enemy's continuing heavy artillery fire kept Higgins boats—also called LCVPs (landing craft, vehicle and personnel)—from landing. LVTs (landing vehicle, tracked; also called "amtracs") were similarly unable to land. Even the LSTs (landing ship, tank), which were oceangoing ships capable of depositing heavy equipment directly on shore, proved unable to land. Normally, those craft would come ashore day and night with ammunition, medicine, food, and water. Then trucks would load everything up and bring it to the front lines while the landing craft went back for more. There was no naturally occurring drinkable water on Peleliu, and in the extreme heat we men were hurting bad. The coral rock that the island was made of seemed to absorb and magnify the heat. We found ourselves longing for rain, something we never would have anticipated after the soggy jungles of Guadalcanal or Bougainville. But rain didn't come.

I found myself constantly wetting my lips with my tongue, until my tongue grew too dry to make a difference.

Some of our ships finally resorted to filling oil barrels with water and dropping them into the sea as close to the island as they could. Usually the waves and the tide carried them in for the last half mile or so. Many of those barrels still had oil in them when they were filled with our drinking water. And the oily water caused cramps. Each man had to decide for himself whether he wanted to chance drinking that water. You couldn't tell someone else what to do any more than he could tell you. That was a lonely feeling, if you let yourself dwell on it.

We all missed the barrel-sized seabags that, on most islands, were filled with clean water and hung where anyone could fill his canteen. Now the bags all hung limp and empty. I drank as little as possible of that oily water, but I did drink it. I tried to just wet my lips, which were dry and cracked. But once my mouth felt that cool water, I just had to drink.

The lack of fresh water wasn't as tough for us men from the reservation area as it was for many other Marines. Accustomed to rationing our food and water, we were no strangers to hunger and thirst. Still, though, it was pretty darn difficult.

The constant enemy barrage was especially rough for the wounded. They couldn't get off the island any more than food, water, and ammunition could get on. I pitied them, lying on stretchers in the sun in 110-degree heat, hoping and praying to be evacuated. Unlike the Japanese, we Americans never abandoned our wounded on the battlefield. Often, dead American bodies accompanied the wounded on Peleliu. Because of the island's coral-rock composition, many of the dead couldn't be buried the way they were on other islands. They, too, were carried to the beach and hauled away when landing boats were able to make it to shore.

Peleliu seemed different from the other islands. I can understand why General Roy Geiger referred to it repeatedly as the worst battle of the Pacific war. The shelling was everywhere and the enemy was invisible, hidden in their caves with metal doors that slid shut when our weapons got too close. It just seemed to rain bullets, and there was nowhere to go that was safe from the Japanese barrages.

The prelanding bombardments that had been carried out from our aircraft carriers had not beaten down the enemy, but the bombs had splintered darn near every tree on or near the beach, effectively eliminating cover. No vegetation stood taller than our knees. It was a nightmare.

September 1944: Angaur

"Chief!" one of the second lieutenants called.

Crouching nearby, I responded, "Yessir."

"The U.S. Army, Eighty-first Division, needs a couple of you guys on Angaur. Their communication specialists need help."

I knew that the Army had no Navajo code talkers at their disposal. Although Philip Johnston—without the consent of his associates in the Marines—did propose that the Army should develop a code talker program, the Army officers who were contacted about it failed to see the benefits offered by the program, so they never complied. They were stuck with the outdated method of communication. And now the Army needed our help in transmitting their plans and strategies during their attack on Angaur.

Angaur was a tiny island, three miles long, east of the Philippines, just southwest of Peleliu, also in the Palau Islands chain. U.S. troops had not yet secured Peleliu, but Marine command agreed to lend some code talkers to the Army. It made sense that we code talkers who were attached to the 3d Marine Division, and merely on loan to the 1st Marine Division on Peleliu, be asked to go.

Francis; my old partner Roy Begay; Roy's new partner, Roy Notah; and I made the trip to Angaur, an island with no airfield, and so accessible only from the water, in a pontoon plane. The plane landed out beyond the surf in full daylight, then taxied in toward the beach, dropping us as close to shore as it could. Luckily, there was very little enemy fire when we reached shore.

The Army communications center on Angaur wasn't much to look at. It was housed in a small tank. The other code talkers and I ventured out from that tiny communications center to relay messages as ordered.

That first night, the voice of Tokyo Rose blasted from Japanese loudspeakers. This wasn't new. It seemed that no matter where we fought, the broadcasts of Tokyo Rose kept us from sleeping at night. Tokyo Rose was actually several different women, all of whom spoke perfect English in a sensual voice. Her messages were calculated to get the troops upset, to make us worry. She talked about American troop movements as though she knew what would happen the next day and the next week.

She gave us gruesome details about how we would die in battle, alone, with no one to care. She told us that our sweethearts were going out with other men, having a good time at home while we fought the Japanese. She told us our families had forgotten about us. Her voice droned on and on. It was impossible not to wonder: Was there any truth to what she said? Sleep eluded us while we struggled with uncertainty.

Several men shouted out dirty jokes, all starring Tokyo Rose. Then angry cries of "Hey! Cut if off!" punctuated the night. But everyone knew the transmissions came from the Japanese, and the Americans couldn't control them, except for shooting out the occasional loudspeaker.

And that night, no one wanted to risk raising his head to shoot.

"She makes it all up," Francis said. "All of it."

"But it still gets you to worrying, doesn't it?" I huddled deeper into the foxhole. "She's a bad woman."

The next evening was hot, as usual. Francis and I walked together, talking quietly in Navajo, as we returned from an assignment. The sun had just set, and we were headed back to the Army communications center.

Suddenly two United States soldiers waylaid us.

"Don't move, Japs," one of them said. "Why are you wearing United States Marine uniforms?"

One soldier held a rifle on Francis, and the other held a .45 pistol to my head.

The soldier with the .45 accused me. "You killed a Marine and stole his uniform, didn't you, Jap?"

I stood my ground. "I *am* a Marine," I said. "Just listen to me. I speak perfect English. How could I be Japanese?"

"Lots of Japs speak perfect English," the soldier said. He looked at his buddy. "Should we shoot these Japs right here?"

My whole body went cold. After surviving Guadalcanal, Bougainville, Guam, and Peleliu, would I die here, killed by an American soldier?

My mouth went dry, but I managed to blurt out, "One of you guys go to the communications center. Get hold of an officer. They'll vouch for us." Because of the secrecy of our mission, Francis and I could not tell those Army men that we were code talkers. Navajos. The soldier with the .45 looked me straight in the eye, and I could feel his hatred.

"C'mon, man," I said. "I'm on your side."

The soldier's eyes wavered, just barely. He turned and nodded at his buddy. "Get someone from communications."

The three of us waited in an uneasy silence. My mind strayed to home. How long would it take for Grandma and Father to find out about my death?

Finally—after what seemed like enough time for the soldier to have circled the island three times—an Army communications officer, a major, arrived. He took one look at Francis and me and yelled, "What the hell are you men doing, capturing our own Marines? Of course these men are U.S. military. You're damn lucky you didn't shoot them."

I breathed a sigh of relief.

"You men"—the officer dragged his icy stare from one Army man to the other—"report to me tomorrow morning for disciplinary action."

The Japanese, once masters of the Pacific, were losing their grip Thanks, in part, to our code, a war that had once seemed unwinnable had now begun to tilt in our favor. On Angaur, like Peleliu, the Japanese had built underground bunkers. This made it difficult to confront the enemy. Angaur's terrain was flatter than that of Peleliu, so U.S. troops used bulldozers. Managing to approach the bunkers and tunnels, they sealed their entrances. Starving and dehydrated, the Japanese gave in. The Army's 81st Division secured Angaur just a few days after our arrival there, on September 20, 1944.

We four Navajo code talkers were sent back to the continuing bloodbath on Peleliu.

September to late November 1944: Back at Peleliu

Nights were tough on Peleliu. As on every other island, we could hear the Japanese Zeros, their sirens wailing, and count how many bombs they dropped. Each bomb made a click. Cramped into the shallow depression that served as a foxhole on the coral island, we'd count the clicks. *Click click click click.* Four bombs. Then we'd wait. The whistle came next as the bomb approached. Wondering whether it would hit us, we'd feel cold sweat breaking out on our foreheads and under our arms. We knew those shells respected no one. Many men hollered to relieve the tension. We Navajo men would usually stay silent. When the bomb finally hit, the ground shook. The concussive noise assaulted and numbed our eardrums like a flash of light blinds your eyes.

Sometimes we took over Japanese foxholes, constructed when the enemy had had time to blast the stubborn coral rock with explosives. These were sometimes linked by tunnels. We'd crawl into the tunnels when the bombs came, but we'd still feel the ground shaking.

The 1st and 7th Marine Regiments, belonging to the 1st Marine Division, attempted to climb up and destroy the Japanese entrenchments on Umurbrogol Mountain. There, the Japanese had hidden artillery positioned so as to produce a deadly cross fire. Men attempting to climb the ridge were easy targets, cut down pretty much at will. Our American fighting men suffered tremendous losses, and Umurbrogol became known to us Marines as "Bloody Nose Ridge."

On September 23, the 321st Regimental Combat Team, members of the Army's 81st Infantry Division, arrived on the island. General Rupertus had resisted calling the Army in to help when it became apparent that we Marines were undermanned, but General Roy Geiger had overruled him.

Fresh from their speedy victory on Angaur, the Army managed to establish and hold an offensive line on the west side of Bloody Nose Ridge. Then the 5th Marine Regiment, also belonging to the 1st Marine

Division, moved northward along the line established by the Army, capturing northern Peleliu on September 30.

In mid-October 1944—a month after our initial landing—III Amphibious Corps commander General Roy Geiger declared Peleliu secured. Although sections of Peleliu were ours, his declaration was premature. Many of the enemy still fought from the island's mountains and ridges, secure in their hidden caves and bunkers. Also, the Palau Islands housed Japan's administrative headquarters for its Pacific island holdings. And Japan's Lieutenant General Sadae Inoue, managing the Peleliu defense from another of the Palau Islands, was not about to let the men under Colonel Nakagawa give up the fight on Peleliu.

I woke up in a bomb crater blasted into the flintlike coral. No munitions noise. I'd arrived back on Peleliu, after helping out on Angaur, three weeks—or was it only a few days?—before. One day had become interchangeable with the next. I sat for a moment, eyes closed, knees pulled up to my chest.

What island would be next?

I nudged Francis. "Time for breakfast."

Francis groaned, then opened one eye.

Someone shouted, "Hey, Chief, did you hear? One of your guys brought in some Jap prisoners. Four of them."

Another Marine yelled, "No, there were half a dozen, at least."

I said nothing, waiting to hear more.

The first Marine gave Marine number two a slantwise look. "Anyway, he walked right into camp with 'em, holding his rifle. Just like John Wayne."

"We thought he was a Jap bringing in his own men," Marine number two added. "We should of said, 'C'mon over here, Chief. Let me see your dog tags.'"

The story of the code talker and his captives spread, giving everyone a good laugh. Like the Army men on Angaur who had detained me and Francis, some of the Marines thought we dark-haired, dark-skinned code talkers resembled the Japanese. At first, I couldn't understand it. In my opinion, the two races—Japanese and Navajo—looked nothing alike. But later, after staring eye to eye with that young Japanese prisoner on Guam, I understood. But I never did understand why so many American troops thought our Navajo transmissions were Japanese. I guess Navajo just sounded foreign to them. Our language and the language of the enemy sounded nothing alike.

The Marines continued to tease us Navajos about our man who had captured the six Japanese. I really didn't mind the ribbing the other Marines often gave us. And I didn't mind the nickname "Chief." We didn't think of it as a slur. We knew we were well respected as fighting men. We laughed and joked with our fellow Marines, giving back as much as we took.

The title "code talker" had not been coined yet, since most of the Marines did not know of our secret function. But other Marines had been warned not to call us Navajos or Indians. No one wanted the Japanese to draw any dangerous conclusions. So "Chief" stuck.

Francis, the two Roys, and I ate cold military rations—packages filled with sardines, a packet of bland crackers that were neither sweet nor salty, and fruit in a can. I used my Ka-bar to open the side of the fruit can. The canned stuff was good, but I especially liked the wild fruits, like coconuts, that dropped from the trees on the islands. A quick stab of the Ka-Bar broke the coconut open. We sliced them like pineapples. They were sweet, delicious.

Now that Peleliu had been declared secured, we had a big mess tent, and the food had taken on more variety. So after eating our cold rations, we walked to the mess for some hot food. After we'd repeatedly gone for days without food, the more we could eat, the better.

I munched on a hunk of nonmoldy bread. *Wait a minute*. I couldn't believe my ears. Did the mail sergeant actually call my name?

"Nez, Chester."

There it was again. I rushed from the mess tent to grab my letter. With all the stamps and crossed-out addresses—sending the innocuous envelope from one battlefield to another, until it finally stopped on Peleliu—I could barely tell that it was from home. But it was.

Letters from the United States routinely took eight months to reach us men on the islands. And, judging from what my family said in the few letters that had reached me, my responses took months to make it home.

I pulled a paper from the open envelope. There were only a few readable lines. The remaining sentences were blacked out. I knew requests from home for inappropriate things, like battle souvenirs, were always censored. But the reasons for much of the other censorship remained a mystery.

At any rate, the readable portions of my letter from home said things like "Hello. How are you?" and "Take care of yourself," with plenty of blacked-out lines in between. I studied the handwriting, knowing that it was my younger sister Dora who wrote the letter, in English, and who read my letters to everyone back home. I hated to have to destroy it after reading it, but those were the orders. Command didn't want to take a chance that the Japanese might get hold of our letters. They didn't want them to be able to infer how things were at home in the United States, how morale was holding up and who was in the service. The Japanese were a smart adversary, and they could surmise things about troop movements from unlikely sources. Of course, our outgoing letters were censored as well as the incoming. Still, just knowing that my family was thinking about me, praying for me, made the day grow brighter.

I joined the other guys who had letters, and quite a few who didn't. We lucky ones all read our messages from home out loud. It's amazing how similar the Navajo letters tended to be, after being censored. Pretty much all of our relatives had to find someone who wrote English in order to send a letter. Our generation had attended school, but our parents generally spoke the unwritten Navajo, not English.

I think hearing them read out loud made the men who had no letter feel almost like they'd received one, too. At least it worked that way for me. And the letter-reading session always turned into a good opportunity to talk and joke. That made everyone less tense.

I would have liked to get more uncensored news—about my family, our neighbors, the sheep. When I answered a letter, I knew my response would arrive, months later, ruthlessly censored as well. No doubt my relatives were just as bewildered by the censoring as we Marines were. I pictured Dora laboring over my letters, trying to make sense out of them, trying to have something meaningful to translate for the others. But I was too busy to let something like mail worry me for long. I had to keep my mind clear. There was too much else to think about.

The 5th Marine Regiment, having taken northern Peleliu, about-faced and attacked the Japanese on Umurbrogol, or Bloody Nose Ridge, from behind. Ferocious battles followed as the 7th Marine Regiment, still attacking from the south, attempted to climb the steep ridges of Umurbrogol. The series of coral ridges seemed endless, rising from the ground like miniature mountains. The coral cut our boots and slashed our bodies when we dove for cover. The coral, in addition to making it impossible to dig foxholes, shattered when hit by Japanese fire, its shards becoming shrapnel. As the Marines climbed Umurbrogol, the Japanese easily picked the climbers off from adjacent pillboxes and caves. Things looked grim.

But another of the Army's 81st Division Regiments—the 323rd Infantry Regiment—arrived on Peleliu near the end of October. We raggedy Marines, decimated in numbers, exhausted, and clutching our sanity with shaky hands, finally left.

A month of slow and painstaking attacks ensued, with the Allies eventually gaining the upper hand. Three days before the 323rd Infantry Regiment finally took the last large Japanese stronghold on Umurbrogol, Colonel Nakagawa shot himself.

Peleliu was finally secured. Most of the Marines had left some weeks before. It was November 27, 1944, six weeks and four days after the island had earlier been "declared" secured. And although the Americans finally had control of the entire island of Peleliu, individual Japanese soldiers continued to wander down from Umurbrogol Mountain for several years.[1]

I sometimes wonder about those Japanese who never learned of the war's end. I think that maybe they chose to go "missing" rather than to be captured and returned to a world where they would be scorned. The families of Japanese prisoners faced dishonor right along with the men. So perhaps, after their buddies died, those men decided to be "missing" or "dead," too. Maybe that was preferable to returning alive and being treated as a coward.

Victory had cost the United States dearly. In terms of deaths per number of fighting men, Peleliu had the highest casualty rate of the Pacific war. I have too many pictures in my head of the Navy "docs" running with stretchers through that hellish coral rock, sliding and falling, the wounded man falling off. Or of the Japanese targeting the men as they struggled with a laden stretcher.

At battle's end, 1,500 U.S. troops were dead, with 6,700 wounded or missing. Close to 11,000 Japanese and Japanese "subjects"—mainly Korean and Okinawan laborers—were killed, with only 19 fighting men and 283 laborers taken prisoner. Many Japanese had committed suicide, preferring that to capture. And, to tell the truth, enemy wounded lying on the battlefield were unlikely to survive. They were generally shot by the Americans. Too many had attacked their rescuers when we attempted to help them.

All of us code talkers remember Peleliu with heavy hearts. Code talker Jimmie King said it was the island where the code talkers suffered

---

1 Olive-drab.com. In April 1947, twenty-seven Japanese troops were discovered on Peleliu. They had to be convinced that the war was over.

the most, but I'm not sure about that. All of the islands were tough. On Peleliu, we did go a long time without water and food. And there weren't enough medical personnel to deal with all the wounded. Normally, the wounded would be brought to a hospital ship, patched up, and returned to battle. Only the severe cases were sent home. But on Peleliu, they couldn't get to the ship, and many died waiting to be taken on board.

Several code talkers were wounded on Peleliu. Code talker Tommy Singer died in the water, making his landing on the island.

In his book *With the Old Breed*, E. B. Sledge describes all war as horrendous. "But there was a ferocious, vicious nature to the fighting on Peleliu that made it unique for me. Many of my veteran comrades agreed."[2] And Major General Roy Geiger maintained that Peleliu was the worst battle of the Pacific war.

In terms of matériel, the losses were huge as well. Estimates say it took more than fifteen hundred rounds of ammunition to kill each Japanese defender of Peleliu, an almost unbelievable number.

And, back in the States, the terrible battle went largely unnoticed and unheralded. General Douglas MacArthur had insisted that the conquest of Peleliu was necessary for his attack on the Philippines. He would use the island as a fighter-plane base. Media attention was diverted by General MacArthur and his famous promise, "I will return," which referred to his retaking the Philippines. He returned to the Philippines on October 20, more than a month before Peleliu was completely secured. But bloody Peleliu was never utilized in that or any other attack.

Despite the United States' insistence upon secrecy, the Japanese somehow learned that the unbreakable code being utilized by the Americans had something to do with the Navajo language. No one knows exactly how or when this information was obtained, but it has been hypothesized that a Japanese translator with the surname Goon first associ-

2 E. B. Sledge, *With the Old Breed*, p. 157.

ated the Navajo language with the unbreakable code while participating in the interrogation of Joe Kieyoomia. Kieyoomia, a Navajo man who had survived the Bataan Death March, was questioned by Goon and tortured by his Japanese captors in their attempt to force him to crack the code. His ribs and wrist were broken, and he was made to stand naked in freezing weather until his bare feet froze to the ground, leaving blood and flesh on the ice when they pulled him back inside. A nail was driven into his head. It was no use. He could not and would not help the enemy. But the constant attempts the Japanese made to force him to crack the code meant that, at least, they kept him alive. Kieyoomia survived the war, still knowing nothing about the Navajo code.

After the war, I read a newspaper article about a Navajo man who'd been stationed in Alaska. He heard his Navajo language over the radio as he was flying in a military craft. He told his buddies, "These are my people talking." But he was never able to make any sense of what was being said in the Navajo code.

Several Navajo prisoners reported, postwar, that the Japanese had tried to get them to figure out the Marine's code. None of these captives were code talkers, and none shed any light on the complicated secret language.

Once the Marines realized that the code was truly a matter of national security, they began to assign bodyguards to us code talkers. I think I had two, although I wasn't actually told that they were bodyguards.[3] We just thought our bodyguards were buddies, guys who hung around with us and followed us—even when we went to use the restroom. Now we know the bodyguards were making sure the code talkers were safe.

If a code talker was injured or killed, one of his bodyguards had to

---

3 Later, when the war was over, some bodyguards revealed their assignments to the Navajos they guarded. I never officially met my bodyguard(s), if, indeed, I had them.

explain to his superior officer exactly what happened. The bodyguards were expected to stay alert, and if one of them took a break, another took over. At night, with Japanese bombs blasting, the bodyguards stayed close to us code talkers, making sure we were taken care of. I guess the theory was that you could replace a fighting man, but you couldn't replace a code talker.

I don't know whether our bodyguards had orders to kill us rather than allow us to be captured. The Marine Corps has been asked if this was so, and they did not deny it. I believe that an American bullet would have been preferable to Japanese torture. At any rate, no code talker was ever executed by his bodyguard.

The 1st Marine Division was sent from Peleliu to R&R in Australia. Once again, Francis and I returned to our 3d Marine Division without that R&R. We went back to Guadalcanal, this time to make preparations for the landing on Iwo Jima.

CHAPTER SEVENTEEN

No Hero's Welcome

January 1945 to October 1945

A forbidding place, covered by black volcanic ash, Iwo Jima was home to no indigenous animal life. Instead, antiaircraft guns, manned by the troops of the Land of the Rising Sun, sat atop Mount Suribachi on Iwo Jima, picking off United States aircraft that overflew the island.

Back on Guadalcanal, we men trained hard, each wanting to be as prepared as possible for the coming conflict. A volcanic island in the Kazan Rettō chain, Iwo Jima was the gateway to an eventual attack on Japan. It had been colonized by the Japanese back in the 1800s, and it was part of Japan's inner-island defense plan.

Iwo Jima was directly in the flight path to Japan from airfields on the islands we had already conquered. Those American-held islands were a little too far from Japan to make a round-trip flight practical. Our pilots declared their need for a refueling base. We needed to secure Iwo Jima, and it promised to be a terrible battle.

I sat, listening to the lieutenant's briefing. My heart raced. Another island assault.

"The Japanese have built a network of tunnels on Iwo Jima," the lieutenant boomed. "They spread out like an ant colony under the entire island."

My heart sank. The Marine sitting next to me turned, met my eyes, and shook his head, a slow motion that spoke of acceptance, but also of the inescapable knowledge of impending danger. *Darn!* I thought. Tunnels, just like Peleliu.

"The enemy positions will be nearly impossible to assault," continued the lieutenant, his enthusiastic voice beginning to grate, given the message it delivered.

A dark cloud hung over the preparations for the landing. Everyone worried.

It was late January 1945, early morning. We men milled around, waiting to board ship. Some had heard that plans had been changed. We would attack Japan, not Iwo Jima. But we code talkers knew better. We had transmitted strategic messages about the coming battle on Iwo Jima. Japan considered Iwo Jima to be a critical island, a buffer in their homeland defenses. The United States, too, saw the island as critical—critical to the conquest of Japan.

Battleships, aircraft carriers, troop carriers, and supply ships all stood ready to depart. A man holding a clipboard moved among us troops, calling out names.

"Nez! Chester Nez!"

My stomach clenched. *Was that me?* I responded, "Over here."

"Congratulations!" the man said. "You've made your points. You're going home."

The point system awarded points for each island invaded and wrested back from the Japanese. Each island was assigned a unique number, and we Marines were stamped with that number when we invaded the island. The stamps, on our fighting jackets, were very bright, like neon, and they wouldn't wash off. I had five of them. I reviewed my point tally in my head. By my calculations, my points actually exceeded the number required to be relieved. Happiness swelled up inside me like a balloon ready to burst. It was the happiest day of my life. Home!

When I climbed aboard the transport ship that would take me to San Francisco, everything had changed. I was a Marine who had fought for my country, a Marine who had contributed in a most unusual way to the war effort. The code I had helped to develop had never been cracked. I had been accepted by the other Marines as a competent combatant. I had been respected and treated as an equal by men who—I'd been warned on the reservation—might look down on Native Americans. And I had seen the world outside the Checkerboard. I'd seen big cities, the ocean, tropical islands, and battle. My life was forever changed.

I had lived through a time that many people never experience, a terrible time of danger and cruelty and fear. But I had done what was needed, and I had proved to myself that I could be depended upon. I never had to wonder about that after I came home from the Pacific war.

And after my war experience, I would never again take the little things, like clean clothes and clean water, for granted. I still appreciate those things every day.

Other Marines who'd made their points sailed with me. It took a couple of weeks to reach stateside. The ship docked in San Francisco. Everything was quiet, with no one there to greet us. The jubilation we returning Marines felt about coming home was mixed with the cold knowledge that the war was not over. Many of our buddies were still in danger. I did not know the whereabouts of Francis, Roy Begay, and Roy Notah.

I was still a private first class. I read later that the Marines had no protocol in place for promoting code talkers, since it was a new specialty. A couple code talkers made it to sergeant, but I don't know of anyone going any higher than that.

I checked into the Naval hospital in San Francisco to prepare for my return to civilian life. At breakfast one morning, not long after my arrival, newspaper headlines and speakers in the hospital dining room screamed of the attack on Iwo Jima. The Marines had landed on the island at 2 A.M. on February 19, 1945.

Major Howard Connor, a 5th Marine Division signal officer, had half-a-dozen code talkers with him when he invaded Iwo Jima. He said that without them, the Americans wouldn't have taken the island. Iwo Jima was the only battle in the Pacific war where Allied casualties outnumbered Japanese casualties.

On World War II Pacific island battlegrounds, Marines gained the reputation that defines them today—fiercely loyal, fiercely determined, and fiercely lethal combatants. Living examples of their motto *semper fi* (shortened from *semper fidelis* or "always faithful"), Marines looked out for each other. And we code talkers, with our secret mission, shared an additional, immeasurable bond with one another. We watched out for our fellow Marines *and* for our fellow code talkers.

Code talkers took part in every Marine battle in the Pacific War. Each of the six Marine divisions had code talkers. We talkers trusted each other without question, and our fellow Marines sought us out for special assignments.

Sergeant Dolph Reeves, with Radio Intelligence, recalled, "During our beach assault and island operations, Navajo talkers were worth their weight in gold and were thoroughly professional . . . Their contributions to Marine operations in the South Pacific were probably unmeasurable."[1]

George Strumm, 25th Regiment chaplain, said, "Of course their task was dangerous . . . They were most courageous in all their duties. The sacrifice for freedom given by these very brave men was incredible. I feel that all the Marines respected them very highly, including the Officers."[2]

---

1 Sally McClain, *Navajo Weapon*, pp. 208–209.

2 Ibid., p. 221.

Davey Baker, attached to a Marine Special Forces group, stated, "Most Marines and Army personnel never had a clue what the 'coders' were and what a major part they played in our war. If God alone may know, they saved thousands of American lives, yet their tale has been hidden by the very role they played."[3]

When the surrender of Germany on May 8, 1945, did not lead to Japan's surrender, the Allies knew they must employ drastic measures. Atomic bombs were dropped on Hiroshima on August 6, 1945, and on Nagasaki on August 9, 1945. When the Japanese military still refused to surrender, Tokyo was bombed on August 13 by 1,600 United States aircraft. The bombs were not atomic, but the devastation was extreme. Emperor Hirohito finally admitted defeat.

American troops studied the destruction of buildings, land, and people resulting from the atomic bomb at the Nagasaki site. The devastating explosion was something never experienced or even anticipated before, and American scientists felt its impact needed to be studied. The men sent their observations back to the United States via Navajo code, some of the final transmissions of the war.

After the halt of hostilities in the Pacific, the *Fuji Evening,* a Tokyo newspaper, admitted, "If the Japanese Imperial Intelligence Team could have decoded the Navajo messages . . . the history of the Pacific War might have turned out completely different."

Back in the San Francisco hospital, I couldn't avoid thinking about the things I'd done that had gone against Navajo belief. I had become so used to the dead bodies that I had pushed them out of the way without thinking, unmindful, like I was doing some household task.

The war had climbed inside my head. On the islands I'd been busy,

---

3 McClain, pp. 221–222.

too busy to dwell on the horror around me. But in the hospital I had no responsibilities. The days stretched out long as a highway, and nightmares invaded both my waking and sleeping hours. I felt lost. Sometimes I actually thought I'd been killed. And the dreams—horrifying dreams of unearthly battles, with Japanese faces leering at me—refused to end.

I looked around. *I'm in better shape than a lot of these guys.* Battle-weary Marines and Naval troops filled the hospital in San Francisco. Some just rolled up in a corner in the fetal position, crying. Many of the men huddled on their beds, refusing or unable to speak. Victims of what was termed "combat fatigue," they couldn't move, couldn't function.

And I couldn't shake the war from my head.

In the Pacific, I'd been surrounded by the other code talkers. We all joked around, talked Navajo, helped each other with the stress. That gave us strength, kept us going. But none of my buddies were with me now. Two other hospitals, one in San Diego and another elsewhere on the California coast, also took in returning combatants to prepare them for their return to civilian life. Those facilities might have housed some of my friends. I wasn't sure. But in my hospital, the silence was filled with the faces of the enemy.

Am I losing my mind?

Loud noises made me jump. I always felt uneasy. Even though, intellectually, I knew I was safe, my reflexes told me I could be shot at any second. A nurse or doctor dropped something, or a car backfired in the parking lot, and I'd be back on the islands, diving into a foxhole.

I met with my doctor.

"We think you're ready to go home," the doc said.

I had been waiting to hear those words for five months. Months that dragged by, filled with the grinding repetition of nightmares, of Japanese enemies appearing even during the day. I looked around at the men lying listless in bed, smelled the hospital disinfectant undercut with a whiff of urine. *I'm lucky.* Many of those men would never be ready to go home.

I boarded a train in San Francisco and returned to the Marine recruiting station in San Diego for several months' additional duty. There, I was briefed by Marine security, warned not to talk about the code or what I had done in the war. I felt a twinge of disappointment when I realized I would not be able to tell Father or Dora or my brothers about my role in developing the code that kept American tactical plans secret. But, of course, that code might be used again in future conflicts.

The war had ended by the time I received my discharge papers and the papers documenting my service, describing me as Private First Class Chester Nez. Those were dated October 11, 1945. The Japanese had signed an armistice agreement on August 14, 1945, shortly after the atomic bombs were dropped on Hiroshima and Nagasaki. They officially surrendered on September 2, four months after the Germans surrendered.

October 1945 through the late 1940s

I boarded a Trailways bus for Albuquerque, New Mexico's largest city, where my older brother Coolidge lived.

En route I stopped at the federal building in Gallup, New Mexico, to get an identification card, a card that was required for Native Americans at that time. Dressed in my spotless Marine uniform, I entered the building with confidence and approached the desk of a civilian paper-pusher. From behind his desk, the man stared at me, the Navajo Marine, and his eyes narrowed.

"You're not a *full* citizen of the United States, you know." Wielding the small power given to him by his position, the man pressed his lips together and raised his brows in a contemptuous expression. "You can't even vote."

"I'm a Marine. I'm on my way home after serving my country in battle," I said. I took a deep breath and told myself to stay calm. This guy didn't know anything. But I didn't much like what the civil servant had to say.

I stared at the smug man. "I wish I had my forty-five with me," I said. I pointed my finger like a gun, aiming at the man's chest. "I'd shoot you right there. Right there." I turned around and walked out, ignoring the protests that followed me out the door.

Although Native Americans were made citizens of the United States in 1924, we weren't finally granted the right to vote in New Mexico until 1948, three years after I finished my service as a Navajo code talker in the Pacific War.

Coolidge met me at the bus stop in Albuquerque.

"Welcome home, brother."

Coolidge was my older brother, but I could see that he was proud of me, his little-brother Marine. We went to Coolidge's small house in the sprawling desert city. Immediately Coolidge's friends began to arrive.

"Let's meet this Marine brother," they'd say. And when I shook their hands, they told me, "Congratulations on returning safe."

Over beers the men always asked, "Well how was it? What did you do in the war?"

I remembered the Marines' warning. I couldn't mention being a code talker, couldn't say anything about helping to develop the top-secret code. "The Marines issued me a gun and some ammunition and told me to go hunt down and kill some Japanese," I said.

For two and a half weeks, Coolidge, various friends, and I celebrated my return.

After celebrating and then spending several months in Albuquerque, I realized that I missed the rest of my family. Grandmother, Grandfather, Father, and Dora still lived on the Checkerboard. I wanted to see them all and to help Dora with the exhausting task of herding Grandma's sheep. I headed west on a Greyhound bus to Gallup, then walked from there, with my thumb stuck out for a ride.

I stepped from the car that dropped me off at *Chichiltah*. Bright red rocks with splashes of purple shadow greeted me. The mesa glowed white and red. A bold turquoise sky, feathered with clouds, arched above me.

With the familiar beauty of home finally surrounding me, I remembered the Navajo prayer:

In beauty I walk.
With beauty before me I walk.
With beauty behind me I walk.
With beauty around me I walk.
With beauty above me I walk.
With beauty below me I walk.
In beauty all is made whole.
In beauty all is restored.
In my youth I am aware of it, and
In old age I shall walk quietly the beautiful trail.
In beauty it is begun.
In beauty it is ended.

A neighbor was holding a "sing" when I first arrived, and my father was helping out. A sing is a ceremony conducted by a medicine man or woman, a person also called a "singer" or *hataathlii*. It is part of the Right Way of life. It puts things back in harmony when something has gone awry.

I stood in the doorway of Grandma's hogan. A figure approached from down the canyon. As it grew larger, I realized it was Uncle, riding a horse. I hadn't ridden a horse since before enlisting back in 1942.

"Climb up," said Uncle when he got near, patting the rump of the horse.

Uncle and I had always been good friends. I swung up behind him, happy to see him and eager to reach the sing and greet my father.

The familiar aroma of juniper smoke announced the gathering, as the smell of popcorn announces a carnival. It reached our noses well before we spotted the site of the ceremonial. Then we gained the top of a piñon-dotted hill and saw hundreds of *Diné* inhabiting a valley between red mesas. The colorful scene moved like an industrious city, all the activity centering on a special hogan that had been built specifically for the occasion. Women stood about in bright crushed-velvet blouses, their turquoise and silver "squash blossom" necklaces hanging heavy around their necks. They talked to friends while small children clung to their long, full skirts. Men sported heavy silver-and-turquoise belt buckles and multiple turquoise rings on each hand. Dense, handwoven blankets, wrapped around shoulders as protection against the cold, turned the open area into a moving tapestry.

A sing, which can be held anywhere in the vast empty miles of Navajo land, is a huge undertaking. Often the host family saves for years in order to afford the mutton to feed a large crowd. They stockpile firewood for the bonfires and gather poles for the ceremonial hogan. They pay the medicine man or woman who performs the ceremony. Dedicated to helping one person with a specific problem—like an illness—the sing benefits all who attend in good heart.

During the sing, the *hataathlii*, singer, and his assistants create several dry paintings. The intricate designs and multiple colors are prescribed by tradition. Rock, sandstone, and charcoal, as well as other locally available substances, are ground to a fine powder to make the colors, which are dribbled carefully onto the hogan floor by hand. Paintings are usually created by several men working together for four or more hours. The person for whom the sing is being held sits on the sand painting while the medicine man prays. At the end of the short ceremony associated with each specific sandpainting, the painting is destroyed. The traditional design represents the unchanging laws of the Right Way, while the destruction of the painting reminds all attendees of the transience of life.

My father, still tall and lean, approached Uncle and me, his face lit by a hundred-watt smile.

"I am relieved to have you home safely, my son. My daily prayers have been answered."

But we Navajos don't celebrate the accomplishments of one who has done his expected duty, so although the homecoming was joyous, there was no reason to celebrate my bravery. And, of course, I could not tell Father about my service as a Marine code talker.

Father had to stay and assist at the sing, which could go on for as many as nine nights. I knew that participants slept during the day, because ceremonial events would keep them up all night. All night, chanting and singing, punctuated with rattles and drums, would fill the dark, the music pounding on until it became the earth's heartbeat.

But I had been gone a long time, and I wanted to be home. I left the sing and rode back to Grandma's hogan. Father would join us there when his duties were fulfilled.

I think everyone was happy to have me back. For them, now that I was home in the box canyon nicknamed Nez Valley by my family, everything returned to normal. I hoped the quiet would be healing. Back among the sheep and goats, with the people I loved, maybe life would return to normal.

I tried to relax, to return to my past self, but my memories were not peaceful like those of my grandparents, father, siblings, and extended family. And the quiet grew increasingly disturbing and unreal.

The adults on the reservation were careful to never discuss the war in front of young kids. No one wanted our children to glorify war in any way. It was okay to speak to other adults about the conflict, but even so, I stayed pretty quiet. The secrecy that the Marines had imposed upon the code talkers stifled me. It wasn't much help to talk about what I'd done and seen in general terms, as I was allowed to do. My memories were very specific and very disturbing, and I decided that it was better not to say much at all if I couldn't reveal my true story.

I knew that other soldiers returning from war had the solace of talking things out if they wanted to—either with their families, with friends, or with other enlisted troops. Their efforts had not been deemed secret, like ours. We code talkers, forbidden to talk about the realities of our war, were largely denied that solace of getting everything out into the open. Even though I knew my family wanted to learn about what I'd faced, and even though I knew they would help me if they could, I couldn't bring myself to talk about the limited things I was allowed to reveal.

The Japanese enemy populated my dreams, continuing to plague me even when I was awake. Our invasions of hostile islands played like an endless film in my head, with me and my buddies exposed to enemy fire as we struggled toward the beach.

When my time at home had passed the half-year mark, I finally broke down and told my sister Dora about these unwelcome visitors. Then I told Father, Grandmother, and Grandfather. The dead Japanese wouldn't let me sleep or function normally during the day. All that blood I had walked through had stained my mind. Just as the island fighting had trapped us soldiers, never letting us get away from the battles, keeping us scared twenty-four hours a day, the devil spirits of my dead enemies now trapped me, never letting me enjoy any peace. My family agreed that if things continued as they were, the Japanese would eventually take me away. I needed a ceremony. They would put up[4] an Enemy Way.

A hand-trembler performed a diagnosis. Although I knew it was the Japanese who plagued me, the hand-trembler was part of the ceremonial protocol.

Grandma brought me to the hand-trembler's home.[5] The trembler, who could be either male or female but in my case was male, held an unpolished crystal in his hand while chanting in my presence. He asked questions, which I answered as accurately and as honestly as I could. The trembler concentrated on the crystal until he fell into a trance. His hand

---

4 The phrases "put on" and "put up" are both used when referring to a ceremony.

5 Traditionally, an older person accompanied the "patient" when he visited the hand-trembler.

began to tremble. He saw the cause of my nightmares revealed in the crystal. This was important, because the trembler would prescribe a specific ceremony, one that would address the causes of my problem, not just the symptoms. His understanding of both my symptoms and of human psychology in general led him to make a diagnosis. He told me which healing ceremony I needed in order to get back in balance.

"I will select a fine singer to perform your ceremony," Father told me. The hand-trembler had diagnosed my problem, but the singer, or medicine man, was the one tasked with fixing it.

The four-day ceremony chosen for me was one of the "Bad Way" ceremonies, one that would rid me of an evil presence.[6] The hand-trembler had determined that the cause of my problem was evil, not good. It involved ghosts, *chindí*, left behind when the Japanese who were haunting me had died. Every person has at least some kernel of evil, and the *chindí* is composed of everything that was evil in the dead person. The specific ceremony chosen, called a sing, like the ceremony my father was attending when I arrived home from the war, was one often performed for children returning from boarding school or men returning from war, the "Enemy Way."

Originally the Enemy Way ceremony was created to destroy the ghosts of the monsters which had plagued the early *Diné*, monsters which had been vanquished by Changing Woman's twin sons. In more modern times, the Enemy Way is used to destroy the ghosts of *any* enemy or outsider, consequently restoring balance and allowing a return to the Right Way, the Good Life.

We Navajos see ourselves as composed of two bodies, the physical and the spiritual. The two are inseparable, and life according to the

---

6 We Navajos practice Bad Way ceremonies as remedies for evil and Good Way ceremonies to help to keep people on the Good Way road of life.

Good Way requires that they be in sync, and that we be in sync with our world. Traditionally we worry more about living life according to the Good Way while we are on this earth than we do about an afterlife. I can't remember any mention of an afterlife in the Navajo Good Way, other than references to the *chindi* left behind by the dead. When someone died, their *chindi* could stay behind in the form of a coyote, or could simply remain in the place where the death occurred.

The diagnosis of the hand-trembler had told me what I would need for the ceremony. The sing would require something personal from a Japanese person. This was called the "scalp" but could be a few hairs from a Japanese head or a scrap of clothing worn by a Japanese person. That kind of thing wasn't easy to find on the reservation, but we were lucky that some of the Navajo soldiers, as I mentioned earlier, had cut hair and clothing from the dead Japanese and sent the items home to be used in ceremonies. The items were purchased by medicine men who utilized them as "scalps" in the Enemy Way ceremonies.

Father asked for advice from friends and neighbors, eventually choosing a medicine man to perform the Enemy Way. Traditional Navajo ceremonies, with their accompanying historical stories, chants, and sand-paintings, are complex. To perform a chant that might last from four to as many as nine nights, a singer must memorize prodigious amounts of material.[7] Although a medicine man or singer might study and learn several ceremonies, many specialized in a specific one. Thus, a specific "sing" or "way" often had a limited number of preferred singers.

It was the medicine man's job to help me figure out why the enemy continued to plague me. Knowing the "why" became the first step to overcoming the problem. Then my body and mind could be cleansed,

---

7 Clyde Kluckhorn and Dorothea Leighton, *The Navajo*, p. 163. Memorizing a nine-night chant is comparable to memorizing an entire Wagnerian opera, including the orchestral score, all vocal parts, and details of staging and costumes.

leaving me free of my Japanese tormentors and bringing me back to the "Good Life."

Father talked to the medicine man at length, telling him about my problems. The medicine man gave Father questions to ask me, and Father relayed the answers back to the medicine man. He told him how my visions grew stronger at night, until they veiled the rest of my world.

In preparation for the ceremony, my family butchered a goat and several sheep. They would feed the people who came to the sing. Wood was chopped, and the ingredients to make mounds of fry bread and tortillas were purchased. The family hosting or "putting up" a sing never knew how many people would attend. Traditionally, Navajos were supposed to take part in at least four sings during their lifetime, so often people heard of a sing and traveled to find it.[8] Of course, people close to the family came. But many others, even people my family didn't know, heard about me—the returned Navajo Marine—and came to lend support and help me reenter the Good Life. Everyone brought food and news to share. And they brought *hozoji:* kindness, compassion, and goodwill.

On the first night, the ceremony was performed near the home of the medicine man. The last night it was held at Grandma's home, and on the intervening nights at a location between the two. The young woman who led the Squaw Dance portion of the sing rode on horseback, carrying the prayer stick—or rattle stick—from one location to another. Several men and boys, also on horseback, accompanied her.

Squaw Dances, part of the Enemy Way sing, are so named because the young women who participate in the dance pick male partners from the audience. After each dance, the male bargains with the female, arranging

---

8 It is said that a person should attend four sings. Some say it is preferred that the sings all be for the same problem, even if the person attending is not the primary patient in all four.

a price he must pay to be released from the dancing. The price—always minimal—is paid, and the young woman chooses another partner. The dance is very popular.

At Grandmother's home, a large fire in a shack provided a place for cooking. My female relatives prepared the food, and everyone who attended was welcome to eat. At night, most of my female relatives slept in the cook shack, and the men in the hogan. Other families camped on the ground overnight, sleeping on sheepskins and blankets. No conjugal relations were allowed during the days of the ceremony.[9] Everyone was supposed to concentrate on the purpose of the sing.

The pot drum, an integral part of the sing, was made of pottery and filled with water. Taut buckskin, stretched over the pot, was punched with eye- and mouth-holes. The drum-with-a-face represented the ghosts, who were beaten into the ground as the drum was played for the Squaw Dance songs.

Dry paintings, or sandpaintings, were created on a skin placed on the floor of Grandma's hogan.[10] Several men, over a period of hours, painstakingly created these paintings from various finely ground colored sands, charcoal, and corn pollen. The *hataathlii* supervised their creation. Every line had to be correctly placed.

Each painting was used in a ceremony involving me, then destroyed afterward. The medicine man told me things I needed to know in order to recover from my bad visions. These things were secret, just between him and me, so I can't talk about them here.

The traditional scalp shooter was hired. He fired at the Japanese items—the "scalp"—that the medicine man had provided for the ceremony, using a sling similar to the one I had played with as a boy, except that this

---

9 Whether or not this restriction was actually observed is questionable.

10 Some families putting on a sing build a ceremonial hogan, separate from the hogan in which the hosting family lives. This was not done in my case.

sling was made from rubber and buckskin instead of string and the tongue of a shoe.[11]

The sing was a success. *Hozoji* was exhibited toward all who attended the ceremony, just as tradition mandated. I reentered the trail of beauty. For a long time afterward, my dreams and visions of the Japanese subsided.

---

11 Scalp shooters often employed a rifle rather than a sling.

CHAPTER EIGHTEEN

Singing, Boxing, and the Korean War

Late 1940s: Haskell

I looked to the east, across the long stretch of box canyon. The last couple years with my family, herding sheep, had been peaceful, but I realized I didn't want to stay on the Checkerboard forever. It was time to get down to the serious business of living.

I had signed up for the Marines before finishing high school, so getting my diploma was goal number one. Like many young men who returned from war, I would go back to school.

But which school? I thought back to Fort Defiance. There was one teacher who stood out, Freddie Richard. I had liked and respected him. Freddie, an eighth-grade teacher at my old school, had grown up in Oklahoma. He was part Native American. The students called him *Hachi Yázha*, the little man. He loved music, and on many nights the notes of Freddie's saxophone had soared out over the grounds of the boarding school like the voice of a mournful bird.

The bus pulled up to the stop where I waited. I boarded, thinking about the many daylong treks I had made to boarding school in the back of a flatbed truck.

"How long to Fort Defiance?" I asked the driver.

"About two and a half hours."

The driver was right. In less than three hours, I arrived at Fort Defiance, where I found my old teacher.

"I liked Haskell," Freddie told me. "It's in Kansas. Far away, but farm country, so not so different. Greener than New Mexico and Arizona."

Freddie's alma mater, the Haskell Institute, was an all-Indian high school in Lawrence, Kansas. With Freddie's help, I applied there.

I arrived at Haskell during the second semester, with the school year already in full swing. I had some catching up to do, but after fighting in the war, school didn't seem so scary.

I found jobs working on several different farms. The wages helped pay for my room and board. Farm families picked me up from the dorm on weekends and returned me in the evenings. I stayed at school all year long to make up for lost time, attending summer classes.

Before long, Haskell High School, which later became Haskell Indian Nations University, felt like home. Members of 179 different Indian tribes attended the school. I made many friends, notably several young Sioux and Cherokee men. But my closest friends were fellow Navajos. Robert Yazzie was an old friend from Fort Defiance. Then there were Lawrence Padaock, Jack Nez, and Ned Hataathlii, whose surname meant "the singer," like a medicine man. Ned was a Navy man, and Jack Nez was a Marine buddy, one of the original code talkers, so I had more than just childhood background and school in common with them.

I dived into school, work, and athletics. I played running back on a veterans' football team. The beautiful uniforms, complete with pads, cleats, and helmets, sported yellow numbers on a gold field. When I slipped the well-made jersey over my head, I had to grin. Things had sure changed since my days at Fort Defiance.

Another sports uniform hung in my closet—basketball. My friends and I played on a veterans' team, again with all the requisite equipment.

This school, which famous Olympic triathlete Jim Thorpe had briefly attended, was a whole different world.

One day a bunch of buddies and I piled into a car owned by a friend from Fort Defiance. I had the entire weekend off—no farmwork. Since the bars in Lawrence did not serve Native Americans, an Anglo friend had bought beer. We loaded a good quantity of beer into the car, stuffing bottles between and under us. We headed out to fish in one of the many good fishing spots on the lakes surrounding Lawrence, armed with homemade fishing rods consisting of a long stick with a string and hook attached. We actually caught a good quantity of fish with those rods.

My group of friends kept things interesting. Depending on the season, we might go to basketball or football games, or watch boxing matches. Sometimes we drove to Kansas City, Missouri, the largest nearby city, to hang out. Some of the bars there served Native Americans.

I had boxed a little at Fort Defiance as a 112-pounder. In the Marines, I took up the gloves occasionally. At Haskell, I played basketball, football, golf, and soccer for fun, but took boxing seriously. My buddies and I watched professional boxing with an eye to improving our own style. Joe Louis, the "Brown Bomber," was a special favorite. He had won the Golden Gloves tournament before becoming a professional boxer.

Haskell's team, a group of twelve or fourteen men, had five Navajo members. The rest were from other Native American tribes. We traveled to meets in places like Topeka, Kansas; Oklahoma City; and Kansas City, Missouri. Other meets were held at home in Lawrence.

Six teammates crowded into the station wagon. I had a good feeling about this meet. And I was looking forward to three or four days in a hotel paid for by the school. Luxurious living. I boxed in the 126-pound weight class, and I was en route to Kansas City for the semifinals in the Golden Gloves tournament, where kids from many different schools competed.

Before the meet, I taped my fingers to protect them from breakage. My hands were steady as I wrapped my bunched fingers. The wrap had to be tight enough so I couldn't bend the fingers into a complete fist, but not so tight that it impeded circulation. I wrapped my wrist and thumb. Then I donned the twelve-ounce gloves. I'd practiced a lot, with small punching bags and heavy body bags. And I'd skipped rope until I could box for hours without feeling exhausted. I wanted to be ready.

In the semifinals of the tournament, an African American kid, a really fine boxer, beat me on a decision.

Once during my boxing career I got knocked out. It happened in Topeka, during another Golden Gloves tournament. It was the third of three rounds when I took a hit to the head. I woke up lying on the mat. Again in Topeka, I had my nose broken, and could never again breathe through my right nostril. After that break, I stayed in the hospital for two weeks, with my face all bruised, and my eyes blackened and swollen nearly shut. That was the worst of my injuries.

Boxing was a tough sport, and I realized that. But it was a sport where real determination could result in an athlete being recognized.

But boxing wasn't my only interest. Alone in my single room, I imitated Bing Crosby, Al Jolson, Perry Como, and Nat King Cole. I had a decent voice, and the very act of singing made me feel free somehow.

I looked at the notice, cut from a newspaper, that sat on my table. *Ted Mack's Amateur Hour,* a popular radio show, was looking for talent. They'd be holding an audition in Topeka.

It was a very un-Navajo thing to do—trying out for a competition like that. Several of my friends told me I shouldn't do it. But I had made up my mind. I would audition.

The audition in Topeka attracted many contestants. I waited to sing my favorite song, not even feeling particularly nervous. Facing the Japanese had changed my perspective on life. After that, facing the audition judges couldn't be half bad.

I stood in front of the judges, and the pianist played an introduction. I launched into "I Love You for Sentimental Reasons," singing into a microphone. My voice was broadcast to Topeka, Lawrence, and Kansas City.

Ted Mack approached me backstage.

"Where were you born, son?" Ted asked.

"In New Mexico," I told him. "I grew up near the Navajo Reservation at *Chichiltah*."

"And what are you doing here in Kansas?"

"I've already fought in the war. A Marine. Now I'm getting an education."

Mack continued to talk with me for a quarter hour or so, asking about my life and my military service. I could not speak about my code talker past, but spoke in generalities about the war.

Although I was not selected to be a finalist on the show, I felt pleased that at least I'd given it a shot. After my experience as a Marine, I expected to fit into mainstream America. Trying out for Ted Mack was only the beginning. I continued to sing at parties and high school events.

I graduated from Haskell, and moved on to the University of Kansas at Lawrence.

Late 1940s and 1950: University of Kansas

The University of Kansas was a Native American–friendly school. I lived in a dorm at my old high school, Haskell, where I worked at various jobs like window washing and cleaning to pay for my room and board. I commuted to the nearby university by bus. There, I majored in fine arts. I planned to become a commercial artist.

The assignments in college fascinated me. I created "storyboards" for advertisements and learned about human anatomy in "life" classes. I utilized many different media—watercolors, oils, pastels, pencil. My favorite subjects were landscapes. Each class taught me something new and expanded the horizons of my artistic knowledge. I studied great artists of the past like Michelangelo and Leonardo da Vinci, learning how to manipulate color, shadow, and light.

We students had to defend our paintings in front of the entire class. I felt that stomach-churning feeling that I'd experienced back in my boarding school days. But I reminded myself that I was a Marine. I relaxed. My southwestern landscapes with powerful skies—done entirely from memory—were well received.

A group of my Native American friends gathered frequently for cookouts, where we prepared and served traditional foods like mutton and fry bread. An intriguing young woman, Ethel Pearl Catron, often accompanied the group. She, too, was Navajo, with jet hair curled and parted in a popular style.

I approached Ethel. She had a lovely smile.

As we talked, I soon learned that she was in trade school, training to become a boarding school matron, like her mother. I couldn't help thinking how matrons had changed since my school days. She and I went to the movies and went dancing together. Ethel was easygoing with a ready laugh. But she knew how to be serious as well. She had definite plans for her future and took her schoolwork seriously.

With Ethel, there were always things to do and things to talk about. And we could talk in Navajo. I was lured by the prospect of continuing to use my native language, which had played such an important part in my life. Although I'd had two other serious girlfriends, one from Wisconsin, a member of the Sac and Fox tribe, and a young Navajo nurse whom I'd known in grade school, I felt Ethel was the woman for me. I was in love.

But after two years at the University, thoughts of a personal life or further education were blotted out by world events. I had joined the Reserves while at Haskell in order to earn some extra money, and I was called to take part in another war.

1950 to 1951: Korean War

I sat outside the hogan at *Chichiltah*. I had received my orders to report for duty in the Korean War. But as I looked at the faces of my family, I didn't have the heart to tell them.

I stayed for a few days, helping with anything that needed doing, talking with Dora and Father, but never revealing my call to war. The man who owned Cousins's Trading Post (not the same trading post my father worked for), Bob Cousins, drove me to the train, stopping to buy me a big steak dinner.

In Albuquerque, I met the other reserves who'd been called to active duty. There were men from the Navy, the Army, and other branches of the service. We men boarded a troop train that delivered us to California.

On September 14, 1950, I returned to my old stomping grounds, Camp Elliott near San Diego. This time a new menace, Korea, threatened my country.

It was a tough time. Although North Korea's aggression against South Korea dominated the news, I had convinced myself that the United States wouldn't enter into a full-fledged war there. I knew I'd done my duty in World War II and had hoped that would be the end of it. But my country needed me again.

At Camp Elliott, I met quite a few World War II veterans. There were some Navajo Marines, and even a couple of code talkers, although none were the men with whom I had developed the code. It was good to be able to discuss our experiences in the war, and even to compare notes with the other code talkers. We were allowed to discuss the code with one another, although not with outsiders.

We were assigned work detail while waiting for transport to our official assignments. I was placed with the other communications men, although I don't believe my superiors knew about my code talker service. The other communications personnel and I were issued M1 30-30 rifles and new uniforms.

"I haven't told my family yet," I confided to one of the other Navajo men.

"Me either," the man replied. "Couldn't face it."

"We'd better write to them before we hit Korea. Who knows what it will be like over there."

I wrote to my family, knowing that Father would resume the ritual he'd begun when I fought in the South Pacific. He prayed three times per day—morning, noon, and evening—for my safe return.

After five days at Camp Elliott, I shipped out to Hawaii!

Not a bad assignment. I admit, I had been worried about being assigned to combat in Korea. After the things I had seen in World War II, that would have been difficult duty to face. But my luck was holding. It didn't look as though that was going to happen.

In Korea, I knew that autumn would be chilly and winter would be cold with deep snow. Hawaii, with its temperatures in the high seventies to the mideighties, was heaven. It rained a lot more than it did in New Mexico, but I didn't live in a foxhole, so that was no problem. The barracks in Pearl Harbor were dry and warm.

I turned in my M1 rifle and was given a pistol, which the brass felt was easier to carry. I alternated between performing guard duty and unloading transport ships. The physical work of unloading ships was a tension-free job that proved particularly relaxing. And the beaches were warm, clean, beautiful—and free of dead bodies.

My next assignment was Pocatello, Idaho.

In Pocatello, as in Hawaii, I performed guard duty—this time at a depot that sent supplies to troops overseas. It was an "all service" base, one that consolidated supplies for the Army, Navy, Air Force, and Coast

Guard. I patrolled on foot at times, but mostly by Jeep, with a partner. The depot was huge.

The war ended in 1953, but I was allowed to go home in late 1951. My discharge papers, dated November 1952, acknowledge my promotion to Marine corporal. After World War II and its bloody Pacific island battles, the Korean War was easy living for me. Our secret Navajo code was never used. Later, we code talkers learned that officers believed the war would end quickly, and they didn't want to risk the code unless it was absolutely necessary. The frantic pressure we lived with during World War II was not present in my role in the Korean War. The bodies of dead buddies and enemies never surrounded me. After my fighting in the Pacific, the Korean War seemed kind of forgotten.

After being discharged, I stood by the side of the road in Pocatello, a Marine in uniform, and stuck out my thumb. A car stopped immediately.

I was heading home.

When my ride dropped me off, I again held out my thumb. Right away, another car pulled over to the side of the road. "Where you headed, son?"

It was like that for two days and one night. Everyone wanted to know about my service in Hawaii and Pocatello and about my part in World War II. Even though I could not divulge my history as a code talker, I enjoyed the conversations.

After two days on the road and the intervening night in Salt Lake City, I arrived at Coolidge's house in Albuquerque much more quickly than I had dared to hope. I thanked both God and the Holy People that my part in the Korean War had held none of the gut-wrenching fear I'd experienced as a Marine fighting the Japanese in the Pacific.

CHAPTER NINETEEN

Wedding and White Man's Work

Early 1950s

Back from the Korean War, I couldn't wait to finish college and to get married. I returned to the University of Kansas, where I again spent a lot of time with Ethel.

I, of course, had inquired about Ethel's clan. She belonged to the "Where Two Waters Meet" people. This was significant, because I could only marry into a clan not related to my own Black Sheep clan or my father's Sleeping Rock clan. The clan is a big part of your identity. When two traditional Navajos meet, they shake hands—avoiding the impolite practice of looking into each other's eyes—and tell each other their clan and also their related clans.

Each clan had three related clans.[1] For Black Sheep people, the related clans were the Salt people, the Canyon people, and the Corn Pollen

---

1 In some areas, clan restrictions may be more complex.

people. My father's clan, the Sleeping Rock people, also had three related clans into which I could not marry.

I remember a girl, back when I was a young kid. I really liked her. But Grandma told me that we were related through our clans, so I'd better not entertain any romantic ideas. That would be incest, as strong a taboo in Navajo culture as it is in Anglo culture. So that's where everything stopped.

Marriage was a very solemn event back then, not to be taken lightly. It's changed a lot nowadays. You can marry your clan half sister. Or she might be your auntie or she might be your grandma through the clan. It doesn't seem to matter now.

At any rate, Ethel's clan, the Where Two Waters Meet people, was not related to my parental clans.

Ethel and I spent every moment we could manage together. After she graduated from her matron's training course at Haskell, she returned to Window Rock, Arizona. I visited her at her sister Flossie's house. There, I asked Ethel to be my wife.

She smiled. "You'll have to talk to my mother." This was traditional among us *Diné*.

We bought tickets on a Greyhound bus to Chilocco, Oklahoma. Ethel's mother worked there, as a matron in a boarding school. All during the trip, I worried about the mother. After all, she was a matron. And my memories of matrons were not good.

When we arrived, Ethel's sister and brother joined us for dinner. The food was good. Mrs. Catron made an effort to make me feel comfortable. I took a deep breath and looked around the table at Ethel's family. I knew it was time to ask for permission to marry her. My jaw clenched as I tried to disconnect Mrs. Catron from the severe matrons in my memory. My heart beat so loudly that I wondered whether the others could hear it.

Finally, I addressed Ethel's mother. "I would like to have your daughter as my wife."

"There she is," said Mrs. Catron, pointing at Ethel. Then she smiled. "I think that's a very wise decision," she said. "You should set a date."

When I completed the year—my third—at the University of Kansas, my GI Bill money ran out. My old friend and eighth-grade teacher from Fort Defiance, Freddie Richard, again helped me. He suggested that I apply to the Navajo tribal administration in Window Rock, Arizona, for a loan. I applied, but the tribal leaders informed me that they had no money to lend.

I continued to do farmwork while contemplating my next step. Ethel was working in Window Rock. We kept in touch by mail and had set a date for our wedding: that summer of 1952. I would need a job. Perhaps Albuquerque was the best place for me. I moved there.

1952: Wedding

I found a little house on Marquette Avenue in downtown Albuquerque. It backed up to an alley, giving me access from the rear. I rented the back half from Mrs. Ross, a widow. We shared the bathroom. Lew Wallace Elementary School sat just across the street. I figured that would be handy when Ethel and I had children.

We decided on a half-Anglo, half–Native American wedding. The modern ceremony was to take place in St. Michaels, Arizona, not far from the New Mexico border. One of Ethel's sisters drove Ethel, who was by then living in Chinle, Arizona, to Albuquerque. The rest of Ethel's family arrived in Albuquerque, staying with me in my little house for a few days. Then we all headed out for St. Michaels.

Standing outside St. Michael's Catholic Church, I brushed a piece of lint from the leg of my Marine uniform. My heart beat a staccato rhythm. I prayed that I was doing the right thing. But when I moved inside to the altar and watched Ethel, dressed in a long white wedding dress, walk slowly toward me down the aisle, my doubts gave way to certainty. She looked beautiful, and I knew that she was just as beautiful a person on the inside as she looked on the outside.

I straightened my shoulders under my uniform. Proud of my service as a Marine, I had forgone the custom of displaying Native American finery on my wedding day: no headband, no white pants with velveteen shirt, no rust-colored moccasins with white soles, no heavy silver concho belt or silver-and-turquoise bracelets and rings, no necklace of turquoise *heishi* beads, enhanced with a drop of turquoise nuggets. Just my Marine uniform.

Ethel approached in her white dress, smiling—no velveteen blouse, no long skirt with sash belt, no turquoise-and-silver jewelry. Her hair was curled in a modern do, not tied into a traditional knot.

Instead of the exchange of a dowry, we stood at the altar and exchanged vows. Instead of Ethel and me drinking water together and feeding each other from a basket holding cornmeal mush,[2] we ate wedding cake.

I relaxed. Everything proceeded smoothly. Ethel tossed the bouquet.

Then, to satisfy tradition, Ethel and I dressed in casual clothing and drove to nearby Hunter's Point, on the reservation, still in Arizona. An outdoor ceremony there was presided over by a medicine man, who blessed us both and blessed our union.

After the blessing, both of our families observed the Navajo tradition of flooding us with advice. Our families, sitting in separate groups, took turns. They talked about things like living according to the Good Way. Grandfather emphasized the responsibilities: caring for each other, caring for the children who would come. Other relatives chipped in with more advice about raising children, and about deciding where to live.

We newlyweds listened carefully. Then we all celebrated with a picnic, reminding me of Ethel's and my courtship days in Lawrence, Kansas.

---

2 A dish resembling cream of wheat.

After the wedding, we returned to my house in Albuquerque, where I looked for work.

I was lucky. During the week, I ate lunch at the unemployment office. It took almost a month, but they finally called me, and I went to interview at the VA Hospital.

The engineering supervisor at the Veterans' Administration Hospital, Mr. Ertman, had some Native American friends of whom he thought highly. When he interviewed me, he gave me a job on the spot.

I was luckier than many. A lot of the code talkers, after gaining the respect of the Marines, figured they would be able to get that same respect back home in white society. But many couldn't find jobs. That sometimes led to drinking. And the drinking spiraled into lost opportunities and vanished self-respect. Too many men died of the diseases— both mental and physical—exacerbated by alcohol. Penniless. But they didn't give away the secret of the code talkers, even to save their own skins.

I worked on the VA maintenance crew. The hospital had its own electric shop, paint shop, and carpentry shop, on-site maintenance for just about everything. I worked in the paint shop. While painting, I discovered that I had a talent for mixing colors to match existing walls and ceilings. Of course, computerized paint mixing had not yet been developed. I guess my fine-arts education helped train my eye. With a spray gun and a paintbrush I painted the entire hospital and the residences surrounding it.

When the chapel needed to be painted, I spent a month designing and executing a mural of *Ye'ii* figures. The twelve *Ye'ii* are powerful spirits who act as mediators between man and his creator. Often portrayed as manlike figures with masks and painted chests, they are roughly the Navajo equivalent of the Pueblo Kachinas. Some wear young, flexible piñon branches around their necks. Some carry a gourd rattle and a feather. Hanging from their elbows like banners are designs that represent the universe and the Good Way of life. My mural contained stylized versions of the *Ye'ii*, because an exact depiction was forbidden according to Navajo tradition. The mural is still there, although the VA chapel was converted into a recreation room some years ago.

I was happy at the VA. I made many friends. One, Benny Gutierrez, was especially close. Benny, a big man, talked a lot and loved to joke. He was also a painter, and he and I worked on many projects together. Occasionally, Benny's wife, Sally, invited Ethel and me over for dinner.

In our rental, the electricity and running water—with a wringer machine to wash clothes—were a luxurious change from the oil lamps and bucket-hauled water of hogan life. I returned to the hogan on occasion to help Dora with the livestock or just to visit. But fighting side by side with white men in the Marines had changed me. Like many Navajo military men, I expected to live in the white man's world, to be accepted and treated with courtesy and respect as a contributing member of mainstream society.

I had a wife, a job, and a life that pleased me. My postmilitary life was in balance, and I knew I "walked in beauty." Like other Navajos, I knew that beauty could be found anywhere if you concentrated on living the Right Way. When things went wrong at work or at home, I set my jaw and determined to do whatever needed to be done to make my life and my family's lives comfortable.

CHAPTER TWENTY

Children

Early to late 1950s

Life flowed smoothly.

As a boy, I had never hunted. The sheep and goats fulfilled my family's need for meat. But living in the city, I missed the open vistas of the countryside. And meat no longer approached me on the hoof. A couple of friends and I decided to go for a hunt. Jake Morgan was a buddy I had known overseas, and Jack Begay had been in the Air Force. As veterans, we three found we had a lot in common.

That first hunt, I was nervous about the other hunters. All those guys with guns. I wondered whether they'd be careless.

We slept outside with no tent. Away from civilization, the New Mexico night sky held brilliant splatters of stars. I had grown to know the constellations as a child. They appeared so close. I could almost reach out and pick them like silvery, mica-laden rocks.

We brought no meat with us. After all, we were hunting meat, and we didn't want the Holy People to think we didn't need it. I knew we'd shoot a deer if we saw one, but never a bear. We Navajos see bears as relatives, and we respect them like a grandfather. Unlike other tribes, we don't use bear claws in our jewelry, and bear "trophies" never appear in Navajo homes.

When I bagged a deer, I immediately gave thanks with corn pollen. My prayer apologized for killing the deer and thanked him for allowing me to use his meat. I ate only the liver during the trip, and removed the entrails. I brought the remainder of the meat home.

Although I didn't take a daylong sweat bath before hunting, as hunters in "the old days" would have done, I left the head and hooves where I'd shot the animal, a sign of respect. There would be no trophies on my wall.

At home I butchered the carcass and saved the pelt. The butchering was done in the "Right Way," according to tradition, so that the deer could return to the place where it had lived and inform the other deer that it had been treated with respect, in keeping with the balance required by nature. No meat was wasted, so the deer knew there had been a purpose in his death. He would tell the other deer of this. Ethel and I had meat for several months from that single deer.

I paced across the visitors' lounge in Gallup's Catholic hospital. How long would this take? Ethel lay somewhere in a delivery room. In a matter of hours, maybe even sooner, I'd be a father. I sat, then stood to resume pacing.

A doctor, his face solemn, approached. "Are you Chester Nez?"

I nodded.

"It was a rough birth," he said. "We had trouble getting your daughter to breathe. I don't think she's going to make it. I'm sorry."

"My wife?"

"She's exhausted, but she should be okay."

I held little Georgann nervously. She seemed perfect, with all ten fingers, all ten toes, and a mop of black hair. But the birth had traumatized her tiny body and she had scratches on her shoulder, cheek, and knees.

She survived for only a half hour in the hospital.

In traditional Navajo culture, girl babies are highly valued. When they marry, their husbands come to live with the family, providing more hands to take care of the animals and crops. When boy children marry, they move away to live with their wife's family, so their labor is lost. I always wanted a girl, and I often think about the little girl who would have been my oldest.

Almost immediately, Ethel became pregnant again. When her time was near, I took her back to the hospital in Gallup—a three-hour drive from Albuquerque. I again paced the hospital floors while she endured labor. What if this baby died, too? But Stanley survived, a healthy boy, who later showed a talent for art, like me.

Michael was born two years later, in 1955, in Bernalillo County Medical Center in Albuquerque. He was followed by Ray and Albert, who we called "Chubby."

Chubby didn't stay with us long. Ethel, older son Stanley, and Chubby went to visit Grandpa Catron on the train. At their stop, two-year-old Chubby jumped off the metal step, then, in high spirits, threw his head back and hit the step, fracturing his skull. He lapsed into a coma and died two weeks later of pneumonia in the Gallup hospital.

Chubby's death, in October, left my family bereft. Ethel couldn't seem to stop crying. I often walked outside our little house by myself. Mike tried to follow.

"Your father needs to be alone," I heard Ethel tell him. But Mike followed me anyway. I tried to wipe the tears from my face before my son saw them.

Then, on December 24, Ethel's teenage niece had a baby boy. Unmarried, Francine didn't want to keep the baby. Ethel and I discussed it. I talked to Ethel's mother, saying we'd like to adopt Tyah.

The baby arrived just after Christmas, when he was only a week or two old. When we placed him in Ethel's arms, she cried from happiness. We told the other kids that he was a wonderful Christmas present. Everyone was thrilled to have him, the little boy Tyah, whose Navajo name meant "he goes among the people." His middle name was Chester. We called him TC for short. Stanley became his protector.

Life settled back into a routine, and I prayed that things were once again in balance, that nothing else bad would happen.

CHAPTER TWENTY-ONE

The Secret Is Out

1968 and Beyond

The secret of our Navajo code was sustained for twenty-three years. In 1968, the military finally proclaimed it declassified. With modern equipment and new encryption methods, they decided they wouldn't be using the code again. We code talkers were released from our silence.

My father was very quiet when I told him that I had been a code talker. I saw the emotion in his face, and it took him a long time to say anything. He was so happy and proud. After our work was declassified, he used to kind of show me off. Many of my relatives and friends died before the code was released from restriction. I am so glad my father lived long enough to learn about my service as a code talker.

He loved that the Navajo language had played such an important part in the war. "I always thought they should use Navajo," he told me after learning of my secret role.

With the release of the secrecy surrounding the Navajo code, I became a bit of a celebrity. That could be embarrassing. I know that I did my duty, nothing more. I had always lived by the Navajo custom which taught that no one should be treated as a hero for doing his duty.

I spoke at Harvard about my World War II experiences. Books about the code talkers began to appear, and I attended book signings, parades, and fairs. In 1971, President Richard Nixon honored us code talkers with a certificate thanking us for our honorable service to our country. In honor of the annual Navajo Tribal Fair that is held every September, he also sent word to Navajo Tribal Council chairman Peter McDonald:

> [It] has come to my attention that the occasion will feature a special tribute to the Marine Corps Navajo Indian Code Talkers. I welcome this opportunity to reinforce the best wishes I extended to you, with special personal tribute to these outstanding citizens whose successful mission earned them the gratitude and admiration of all Americans. Their resourcefulness, tenacity, integrity and courage saved the lives of countless men and women and sped the realization of peace for war-torn lands. In the finest spirit of the Marine Corps, their achievements form a proud chapter in American military history. My congratulations to them on behalf of all their fellow citizens.

But somehow my sleeping enemy awoke. The nightmares returned. They quickly grew more frequent, until I again dreaded sleep.

"You need a ceremony," Ethel told me. "Chinle is a place with a lot of magic. We can put up an Enemy Way there." Ethel's relatives lived in Chinle, Arizona.

Another Enemy Way sing would combat the bad dreams, so my oldest brother, Charlie Gray, traveled to Chinle. There, he directed preparations for the sing. A cookhouse—a type of lean-to with a tent at the back—was built with two east-facing doors, one for my family and one for Ethel's family.

A hogan was prepared for use in the ceremony. Each person entering the hogan had to move clockwise around the room, careful not to step over anyone. That was considered disrespectful, bad manners.

Charlie Gray acted as my guide during the ceremony, telling me where to go and what to do next. By tradition, as the patient, I did not sing and pray with the others during the ceremony. Also, no one could touch me, although they could acknowledge my presence by a nod or a *yá'át'ééh* greeting.[1]

Despite Charlie Gray's best efforts, things went wrong. Somehow, the balance was off.

First, the pot drum broke. The man in charge of the drum had soaked the skin used for the drumhead to keep it supple. But when he checked the drum, the taut skin was cracked, as was the base. My relatives took the unusable drum way off into the mesa and left it there. Somewhere they managed to get another.

A young girl led the Squaw Dance, carrying a prayer stick with a gourd rattle, called a rattle stick. No one was allowed to dance unless the young girl was dancing, holding the prayer stick. When the afternoon sun grew hot, she fainted. The dance was stopped until she recovered, got back onto her feet, and was able to again lead.

Young kids drank alcohol under the cover of night—something strictly forbidden in any ceremony. Their lack of respect further damaged the efficacy of the sing.

A rattlesnake attempted to enter the hogan where my family and I stayed. The man assigned to guard the door stepped on the snake's head, killing it. That conflicted with the Navajo belief that all things should be respected. The guard should have caught the snake and released it somewhere away from the participants.

---

1 *Yá'át'ééh* can be used to mean "hello" or "good-bye." It can also mean "good"—or "not good" when used with the negative *dooda*. *Doo shil yá'át'ééh da* means "I do not like" someone or something.

Those unorthodox happenings worried me. Someone who didn't like me or my family had undoubtedly caused the bad things to happen. I worried all the way through the Enemy Way sing, knowing there was something wrong somewhere. I didn't say anything to anyone, though, just kept it to myself. I reasoned that the bad things happened because someone hadn't come to the ceremony with a good heart. Negativity always threw everything out of balance.

After the disappointing Enemy Way, my relatives decided to put on a Good Way ceremony to set things right. The ceremony, the Holy Way, was held immediately. It lasted for another two or three days, with many participants.

By the end of the Holy Way ceremony, I felt that the unfortunate things that had occurred during the Enemy Way had been cleared. After that, my bad dreams, for the most part, disappeared. I believed in the power of the ceremony, knowing that if one believed, it would work.

As Stanley, Mike, Ray, and Tyah got older, Ethel grew discontent. While they were young, she had worked from home, making jewelry and taking in laundry.

With the children all in school, she started to work outside the home. Over time, she worked at several different jobs—a car mechanic, a secretary, and a waitress at a local bar. Sometimes she partied with the people she met at work. She and I began to pull away from each other.

I spent more and more time with my kids.

One sunny afternoon, I nailed a basketball backboard to the back of the house while Uncle George held the ladder. I climbed down and stood back. Good. The rim looked level. George and I waited impatiently for the boys to get home from school. A few hours later, the children arrived.

"Come on out back," I said, barely able to contain my smile.

"Whoa! Look at this," Mike said. "This is great."

Mike, Stanley, and a group of friends played basketball for hours.

Although I worked, I made sure to spend lots of time with my children and their friends. Our family had moved to a house on Sixty-first Street Southwest, in Albuquerque, a quiet area. On weekends, the children and I played football and baseball out in the street. I never tired of their company. We generally played until sundown, with Ethel sitting on the porch and watching while she crocheted.

I guess I never grew up completely, because I was always ready to get down on my hands and knees to play marbles. Sometimes I let the boys try out my boxing gloves. Our house became the hangout for all of Mike's friends.

Mike told me that his friends said they wished they had a dad like me. I figured I was lucky to have great kids of my own and a neighborhood of their friends who enjoyed hanging out.

Even when our family took trips, we took the children's friends along. I had learned to drive an old stick shift, after graduating high school, by watching how other people did it. I learned how a clutch and a gearshift worked, before actually trying them out. I put this knowledge to good use once I had a family. Ethel and I took them camping and to visit Aunt Dora. Everyone had a good time, and the tagalong buddies always wanted to go again. I viewed several of the children as honorary sons.

But I was strict. I expected my sons to do well in school. They could miss class only if they had a very good reason. They were expected to obey their mother and me without argument.

Soon, however, their mother was no longer there to watch over them. I didn't know how to tell the boys. I gathered them in the living room.

"Your mother and I are going to get a divorce," I told them. Our relationship hadn't improved, and Ethel had moved out.

"Why a divorce? I never even heard you argue," Mike asked.

"We're just not happy together," I told him.

I scheduled court proceedings to make the divorce final. The boys and I waited in court, but Ethel never appeared. The judge allowed me to keep my four boys. They were good kids. We divided up all the chores, and everyone did his part. I was happy to have them with me.

1974 to 1990s

I woke up and checked on the kids. Stanley, my oldest, wasn't home. Where had he gone last night? Oh yeah, a powwow. Stanley was twenty-one, a man, so I didn't worry.

That same day a policeman knocked at the door. My gut clenched. Why would the police come to my house?

"Mr. Nez? Father of Stanley Nez?" the officer asked.

"Yes." I felt my heart weighing heavy in my body.

"I'm sorry to tell you this, Mr. Nez, but Stanley was killed in a car accident."

It wasn't until a week later, when one of the men involved in the accident came forward, that I pieced together the events leading up to Stanley's death.

Stanley had attended a powwow. Afterward, he joined a bunch of friends for a party out on Albuquerque's West Mesa. The land was an empty expanse of desert, populated by Native American petroglyphs— carvings in stone—but not by people or houses.

There was no drinking allowed at the powwow, but the "after" party was not so strict. Stanley and his friends drank and sang songs. The gathering, termed a "49-er," grew lively as the young people sang forty-nine songs.[2]

Apparently, Stanley left the party on foot. A car sped up on one of the many dirt tracks that crisscrossed the mesa, and Stanley hitched a

---

2 The songs commemorated fifty ancient Navajo warriors. No one seems to remember whether forty-nine of these warriors were killed in battle, or whether forty-nine survived.

ride. The driver was drunk, and someone in another car chased them. They smashed into a cement culvert, killing Stanley in the passenger's seat and the driver. Someone in the backseat survived, but he hitched another ride and told no one about the accident. Not until the next day were the car and the two bodies found.

A week passed before the third man gave the facts of the accident to the police, facts that wouldn't bring Stanley or the dead driver back.

I remembered what a good boy Stanley had been, how he'd protected his little brother Mike, walking him to elementary school every day.

Stanley had inherited the artistic talent that had inspired me to be a fine-arts major in college. At twenty-one, full of ideas, he already had a collection of paintings and drawings that he'd created over the years. I thought about a drawing that Stanley had started, one that brother Mike—then a senior in high school—especially loved. In it, a Native American man rode on a white horse. In the background an American flag faded into the clouds.

For some reason, just days before his death, Stanley had talked with me about the picture. "You'll have to finish this drawing for me," he said.

The drawing was never finished. For a long time after Stanley died, I couldn't make myself care about life. My sons Michael, Ray, and Tyah graduated and moved out of our home. I felt the need to escape the city of Albuquerque, where I'd lived when three of my children had died. In the mid-1970s, after suffering from a series of blackouts so that I could no longer climb a ladder safely, I had retired from the VA. I moved back to *Chichiltah* to help Dora with the heavy tasks of living on the Checkerboard. There was wood to cut and split and livestock to tend.

In 1982, President Ronald Reagan gave the code talkers a certificate of recognition and declared August 14 to be National Code Talkers Day.

Ethel, my ex-wife, died in the late 1980s. A year or two after her death, I moved back to Albuquerque, living with my son Michael (Mike); Mike's beautiful wife, Rita; and their three children, Latham, Shawnia, and Michael.

On September 17, 1992, an exhibit honoring the code talkers of World War II was dedicated at the Pentagon in Washington, D.C. Slowly, over the period of years since the declassifying of the code in 1968, more and more people learned of our wartime story.

2000 to 2001

Once our code secret had been out for a while, many people began to see us code talkers as heroes and as one of the most effective weapons the United States had utilized in fighting the Japanese. In April 2000, Senator Jeff Bingaman of New Mexico proposed the "Honoring the Navajo Code Talkers Act," Senate Bill 2408. It was signed into law on December 21, 2000, by President Bill Clinton. The act called for the recognition of the code talkers, and authorized the awarding of gold medals to the twenty-nine original code talkers and silver medals to the ones who followed. Soon, those honors were bestowed

We "original twenty-nine"[3] and our families boarded a Marine jet in Albuquerque. Four of the five surviving original code talkers were making the trip: John Brown Jr., Lloyd Oliver, Allen Dale June, and myself. All four of us were in our seventies or eighties. Within hours, we arrived in Washington, D.C.

My son Mike; Mike's wife, Rita; and their three children, Shawnia, Latham, and Michael, waited with me in the Capitol Rotunda. The other three code talkers and their families waited, too. A fifth living code talker, Joe Palmer (formerly Balmer Slowtalker), was in the hospital and too frail to attend. He was represented by his son, Kermit.

---

3 I wish that the three additional men who helped develop the code—Felix Yazzie, Ross Haskie, and Wilson Price—had also been awarded gold medals.

As we anticipated the arrival of the president, the Rotunda filled with people. I wiped sweat from my brow. This award would bring the events started in 1941 at Pearl Harbor full circle. It was July 26, 2001, just forty-seven days before our country endured another brutal attack—the 9/11 terrorist assault on New York and Washington, D.C.

We craned our necks, watching for President George W. Bush. I surveyed the room from the head table where we were seated. It was a standing-room-only audience. I wondered about the men who had died never having told their families that they were code talkers. Some of them had not been identified in their Marine records as being code talkers and so they received no recognition. How strange it must have felt to be a code talker and to die with that secret, knowing your family would never know.

When President Bush arrived, he gave a speech praising us—our character and service. I listened carefully as the president spoke.

. . . Today, America honors 29 Native Americans who, in a desperate hour, gave their country a service only they could give. In war, using their native language, they relayed secret messages that turned the course of battle . . .

At home, they carried for decades the secret of their own heroism. Today, we give these exceptional Marines the recognition they earned so long ago . . .

In presenting gold medals to each of them, the Congress recognizes their individual service, bravely offered and flawlessly performed . . .

With silver medals, we also honor the dozens more who served later, with the same courage and distinction . . .

Above all, it's a story of young Navajos who brought honor to their nation and victory to their country . . . On active duty, their value was so great, and their order so sensitive, that they were closely guarded. By war's end, some 400 Navajos had served as Code Talkers. Thirteen were killed in action, and their names, too, are on today's roll of honor . . .

Native Americans have served with the modesty and strength and quiet valor their tradition has always inspired.

That tradition found full expression in the Code Talkers, in those absent, and in those with us today. Gentlemen, your service inspires the respect and admiration of all Americans, and our gratitude is expressed for all time, in the medals it is now my honor to present.

May God bless you all.

After speaking, the president awarded us the Congressional Gold Medal, the highest civilian honor Congress can bestow. The first recipient of that medal had been George Washington, back in 1776. When it was my turn, I snapped to attention and saluted. The president saluted back. The audience cheered.

"Why did you salute instead of shaking his hand, Pops?" Mike asked me later.

The other four men had shaken the president's hand when they received their medals.

"He's our commander in chief," I said, "and you salute your commander in chief. You don't shake his hand."

A reception, hosted by MGM Studios, followed the ceremony. MGM announced their soon-to-be-released epic movie *Windtalkers*, a war movie involving the World War II code talkers.

Harry Tsosie was the only one of the first 29 code talkers to die during the war. Of the approximately 390 code talkers who followed the original 29, 12 were killed in the war, bringing the total deaths to 13. Given the deadly Pacific arena where we all fought, and given the fact that we were in the thick of every battle, we men did well. The fatality numbers are not as large as might have been expected.

Later that year, the 320 documented code talkers who followed us original 29 were awarded Congressional Silver Medals, many of them posthumously. Quite a few code talkers—a number estimated to be from 70 to as high as 100 by some—are thought to have been undocumented and, subsequently, unrecognized.

After the gold medal presentation, I was in even greater demand as a speaker. I traveled all over for interviews, wearing my official code talkers' uniform. A red peaked cap represented the Marines. A gold shirt, with a 3d Division patch on the arm, stood for corn pollen. Navajo jewelry showed respect for the Navajo people, the *Diné*. Light-colored pants recalled the earth and all of its inhabitants.

Among the places I visited were Washington, D.C., Boston, New York City, Dallas, Georgia, and California. My son Mike accompanied me. In addition to speaking engagements, I appeared on *Larry King Weekend* on June 8, 2002, with another code talker, Roy Hawthorne. I also appeared on the television show *60 Minutes* and was interviewed by Hoda Kotb for the *Today* show. *National Geographic* magazine interviewed me twice. In 2004, the Boston Red Sox—who had suffered from the "Curse of the Bambino" since the Red Sox sold Babe Ruth to the Yankees—asked me to bless their team. Major David Flores, who had arranged several speaking tours for me in the Boston area, and his son rode with Mike, Rita, and me in the car approaching Fenway Park. A police motorcycle escort accompanied us, sirens blaring and lights flashing. We navigated the Boston traffic, and I arrived in time to give the team a Navajo blessing and toss out the game ball. It was April, and for the first time since 1918, eighty-six years, the Red Sox won the World Series.

CHAPTER TWENTY-TWO

Celebration

June 28, 2009

Sunday dawned cloudy, with the promise of wind and rain. I woke early. My family—son Mike, daughter-in-law Rita, grandson Michael, and great-grandson Emery—dressed in party clothes, and helped me to dress in the red cap, gold shirt, and tan pants of my code talker uniform.

I had been honored by the U.S. Congress, but on this day my extended family was hosting a celebration in my honor. It was a big deal, something for which they'd planned and done fund-raising. It was to be held in *Chichiltah*, the Checkerboard Area where I had grown up. I wanted to get there early so I could socialize with my relatives before the other guests arrived.

Outside the truck window, en route to the reservation, were sweeping vistas of mesas and distant mountains, all colored in a thousand shades of red and purple and tan. The sun, slanting through heavy cloud cover, transformed familiar landmarks into burnished jewels. As we approached *Chichiltah*, the piñon pines grew taller and more abundant, occasionally interspersed with regal ponderosa pines. Rock outcroppings emerged from hills like fabulous sculptures.

We spied the blue-and-white-striped tent from the main road. It sat on the side of a hill, and we approached it on a dirt track through sparse grass. Scattered around were small houses and outbuildings of indeterminate purpose. A lone outhouse, its door lying on the ground, sat near the top of the hill.

I was eighty-eight years old, with my left leg amputated at midcalf. Mike helped me move from the truck into the wheelchair that had become my transport back in March of that year. The two nephews who had arranged the gathering, Raymond and Johnny Gray, greeted us. Inside, chairs and tables filled the circus-sized tent. American flag pennants graced the dais in front, and the U.S. flag popped up everywhere—on people's clothing, decorating the tables laden with food, arranged in patriotic "bouquets," and splashed across the napkin ties.

People arrived, singly and in small groups. Older women were dressed in the traditional velvets with squash-blossom necklaces; younger men and women wore jeans and bright shirts; children dressed in jeans and T-shirts.

Four Navajo military men wearing camouflage marched in, carrying the U.S. flag, the New Mexico flag, the Navajo Nation flag, and the black POW/MIA flag. Everyone jumped up from their chairs. I stood, trying not to waver, on my one whole leg, my right arm raised in a salute, while Miss Navajo Nation, Yolanda Jane Charley, sang the "Star-Spangled Banner" in Navajo.

I looked out at the more than one hundred attendees. *They arranged this all for me.* Sometimes my own celebrity surprised me. People lined up and filed past, shaking my hand and thanking me for my military service.

Various men and women joined me and Mike on the dais. Zonnie Gorman, daughter of deceased code talker Carl Gorman and a fine historian, spoke about our World War II mission. Although Zonnie used

English, most who followed her spoke in Navajo, a language I often spoke with my daughter-in-law Rita. My own children were not fluent.

A small army of women and girls served up a sumptuous home-cooked dinner, complete with fry bread, corn pudding, and mutton stew. The more than one hundred guests ate, and each plate was heavily laden. After the meal, mints were passed out in tiny packets adorned with American flags.

Families posed with me for photos, with everyone looking proud. People brought colorful gifts, including a plaque of thanks from Navajo tribal chairman Joe Shirley.

A live band struck up country-western songs outside the tent's wide entrance. Sudden thunder, a quick shower, and winds that shook the tent dampened no spirits. As the sun reappeared, a small herd of sheep and goats calmly climbed the hill.

Everywhere people laughed and joked. The famous Navajo sense of humor was evident in the frequent laughter and the good-hearted ribbing.

Sitting at the center of the dais, I felt tired but much too excited to think about sleep. I glanced around the room and smiling faces turned toward me.

Someone asked whether I was ready to leave.

I shook my head. "I'd like to stay awhile longer."

CHAPTER TWENTY-THREE

Legacy

Recalling the gold medal ceremony and the recognition following it, I can't help but become reflective.

When I was a little boy growing up, I didn't know a word of English, and that was one thing I hungered to learn. I wanted to get a good education, have a good job, raise a family.

Life has been better than I could ever have expected. It has been one hundred percent. If I'd stayed on the reservation, that probably wouldn't have happened. It would have been maybe thirty, forty percent.

I think about how, in my life, cultures have collided—the quiet of Navajo land giving way to military training, the strict order of military training exploding into the chaos of battle. Then a marriage, dying, the marriage ending.

Somehow I weathered all the challenges my life, managing to survive, trying

But there's one thing that's especia and I have become part of a new oral victory, with our culture contributing to foe. The story of the code talkers has been t the reservation and recorded in the pages of history books forever. Our story is not one of sorrow, like the Long Walk and the Great Livestock Massacre, but one of triumph.

As of January 2011

My adult son Ray died in May of 2008, and my sister Dora died during the Christmas holidays that same year. Sons Mike and Tyah are the sole survivors of my six children.

A second celebration was held in *Chichiltah* on Fathers' Day, June 20, 2010. Three of us code talkers—Thomas Begay, Robert Walley, and myself—were honored. (Robert Walley was the same Robert Walley who'd been my friend at Fort Defiance boarding school.) Navajo tribal chairman Joe Shirley attended. He awarded a plaque and a chief's blanket to us men. I was the only one of the "original twenty-nine" code talkers attending.

Recently I gave a talk to some kindergartners. I tried to make the little kids understand why we used the Navajo language for our code. They listened really carefully. I hope they got something out of it that they will remember. Maybe they will tell their own children someday.

Now, in 2011, my memoir is being published. I hope my words will help to keep the memory of the code talkers alive.

Despite the midcalf amputation of my left leg in March 2009, and of my right leg in April 2010, both due to complications from diabetes, I continue to do book signings, attend award ceremonies, and give speeches.

I still travel with my medicine bag in my pocket.

It's been a good life—so far.

ACKNOWLEDGMENTS

Many thanks:

Chester wishes to thank his son Mike, who drove him to all of our interviews, his daughter-in-law Rita, who speaks Navajo and helps him keep his language alive, and granddaughter Shawnia, grandsons Michael and Latham, and great-grandson Emery, Shawnia's son. He hopes that his son Tyah, who lives in Boise, Idaho, will enjoy this book. And many thanks to retired Marine major David Samuel Flores from Berwick, Maine, who helped spread word of the code talkers and who booked several speaking tours for Chester in New England.

Both Chester and I thank Melody and Myke Groves, who cheered us on, especially in the final stretch. I thank Beverly and Lloyd Hoover, who edited an earlier version of this memoir. Unhappily, Beverly will never get to see the finished product. Donn A. Byrnes and Patricia Sutton first told me about Chester. Many, many thanks. I am grateful to fellow writers Lynn Paskind, Phil Jackson, Dr. Sue Brown, Dale Atkinson, Carla Danahey, Bruno Hannemann, Lila Anastas, Keith Pyeatt, and Sherri Burr for their constant friendship, their suggestions and encouragement. Thank you, Dennis Winter, for sending all those great books on Native Americans. My brother, Gary Schiess, and sister, Dr. Nancy Schiess, read *Code Talker* and gave cogent, kind input. My mother, Angela Garrett Schiess, read and reread this manuscript without complaint, always giving wise counsel. My dad, Charles Schiess, a World War II veteran himself, especially enjoyed Chester's story. Thanks, Dad. For constant moral support, my thanks go out to my daughter, Krystal Avila Cacicia, my sister Caryl (Kai) Colombo, and my brothers, Peter Schiess and Ed McLaughlin. And many thanks to SouthWest Writers, a fine organization in Albuquerque, New Mexico.

I send heartfelt thanks to my late husband, Andrew James Avila, who never doubted that my writing efforts would lead to publication. I hope you know that this is happening, Jimmy. You're my angel, now.

Thanks, too, to our agent, Scott Miller, who sold *Code Talker* four days after agreeing to represent us. And many thanks to Natalee Rosenstein, our editor at Berkley, who saw the potential in Chester's story.

AUTHOR'S NOTE

The Navajo Language and Customs

When Navajo words are used in this book, the *Navajo-English Dictionary* by Leon Wall and William Morgan and *Navajo Made Easier: A Course in Conversational Navajo* by Irvy W. Goossen have provided the spelling.

Some of the names of Chester's acquaintances are spelled phonetically. There are isolated cases where he wasn't sure of some names, but we tried to make a stab at them. I apologize for any inaccuracies.

This is the memoir of one man who, in numerous ways, represents many. It is a book about determination, courage, and knowledge. However, although Chester and I have taken great pains to report his experiences accurately, this book does not purport to be the definitive reference for Navajo customs and ceremonials.

That is another book. Surely a Navajo will write it.

Judith Schiess Avila, May 2011

APPENDIX

The Navajo Code Talkers' Dictionary

This is the final form of the dictionary, revised June 15, 1945, per the Department of the Navy. The Navajo words are spelled phonetically. Courtesy of Naval History and Heritage Command.

NOTE:

The thirty-two alternate phonetic Navajo spellings listed below are from *Our Fathers, Our Grandfathers, Our Heroes,* Circle of Light Navajo Educational Project, pp. 38–55.

I corrected some problems with the month names.

Numerals were transmitted in Navajo, using the Navajo word for each numeral.

LETTER	NAVAJO WORD	LITERAL TRANSLATION
A	WOL-LA-CHEE	ANT
A	BE-LA-SANA	APPLE
A	TSE-NILL	AXE
B	A-HASH-CHID	BADGER
B	SHUSH	BEAR
B	TOISH-JEH	BARREL

C	MOASI	CAT
C	TLA-GIN	COAL
C	BA-GOSHI	COW
D	BE	DEER
D	CHINDI	DEVIL
D	LHA-CHA-EH	DOG
E	AH-JAH	EAR
E	DZEH	ELK
E	AH-NAH	EYE
F	CHUO	FIR
F	TSA-E-DONIN-EE	FLY
F	MA-E	FOX
G	AH-TAD	GIRL
G	KLIZZIE	GOAT
G	JEHA	GUM
H	TSE-GAH	HAIR
H	CHA	HAT
H	LIN	HORSE
I	TKIN	ICE
I	YEH-HES	ITCH
I	A-CHI	INTESTINE
J	TKELE-CHO-GI	JACKASS
J	AH-YA-TSINNE	JAW
J	YIL-DOI	JERK
K	AD-HO-LONI	KETTLE
K	BA-AH-NE-DI-TININ	KEY
K	KLIZZIE-YAZZIE	KID
L	DIBEH-YAZZIE	LAMB
L	AH-JAD	LION
M	TSIN-TLITI	MATCH
M	BE-TAS-TNI	MIRROR
M	NA-AS-TSO-SI	MOUSE
N	TSAH	NEEDLE
N	A-CHIN	NOSE
O	A-KHA	OIL
O	TLO-CHIN	ONION
O	NE-AHS-JAH	OWL

P	CLA-GI-AIH	PANT
P	BI-SO-DIH	PIG
P	NE-ZHONI	PRETTY
Q	CA-YEILTH	QUIVER
R	GAH	RABBIT
R	DAH-NES-TSA	RAM
R	AH-LOSZ	RICE
S	DIBEH	SHEEP
S	KLESH	SNAKE
T	D-AH	TEA
T	A-WOH	TOOTH
T	THAN-ZIE	TURKEY
U	SHI-DA	UNCLE
U	NO-DA-IH	UTE
V	A-KEH-DI-GLINI	VICTOR
W	GLOE-IH	WEASEL
X	AL-NA-AS-DZOH	CROSS
Y	TSAH-AS-ZIH	YUCCA
Z	BESH-DO-TLIZ	ZINC

VARIOUS MILITARY TERMS

ORGANIZATION	NAVAJO WORD	LITERAL TRANSLATION
CORPS	DIN NEH IH	CLAN
DIVISION	ASHIH-HI/ASHI-HI	SALT
REGIMENT	TABAHA	EDGE WATER
BATTALION	TACHEENE	RED SOIL
COMPANY	NAKIA	MEXICAN
PLATOON	HAS-CLISH-NIH	MUD
SECTION	YO-IH	BEADS
SQUAD	DEBEH-LI-ZINI	BLACK SHEEP

OFFICERS	NAVAJO WORD	LITERAL TRANSLATION
COMM. GEN.	BIH-KEH-HE	WAR CHIEF
MAJOR GEN.	SO-NA-KIH	TWO STAR

BRIGADIER GEN.	SO-A-LA-IH	ONE STAR
COLONEL	ATSAH-BESH-LE-GAI	SILVER EAGLE
LT. COLONEL	CHE-CHIL-BE-TAH-BESH-LEGAI	SILVER OAK LEAF
MAJOR	CHE-CHIL-BE-TAH-OLA	GOLD OAK LEAF
CAPTAIN	BESH-LEGAI-NAH-KIH	TWO SILVER BARS
LIEUTENANT	BESH-LEGAI-A-LAH-IH	ONE SILVER BAR
COMM. OFFICER	HASH-KAY-GI-NA-TAH	WAR CHIEF
EXEC. OFFICER	BIH-DA-HOL-NEHI	THOSE IN CHARGE

NAMES OF COUNTRIES

COUNTRY	NAVAJO WORD	LITERAL TRANSLATION
AFRICA	ZHIN-NI	BLACKIES
ALASKA	BEH-HGA	WITH WINTER
AMERICA	NE-HE-MAH	OUR MOTHER
AUSTRALIA	CHA-YES-DESI or CHAH-YES-DESI	ROLLED HAT
BRITAIN	TOH-TA	BETWEEN WATERS
CHINA	CEH-YEHS-BESI	BRAIDED HAIR
FRANCE	DA-GHA-HI	BEARD
GERMANY	BESH-BE-CHA-HE	IRON HAT
ICELAND	TKIN-KE-YAH	ICE LAND
INDIA	AH-LE-GAI	WHITE CLOTHES
ITALY	DOH-HA-CHI-YALI-TCHI	STUTTER
JAPAN	BEH-NA-ALI-TSOSIE	SLANT EYE
PHILIPPINES	KE-YAH-DA-NA-LHE	FLOATING ISLAND
RUSSIA	SILA-GOL-CHI-IH	RED ARMY
SOUTH AMERICA	SHA-DE-AH-NE-HI-MAH	SOUTH OUR MOTHER
SPAIN	DEBA-DE-NIH	SHEEP PAIN

NAMES OF AIRCRAFT

AIRCRAFT	NAVAJO WORD	LITERAL TRANSLATION
PLANES	WO-TAH-DE-NE-IH	AIR FORCE
DIVE BOMBER	GINI	CHICKEN HAWK

TORPEDO PLANE	TAS-CHIZZIE	SWALLOW
OBSERVATION PLANE	NE-AS-JAH	OWL
FIGHTER PLANE	DA-HE-TIH-HI	HUMMING BIRD
BOMBER PLANE	JAY-SHO	BUZZARD
PATROL PLANE	GA-GIH	CROW
TRANSPORT	ATSAH	EAGLE

NAMES OF SHIPS

SHIP	NAVAJO WORD	LITERAL TRANSLATION
SHIPS	TOH-DINEH-IH	SEA FORCE
BATTLESHIP	LO-TSO	WHALE
AIRCRAFT CARRIER	TSIDI-MOFFA-YE-HI	BIRD CARRIER
	or TSIDI-HEY-YE-HI	
SUBMARINE	BESH-LO	IRON FISH
MINE SWEEPER	CHA	BEAVER
DESTROYER	CA-LO	SHARK
TRANSPORT	DINEH-NAY-YE-HI	MAN CARRIER
CRUISER	LO-TSO-YAZZIE	SMALL WHALE
MOSQUITO BOAT	TSE-E	MOSQUITO

NAMES OF MONTHS

MONTH	NAVAJO WORD	LITERAL TRANSLATION
JANUARY	YAS-NIL-TES	CRUSTED SNOW
FEBRUARY	ATSAH-BE-YAZ	SMALL EAGLE
MARCH	WOZ-CHEIND	SQUEAKY VOICE
APRIL	TAH-CHILL	SMALL PLANT
MAY	TAH-TSO	BIG PLANT
JUNE	BE-NE-EH-EH-JAH-TSO	BIG PLANTING
JULY	BE-NE-TA-TSOSIE	SMALL HARVEST
AUGUST	BE-NEEN-TA-TSO	BIG HARVEST
SEPTEMBER	GHAW-JIH	HALF
OCTOBER	NIL-CHI-TSOSIE	SMALL WIND

NOVEMBER	NIL-CHI-TSO	BIG WIND
DECEMBER	KESH-MESH	CHRISTMAS

VOCABULARY

WORD	NAVAJO WORD	LITERAL TRANSLATION
ABANDON	YE-TSAN	RUN AWAY FROM
ABOUT	WOLA-CHI-A-MOFFA-GAHN	ANT FIGHT
	or WOLA-CHEE-A-HE-GAHN	
ABREAST	WOLA-CHEE-BE-YIED	ANT BREAST
ACCOMPLISH	UL-SO	ALL DONE
ACCORDING	BE-KA-HO	ACCORDING TO
ACKNOWLEDGE	HANOT-DZIED	ACKNOWLEDGE
ACTION	AH-HA-TINH	PLACE OF ACTION
ACTIVITY	AH-HA-TINH-Y	ACTION ENDING IN Y
ADEQUATE	BEH-GHA	ENOUGH
ADDITION	IH-HE-DE-NDEL	ADDITION
ADDRESS	YI-CHIN-HA-TSE	ADDRESS
ADJACENT	BE-GAHI	NEAR
ADJUST	HAS-TAI-NEL-KAD	ADJUST
ADVANCE	NAS-SEY	AHEAD
ADVISE	NA-NETIN	ADVISE
AERIAL	BE-ZONZ	STINGER
AFFIRMATIVE	LANH	AFFIRMATIVE
AFTER	BI-KHA-DI	AFTER
AGAINST	BE-NA-GNISH	AGAINST
AID	EDA-ELE-TSOOD	AID
AIR	NILCHI	AIR
AIRDROME	NILCHI-BEGHAN	ROME
	or NILCHI-BEGAN AIRD	
ALERT	HA-IH-DES-EE	ALERT
ALL	TA-A-TAH	ALL
ALLIES	NIH-HI-CHO	ALLIES
ALONG	WOLACHEE-SNEZ	LONG ANT
ALSO	EH-DO	ALSO

ALTERNATE	NA-KEE-GO-NE-NAN-DEY-HE	SECOND POSITION
AMBUSH	KHAC-DA	AMBUSH
AMMUNITION	BEH-ELI-DOH-BE-CAH-ALI-TAS-AI	AMMUNITION
	or BEH-ELI-DOH-BE-CAH-ALI-TAS-AH	
AMPHIBIOUS	CHAL	FROG
AND	DO	AND
ANGLE	DEE-CAHN	SLANTING
ANNEX	IH-NAY-TANI	ADDITION
ANNOUNCE	BEH-HA-O-DZE	ANNOUNCE
ANTI	WOL-LA-CHEE-TSIN	ANT ICE
ANTICIPATE	NI-JOL-LIH	ANTICIPATE
ANY	TAH-HA-DAH	ANY
APPEAR	YE-KA-HA-YA	APPEAR
APPROACH	BI-CHI-OL-DAH	APPROACH
APPROXIMATE	TO-KUS-DAN	APPROXIMATE
ARE	GAH-TSO	BIG RABBIT
AREA	HAZ-A-GIH	AREA
ARMOR	BESH-YE-HA-DA-DI-TEH	IRON PROTECTOR
ARMY	LEI-CHA-IH-YIL-KNEE-IH	DOG FACES
ARRIVE	IL-DAY	CAME
ARTILLERY	BE-AL-DOH-TSO-LANI	MANY BIG GUNS
AS	AHCE	AS
ASSAULT	ALTSEH-E-JAH-HE	FIRST STRIKER
ASSEMBLE	DE-JI-KASH	BUNCH TOGETHER
ASSIGN	BAH-DEH-TAHN	ASSIGN
AT	AH-DI	AT
ATTACK	AL-TAH-JE-JAY	ATTACK
ATTEMPT	BO-O-NE-TAH	TRY
ATTENTION	GIHA	ATTENTION
AUTHENTICATOR	HANI-BA-AH-HO-ZIN	KNOW ABOUT
AUTHORIZE	BE-BO-HO-SNEE	AUTHORIZE
AVAILABLE	TA-SHOZ-TEH-IH	AVAILABLE
BAGGAGE	KLAILH	BAGGAGE
BANZAI	NE-TAH	FOOL THEM
BARGE	BESH-NA-ELT	BARGE
BARRAGE	BESH-BA-WA-CHIND	BARRAGE
BARRIER	BIH-CHAN-NI-AH	IN THE WAY

BASE	BIH-TSEE-DIH	BASE
BATTERY	BIH-BE-AL-DOH-TKA-IH	THREE GUNS
BATTLE	DA-AH-HI-DZI-TSIO	BATTLE
BAY	TOH-AH-HI-GHINH	BAY
BAZOOKA	AH-ZHOL	BAZOOKA
BE	TSES-NAH	BEE
BEACH	TAH-BAHN	BEACH
BEEN	TSES-NAH-NES-CHEE	BEE NUT
BEFORE	BIH-TSE-DIH	BEFORE
BEGIN	HA-HOL-ZIZ	COMMENCE FROM
BELONG	TSES-NAH-SNEZ	LONG BEE
BETWEEN	BI-TAH-KIZ	BETWEEN
BEYOND	BILH-LA DI	DOWN BELOW
BIVOUAC	EHL-NAS-TEH	BRUSH SHELTER
BOMB	A-YE-SHI	EGGS
BOOBY TRAP	DINEH-BA-WHOA-BLEHI	MAN TRAP
BORNE	YE-CHIE-TSAH	BORN ELK
BOUNDARY	KA-YAH-BI-NA-HAS-DZOH	BOUNDARY
BULL DOZER	DOLA-ALTH-WHOSH	BULL SLEEP
BUNKER	TSAS-KA	SANDY HOLLOW
BUT	NEH-DIH	BUT
BY	BE-GHA	BY
CABLE	BESH-LKOH	WIRE ROPE
CALIBER	NAHL-KIHD	MOVE AROUND
CAMP	TO-ALTSEH-HOGAN	TEMPORARY PLACE
CAMOUFLAGE	DI-NES-IH	HID
CAN	YAH-DI-ZINI	CAN
CANNONEER	BE-AL-DOH-TSO-DEY-DIL-DON-IGI	BIG GUN OPERATOR
CAPACITY	BE-NEL-AH	CAPACITY
CAPTURE	YIS-NAH	CAPTURE
CARRY	YO-LAILH	CARRY
CASE	BIT-SAH	CASE
CASUALTY	BIH-DIN-NE-DEY	PUT OUT OF ACTION
CAUSE	BI-NIH-NANI	CAUSE
CAVE	TSA-OND	ROCK CAVE
CEILING	DA-TEL-JAY	SEAL
CEMETERY	JISH-CHA	AMONG DEVILS

CENTER	ULH-NE-IH	CENTER
CHANGE	THLA-GO-A-NAT-ZAH	CHANGE
CHANNEL	HA-TALHI-YAZZIE	SMALL SINGER
CHARGE	AH-TAH-GI-JAH	CHARGE
CHEMICAL	TA-NEE	ALKALI
CIRCLE	NAS-PAS	CIRCLE
CIRCUIT	AH-HEH-HA-DAILH	CIRCUIT
CLASS	ALTH-AH-A-TEH	CLASS
CLEAR	YO-AH-HOL-ZHOD	CLEAR
CLIFF	TSE-YE-CHEE	CLIFF
CLOSE	UL-CHI-UH-NAL-YAH	CLOSE
COAST GUARD	TA-BAS-DSISSI	SHORE RUNNER
CODE	YIL-TAS	PECK
COLON	NAKI-ALH-DEH-DA-AL-ZHIN	TWO SPOTS
COLUMN	ALTH-KAY-NE-ZIH	COLUMN
	or ALTH-KAY-NI-ZIH	
COMBAT	DA-AH-HI-JIH-GANH	FIGHTING
COMBINATION	AL-TKAS-EI	MIXED
COME	HUC-QUO	COME
COMMA	TSA-NA-DAHL	TAIL DROP
COMMERCIAL	NAI-EL-NE-HI	COMMERCIAL
COMMIT	HUC-QUO-LA-JISH	COME GLOVE
COMMUNICATION	HA-NEH-AL-ENJI	MAKING TALK
CONCEAL	BE-KI-ASZ-JOLE	CONCEAL
CONCENTRATION	TA-LA-HI-JIH	ONE PLACE
CONCUSSION	WHE-HUS-DIL	CONCUSSION
CONDITION	AH-HO-TAI	HOW IT IS
CONFERENCE	BE-KE-YA-TI	TALK OVER
CONFIDENTIAL	NA-NIL-IN	KEPT SECRET
CONFIRM	TA-A-NEH	MAKE SURE
CONQUER	A-KEH-DES-DLIN	WON
CONSIDER	NE-TSA-CAS	THINK IT OVER
CONSIST	BILH	CONSIST
CONSOLIDATE	AH-HIH-HI-NIL	PUT TOGETHER
CONSTRUCT	AHL-NEH	TO MAKE
CONTACT	AH-HI-DI-DAIL	COME TOGETHER
CONTINUE	TA-YI-TEH	CONTINUE

CONTROL	NAI-GHIZ	CONTROL
CONVOY	TKAL-KAH-O-NEL	MOVING ON WATER
COORDINATE	BEH-EH-HO-ZIN-NA-AS-DZOH	KNOWN LINES
COUNTER ATTACK	WOLTAH-AL-KI-GI-JEH	COUNTER ACT
COURSE	CO-JI-GOH	COURSE
CRAFT	AH-TOH	NEST
CREEK	TOH-NIL-TSANH	VERY LITTLE WATER
CROSS	AL-N-AS-DZOH	CROSS
CUB	SHUSH-YAHZ or SHUSH-YAZ	CUB
DASH	US-DZOH	DASH
DAWN	HA-YELI-KAHN	DAWN
DEFENSE	AH-KIN-CIL-TOH	DEFENSE
	or AH-KIN-GIL-TOH	
DEGREE	NAHL-KIHD	DEGREE
DELAY	BE-SITIHN	DEER LIVER
DEMOLITION	AH-DEEL-TAHI	BLOW UP
	or AL-DEEL-TAHI	
DENSE	HO-DILH-CLA	WET
DEPART	DA-DE-YAH	DEPART
DEPARTMENT	HOGAN	DWELLING HOUSE
DESIGNATE	YE-KHI-DEL-NEI	POINT OUT
DESPERATE	AH-DA-AH-HO-DZAH	DOWN TO LAST
DETACH	AL-CHA-NIL	DETACHED
DETAIL	BE-BEH-SHA	DEER TAIL
DETONATOR	AH-DEEL-TAHI	BLOWN UP
DIFFICULT	NA-NE-KLAH	DIFFICULT
DIG IN	LE-EH-GADE	DIG IN
DIRECT	AH-JI-GO	DIRECT
DISEMBARK	EH-HA-JAY	GET OUT
DISPATCH	LA-CHAI-EN-SEIS-BE-JAY	DOG IS PATCH
DISPLACE	HIH-DO-NAL	MOVE
DISPLAY	BE-SEIS-NA-NEH	DEER IS PLAY
DISPOSITION	A-HO-TEY or A-HO-TAY	DISPOSITION
DISTRIBUTE	NAH-NEH	DISTRIBUTE
DISTRICT	BE-THIN-YA-NI-CHE	DEER ICE STRICT
DO	TSE-LE	SMALL PUP
DOCUMENT	BEH-EH-HO-ZINZ	DOCUMENT

DRIVE	AH-NOL-KAHL	DRIVE
DUD	DI-GISS-YAHZIE	SMALL DUMMY
DUMMY	DI-GISS-TSO	BIG DUMMY
EACH	TA-LAHI-NE-ZINI-GO	EACH
ECHELON	WHO-DZAH or WHO-DZOH	LINE
EDGE	BE-BA-HI	EDGE
EFFECTIVE	BE-DELH-NEED	EFFECTIVE
EFFORT	YEA-GO	WITH ALL YOUR MIGHT
ELEMENT	AH-NA-NAI	TROOP REPRESENTING OTHERS
ELEVATE	ALI-KHI-HO-NE-OHA	ELEVATE
ELIMINATE	HA-BEH-TO-DZIL or HA-BEH-DO-DZIL	ELIMINATE
EMBARK	EH-HO-JAY	GET ON
EMERGENCY	HO-NEZ-CLA	EMERGENCY
EMPLACEMENT	LA-AZ-NIL	EMPLACEMENT
ENCIRCLE	YE-NAS-TEH	ENCIRCLE
ENCOUNTER	BI-KHANH	GO AGAINST
ENGAGE	A-HA-NE-HO-TA	AGREED
ENGINE	CHIDI-BI-TSI-TSINE	ENGINE
ENGINEER	DAY-DIL-JAH-HE or DAY-DIL-JAH-HI	FIRE BUILDER
ENLARGE	NIH-TSA-GOH-AL-NEH	MAKE BIG
ENLIST	BIH-ZIH-A-DA-YI-LAH	WRITTEN SIGNATURE
ENTIRE	TA-A-TAH	ENTIRE [ALL]
ENTRENCH	E-GAD-AH-NE-LIH	MAKE DITCH
ENVELOP	A-ZAH-GI-YA	ENVELOP
EQUIPMENT	YA-HA-DE-TAHI	EQUIPMENT
ERECT	YEH-ZIHN	STAND UP
ESCAPE	A-ZEH-HA-GE-YAH	ESCAPE
ESTABLISH	HAS-TAY-DZAH	SET UP
ESTIMATE	BIH-KE-TSE-HOD-DES-KEZ or BIH-KE-TSE-SHOD-DES-KEZ	ESTIMATE
EVACUATE	HA-NA	EVACUATE
EXCEPT	NEH-DIH	EXCEPT
EXPECT	NA-WOL-NE	EXCHANGE
EXECUTE	A-DO-NIL	WILL HAPPEN

EXPLOSIVE	AH-DEL-TAHI	EXPLOSIVE
EXPEDITE	SHIL-LOH	SPEED UP
EXTEND	NE-TDALE	MAKE WIDE
EXTREME	AL-TSAN-AH-BAHM	EACH END
FAIL	CHA-AL-EIND	FAIL
FAILURE	YEES-GHIN	FAILURE
FARM	MAI-BE-HE-AHGAN	FOX ARM
FEED	DZEH-CHI-YON	FEED
FIELD	CLO-DIH	FIELD
FIERCE	TOH-BAH-HA-ZSID	AFRAID
FILE	BA-EH-CHEZ	FILE
FINAL	TAH-AH-KWO-DIH	THAT IS ALL
FLAME THROWER	COH-AH-GHIL-TLID	FLAME THROWER
FLANK	DAH-DI-KAD	FLANK
FLARE	WO-CHI	LIGHT STREAK
FLIGHT	MA-E-AS-ZLOLI	FOX LIGHT
FORCE	TA-NA-NE-LADI	WITHOUT CARE
FORM	BE-CHA	FORM
FORMATION	BE-CHA-YE-LAILH	FORMATION
FORTIFICATION	AH-NA-SOZI	CLIFF DWELLING
FORTIFY	AH-NA-SOZI-YAZZIE	SMALL FORTIFICATION
FORWARD	TEHI	LET'S GO
FRAGMENTATION	BESH-YAZZIE	SMALL METAL
FREQUENCY	HA-TALHI-TSO	BIG SINGER
FRIENDLY	NEH-HECHO-DA-NE	FRIENDLY
FROM	BI-TSAN-DEHN	FROM
FURNISH	YEAS-NIL	FURNISH
FURTHER	WO-NAS-DI	FURTHER
GARRISON	YAH-A-DA-HAL-YON-IH	TAKE CARE OF
GASOLINE	CHIDI-BI-TOH	GASOLINE
GRENADE	NI-MA-SI	POTATOES
GUARD	NI-DIH-DA-HI	GUARD
GUIDE	NAH-E-THLAI	GUIDE
HALL	LHI-TA-A-TA	HORSE ALL
HALF TRACK	ALH-NIH-JAH-A-QUHE	RACE TRACK
HALT	TA-AKWAI-I	HALT

HANDLE	BET-SEEN	HANDLE
HAVE	JO	HAVE
HEADQUARTER	NA-HA-TAH-TA-BA-HOGAN	HEADQUARTER
HELD	WO-TAH-TA-EH-DAHN-OH	HELD
HIGH	WO TAH	HIGH
HIGH EXPLOSIVE	BE-AL-DOH-BE-CA-BIH-DZIL-IGI	POWERFUL SHELL
HIGHWAY	WO-TAH-HO-NE-TEH	HIGH WAY
HOLD	WO-TKANH	HOLD
HOSPITAL	A-ZEY-AL-IH	PLACE OF MEDICINE
HOSTILE	A-NAH-NE-DZIN	NOT FRIENDLY
HOWITZER	BE-EL-DON-TS-QUODI	SHORT BIG GUN
ILLUMINATE	WO-CHI	LIGHT UP
IMMEDIATELY	SHIL-LOH	IMMEDIATELY
IMPACT	A-HE-DIS-GOH	IMPACT
IMPORTANT	BA-HAS-TEH or BA-HAS-THE	IMPORTANT
IMPROVE	HO-DOL-ZHOND	IMPROVE
INCLUDE	EL-TSOD	INCLUDE
INCREASE	HO-NALH	INCREASE
INDICATE	BA-HAL-NEH	TELL ABOUT
INFANTRY	TA-NEH-NAL-DAHI	INFANTRY
INFILTRATE	YE-GHA-NE-JEH	WENT THROUGH
INITIAL	BEH-ED-DE-DLID	BRAND
INSTALL	EHD-TNAH	INSTALL
INSTALLATION	NAS-NIL	IN PLACE
INSTRUCT	NA-NE-TGIN	TEACH
INTELLIGENCE	HO-YA	SMART
INTENSE	DZEEL	STRENGTH
INTERCEPT	YEL-NA-ME-JAH	INTERCEPT
INTERFERE	AH-NILH-KHLAI	INTERFERE
INTERPRET	AH-TAH-HA-NE	INTERPRET
INVESTIGATE	NA-ALI-KA	TRACK
INVOLVE	A-TAH	INVOLVE
IS	SEIS	SEVEN
ISLAND	SEIS-KEYAH	SEVEN ISLAND
ISOLATE	BIH-TSA-NEL-KAD	SEPARATE
JUNGLE	WOH-DI-CHIL	JUNGLE

KILL	NAZ-TSAID	KILL
KILOCYCLE	NAS-TSAID-A-KHA-AH- YEH-HA-DILH	KILL OIL GO AROUND
LABOR	NA-NISH	LABOR
LAND	KAY-YAH	LAND
LAUNCH	TKA-GHIL-ZHOD	LAUNCH
LEADER	AH-NA-GHAI	LEADER
LEAST	DE-BE-YAZIE-HA-A-AH	LAMB EAST
LEAVE	DAH-DE-YAH	HE LEFT
LEFT	NISH-CLA-JIH-GOH	LEFT
LEFT SIDE	NISH-CLA-JIH-NA-NAE-GOH	LEFT SIDE [1]
LESS	BI-OH	LESS
LEVEL	DIL-KONH	LEVEL
LIAISON	DA-A-HE-GI-ENEH	KNOW OTHER'S ACTION
LIMIT	BA-HAS-AH	LIMIT
LITTER	NI-DAS-TON	SCATTER
LOCATE	A-KWE-EH	SPOT
LOSS	UT-DIN	LOSS
MACHINE GUN	A-KNAH-AS-DONIH	RAPID FIRE GUN
MAGNETIC	NA-E-LAHI	PICK UP
MANAGE	HASTNI-BEH-NA-HAI	MAN AGE
MANEUVER	NA-NA-O-NALTH	MOVING AROUND
MAP	KAH-YA-NESH-CHAI	MAP
MAXIMUM	BEL-DIL-KHON	FILL TO TOP
MECHANIC	CHITI-A-NAYL-INIH	AUTO REPAIRMAN
MECHANIZED	CHIDI-DA-AH-HE-GONI	FIGHTING CARS
MEDICAL	A-ZAY	MEDICINE
MEGACYCLE	MIL-AH-HEH-AH-DILH	MILLION GO AROUND
MERCHANT SHIP	NA-EL-NEHI-TSIN-NA-AILH	MERCHANT SHIP
MESSAGE	HANE-AL-NEH	MESSAGE
MILITARY	SILAGO-KEH-GOH	MILITARY
MILLIMETER	NA-AS-TSO-SI-A-YE-DO-TISH	DOUBLE MOUSE
MINE	HA-GADE	MINE

---

1 Circle of Light Navajo Educational Project, *Our Fathers, Our Grandfathers, Our Heroes.* Includes "Left Side," although it is not in the Navy's version of the dictionary.

MINIMUM	BE-OH	MINIMUM
MINUTE	AH-KHAY-EL-KIT-YAZZIE	LITTLE HOUR
MISSION	AL-NESHODI or AI-NESHODI	MISSION
MISTAKE	O-ZHI	MISS
MOPPING	HA-TAO-DI	MOPPING
MORE	THLA-NA-NAH	MORE
MORTAR	BE-AL-DOH-CID-DA-HI	SITTING GUN
MOTION	NA-HOT-NAH	MOTION
MOTOR	CHIDE-BE-TSE-TSEN	CAR HEAD
NATIVE	KA-HA-TENI	NATIVE
NAVY	TAL-KAH-SILAGO	SEA SOLDIER
NECESSARY	YE-NA-ZEHN	WANT
NEGATIVE	DO-YA-SHO-DA	NO GOOD
NET	NA-NES-DIZI or NA-NES-TIZI	NET
NEUTRAL	DO-NEH-LINI	NEUTRAL
NORMAL	DOH-A-TA-H-DAH	NORMAL
NOT	NI-DAH-THAN-ZIE	NO TURKEY
NOTICE	NE-DA-TAZI-THIN	NO TURKEY ICE
NOW	KUT	NOW
NUMBER	BEH-BIH-KE-AS-CHINIGH	WHAT'S WRITTEN
OBJECTIVE	BI-NE-YEI	GOAL
OBSERVE	HAL-ZID	OBSERVE
OBSTACLE	DA-HO-DESH-ZHA	OBSTACLE
OCCUPY	YEEL-TSOD	TAKEN
OF	TOH-NI-TKAL-LO	OCEAN FISH
OFFENSIVE	BIN-KIE-JINH-JIH-DEZ-JAY	OFFENSIVE
ONCE	TA-LAI-DI	ONCE
ONLY	TA-EI-TAY-A-YAH	ONLY
OPERATE	YE-NAHL-NISH	WORK AT
OPPORTUNITY	ASH-GA-ALIN	OPPORTUNITY
OPPOSITION	NE-HE-TSAH-JIH-SHIN	OPPOSITION
OR	EH-DO-DAH-GOH	EITHER
ORANGE	TCHIL-LHE-SOI or TCHIL-HE-SOI	ORANGE
ORDER	BE-EH-HO-ZINI	ORDER
ORDNANCE	LEI-AZ-JAH	UNDER GROUND
ORIGINATE	DAS-TEH-DO	BEGIN

OTHER	LA-E-CIH	OTHER
OUT	CLO-DIH	OUT SIDE
OVERLAY	BE-KA-HAS-TSOZ	OVERLAY
PARENTHESIS	ATSANH	RIB
PARTICULAR	A-YO-AD-DO-NEH	PARTICULAR
PARTY	DA-SHA-JAH	PARTY
PAY	NA-ELI-YA	PAY
PENALIZE	TAH-NI-DES-TANH	SET BACK
PERCENT	YAL	MONEY
PERIOD	DA-AHL-ZHIN	PERIOD
PERIODIC	DA-AL-ZHIN-THIN-MOASI	PERIOD ICE CAT
PERMIT	GOS-SHI-E	PERMIT
PERSONNEL	DA-NE-LEI	MEMBER
PHOTOGRAPH	BEH-CHI-MA-HAD-NIL	PHOTOGRAPH
PILL BOX	BI-SO-DIH-DOT-SAHI-BI-TSAH	SICK PIG BOX
PINNED DOWN	BIL-DAH-HAS-TANH-YA	PINNED DOWN
PLANE	TSIDI	BIRD
PLASMA	DIL-DI-GHILI	PLASMA
POINT	BE-SO-DE-DEZ-AHE	PIG POINT
PONTOON	TKOSH-JAH-DA-NA-ELT	FLOATING BARREL
POSITION	BILH-HAS-AHN	POSITION
POSSIBLE	TA-HA-AH-TAY	POSSIBLE
POST	SAH-DEI	POST
PREPARE	HASH-TAY-HO-DIT-NE	PREPARE
	or HAS-TAY-HO-DIT-NE	
PRESENT	KUT or CUT	PRESENT, NOW
PREVIOUS	BIH-TSE-DIH	PREVIOUS
PRIMARY	ALTSEH-NAN-DAY-HI-GIH	FIRST POSTION
PRIORITY	HANE-PESODI	PRIORITY
PROBABLE	DA-TSI	PROBABLE
PROBLEM	NA-NISH-TSOH	BIG JOB
PROCEED	NAY-NIH-JIH	GO
PROGRESS	NAH-SAI	PROGRESS
PROTECT(ION)	AH-CHANH	SELF DEFENSE
PROVIDE	YIS-NIL	PROVIDE, FURNISH
PURPLE	DINL-CHI	PURPLE
PYROTECHNIC	COH-NA-CHANH	FANCY FIRE

QUESTION	AH-JAH	EAR
QUICK	SHIL-LOH	QUICK
RADAR	ESAT-TSANH	LISTEN
RAID	DEZJAY	RAID
RAILHEAD	A-DE-GEH-HI or A-DO-GEH-HI	SHIPPING POINT
RAILROAD	KONH-NA-AL-BANSI-BI-THIN	RAILROAD
RALLYING	A-LAH-NA-O-GLALIH or A-LAH-NA-O-GLALTH	GATHERING
RANGE	AN-ZAH	DISTANCE
RATE	GAH-EH-YAHN	RABBIT ATE
RATION	NA-A-JAH	RATION
RAVINE	CHUSH-KA	RAVINE
REACH	IL-DAY	REACH, ARRIVE
READY	KUT	READY
REAR	BE-KA-DENH	REAR, BEHIND
RECEIPT	SHOZ-TEH	RECEIPT
RECOMMEND	CHE-HO-TAI-TAHN	RECOMMEND
RECONNAISSANCE	HA-A-CIDI	INSPECTOR
RECONNOITER	TA-HA-NE-AL-YA	MAKE SURE
RECORD	GAH-AH-NAH-KLOLI	R-E-ROPE
RED	LI-CHI	RED
REEF	TSA-ZHIN	BLACK ROCK
RE-EMBARK	EH-NA-COH	GO IN
REFIRE	NA-NA-COH	REFIRE
REGULATE	NA-YEL-N or NA-YEL-NA	REGULATE
REINFORCE	NAL-DZIL	REINFORCE
RELIEF	AGANH-TOL-JAY	RELIEF
RELIEVE	NAH-JIH-CO-NAL-YA	REMOVE
REORGANIZE	HA-DIT-ZAH	REORGANIZE
REPLACEMENT	NI-NA-DO-NIL	REPLACEMENT
REPORT	WHO-NEH	GOT WORD
REPRESENTATIVE	TKA-NAZ-NILI	TRIPLE MEN
REQUEST	JO-KAYED-GOH	ASK FOR
RESERVE	HESH-J-E	RESERVE
RESTRICT	BA-HO-CHINI	RESTRICT
RETIRE	AH-HOS-TEEND or AH-HOS-TSEND	RETIRE

RETREAT	JI-DIN-NES-CHANH	RETREAT
RETURN	NA-DZAH	CAME BACK
REVEAL	WHO-NEH	REVEAL
REVERT	NA-SI-YIZ	TURN ABOUT
REVETMENT	BA-NAS-CLA	CORNER
RIDGE	GAH-GHIL-KEID	RABBIT RIDGE
RIFLEMAN	BE-AL-DO-HOSTEEN	RIFLEMEN
RIVER	TOH-YIL-KAL	MUCH WATER
ROBOT BOMB	A-YE-SHI-NA-TAH-IH	EGG FLY
ROCKET	LESZ-YIL-BESHI	SAND BOIL
ROLL	YEH-MAS	ROLL
ROUND	NAZ-PAS	ROUND, CIRCLE
ROUTE	GAH-BIH-TKEEN	RABBIT TRAIL
RUNNER	NIH-DZID-TEIH	RUNNER
SABOTAGE	A-TKEL-YAH	HINDERED
SABOTEUR	A-TKEL-EL-INI	TROUBLE MAKER
SAILORS	CHA-LE-GAI	WHITE CAPS
SALVAGE	NA-HAS-GLAH	PICK THEM UP
SAT	BIH-LA-SANA-CID-DA-HI	APPLE SITTING
SCARLET, RED	LHE-CHI	RED
SCHEDULE	BEH-EH-HO-ZINI	SCHEDULE
SCOUT	HA-A-SID-AL-SIZI-GIH	SHORT RECONNAISSANCE
SCREEN	BESH-NA-NES-DIZI	SCREEN
SEAMAN	TKAL-KAH-DINEH-IH	SEAMAN
SECRET	BAH-HAS-TKIH	SECRET
SECTOR	YOEHI	SECTOR
SECURE	YE-DZHE-AL-TSISI	SMALL SECURITY
SEIZE	YEEL-STOD	SEIZE
SELECT	BE-TAH-HAS-GLA	TOOK OUT
SEMI COLON	DA-AHL-ZHIN-BI-TSA-NA-DAHL	DOT DROP
SET	DZEH-CID-DA-HI	ELK SITTING
SHACKLE	DI-BAH-NESH-GOHZ	SHACKLE
SHELL	BE-AL-DOH-BE-CA	SHELL
SHORE	TAH-BAHN	SHORE
SHORT	BE-OH	SHORT
SIDE	BOSH-KEESH	SIDE
SIGHT	YE-EL-TSANH	SEEN

SIGNAL	NA-EH-EH-GISH	BY SIGNS
SIMPLEX	ALAH-IH-NE-TIH	INNER WIRE
SIT	TKIN-CID-DA-HI	ICE SITTING
SITUATE	A-HO-TAY	SITUATE
SMOKE	LIT	SMOKE
SNIPER	OH-BEHI	PICK 'EM OFF
SPACE	BE-TKAH	BETWEEN
SPECIAL	E-YIH-SIH	MAIN THING
SPEED	YO-ZONS	SWIFT MOTION
SPORADIC	AH-NA-HO-NEIL	NOW AND THEN
SPOTTER	EEL-TSAY-I	SPOTTER
SPRAY	KLESH-SO-DILZIN	SNAKE PRAY
SQUADRON	NAH-GHIZI	SQUASH
STORM	NE-OL	STORM
STRAFF	NA-WO-GHI-GOID	HOE
STRAGGLER	CHY-NE-DE-DAHE	STRAGGLER
STRATEGY	NA-HA-TAH	STRATEGY
STREAM	TOH-NI-LIH	RUNNING WATER
STRENGTH	DZHEL	STRENGTH
STRETCH	DESZ-TSOOD	STRETCH
STRIKE	NAY-DAL-GHAL	STRIKE
STRIP	HA-TIH-JAH	STRIP
STUBBORN	NIL-TA	STUBBORN
SUBJECT	NA-NISH-YAZZIE	SMALL JOB
SUBMERGE	TKAL-CLA-YI-YAH	WENT UNDER WATER
SUBMIT	A-NIH-LEH	SEND
SUBORDINATE	AL-KHI-NAL-DZL	HELPING EACH OTHER
SUCCEED	YAH-TAY-GO-E-ELAH	MAKE GOOD
SUCCESS	UT-ZAH	IT IS DONE
SUCCESSFUL	UT-ZAH-HA-DEZ-BIN	IT IS DONE WELL
SUCCESSIVE	UT-ZAH-SID	SUCCESS SCAR
SUCH	YIS-CLEH	SOX [SOCKS]
SUFFER	TO-HO-NE	SUFFER
SUMMARY	SHIN-GO-BAH	SUMMER MARY
SUPPLEMENTARY	TKA-GO-NE-NAN-DEY-HE	THIRD POSITION
SUPPLY	NAL-YEH-HI	SUPPLY
SUPPLY SHIP	NALGA HI TSIN-NAH-AILH	SUPPLY SHIP

SUPPORT	BA-AH-HOT-GLI	DEPEND
SURRENDER	NE-NA-CHA	SURRENDER
SURROUND	NAZ-PAS	SURROUND
SURVIVE	YIS-DA-YA	SURVIVE
SYSTEM	DI-BA-TSA-AS-ZHI-BI-TSIN	SYSTEM
TACTICAL	E-CHIHN	TACTICAL
TAKE	GAH-TAHN	TAKE
TANK	CHAY-DA-GAHI	TORTOISE
TANK DESTROYER	CHAY-DA-GAHI-NAIL-TSAIDI	TORTOISE KILLER
TARGET	WOL-DONI	TARGET
TASK	TAZI-NA-EH-DIL-KID	TURKEY ASK
TEAM	DEH-NA-AS-TSO-SI	TEA MOUSE
TERRACE	ALI-KHI-HO-NE-OHA	TERRACE
TERRAIN	TASHI-NA-HAL-THIN	TURKEY RAIN
TERRITORY	KA-YAH or KE-YAH	LAND
THAT	TAZI-CHA or TKANZIE-CHA	TURKEY HAT
THE	CHA-GEE	BLUE-JAY
THEIR	BIH	THEIR
THEREAFTER	TA-ZI-KWA-I-BE-KA-DI	TURKEY HERE AFTER
THESE	CHA-GI-O-EH	THE SEE
THEY	CHA-GEE or NI-GHAI	THEY
THIS	DI	THIS
TOGETHER	TA-BILH or TA-BIL	TOGETHER
TORPEDO	LO-BE-CA	FISH SHELL
TOTAL	TA-AL-SO	TOTAL
TRACER	BEH-NA-AL-KAH-HI	TRACER
TRAFFIC DIAGRAM	HANE-BA-NA-AS-DZOH	DIAGRAM STORY LINE
TRAIN	COH-NAI-ALI-BAHN-SI	TRAIN
TRANSPORTATION	A-HAH-DA-A-CHA or A-HAHDA-S-GHA	TRANSPORTATION
TRENCH	E-GADE	TRENCH
TRIPLE	TKA-IH	TRIPLE
TROOP	NAL-DEH-HI	TROOP
TRUCK	CHIDO-TSO	BIG AUTO
TYPE	ALTH-AH-A-TEH	TYPE
UNDER	BI-YAH	UNDER
UNIDENTIFIED	DO-BAY-HOSEN-E	UNIDENTIFIED

UNIT	DA-AZ-JAH	UNIT
UNSHACKLE	NO-DA-EH-NESH-GOHZ	UNSHACKLE
UNTIL	UH-QUO-HO	UNTIL
VICINITY	NA-HOS-AH-GIH	THERE ABOUT
VILLAGE	CHAH-HO-OH-LHAN-IH	MANY SHELTER
VISIBILITY	NAY-ES-TEE	VISIBILITY
VITAL	TA-EH-YE-SY	VITAL
WARNING	BILH-HE-NEH	WARNING
WAS	NE-TEH	WAS
WATER	TKOH	WATER
WAVE	YILH-KOLH	WAVE
WEAPON	BEH-DAH-A-HI-JIH-GANI	FIGHTING WEAPON
	or BEH-DAH-A-HI-JAH-GANI	
WELL	TO-HA-HA-DLAY	WELL
WHEN	GLOE-EH-NA-AH-WO-HAI	WEASEL HEN
WHERE	GLOE-IH-QUI-AH	WEASEL HERE
WHICH	GLOE-IH-A-HSI-TLON	WEASEL TIED TOGETHER
	or GLOE-A-HIS-TLON	
WILL	GLOE-IH-DOT-SAHI	SICK WEASEL
WIRE	BESH-TSOSIE	SMALL WIRE
WITH	BILH	WITH
WITHIN	BILH-BIGIH	WITH IN
WITHOUT	TA-GAID	WITHOUT
WOOD	CHIZ	FIRE WOOD
WOUND	CAH-DA-KHI	WOUND
YARD	A-DEL-TAHL	YARD
ZONE	BIH-NA-HAS-DZOH	ZONE

BIBLIOGRAPHY

NONFICTION BOOKS

Aaseng, Nathan. 1992. *Navajo Code Talkers: America's Secret Weapon in World War II.* New York: Walker Publishing Company. Excellent insights into Navajo culture.

Bailey, Lynn R. 1998. *Bosque Redondo: The Navajo Internment at Fort Sumner, New Mexico, 1863–68.* Tucson, Ariz.: Westernlore Press. Pre–code talker Navajo history.

Bradley, James, with Ron Powers. 2000. *Flags of Our Fathers.* New York: Bantam Books. Not about the code talkers, but a compelling account of the flag raising on Iwo Jima and its aftermath.

Circle of Light Navajo Educational Project. 2004. *Our Fathers, Our Grandfathers, Our Heroes . . . The Navajo Code Talkers of World War II, A Photographic Exhibit.* Gallup, N. Mex. A wonderful book, put together by Navajo schoolchildren.

Durrett, Deanne. 1998. *Unsung Heroes of World War II.* New York: Facts on File. A compact book full of interesting facts about the code talkers.

Goossen, Irvy W. 1967. *Navajo Made Easier, A Course in Conversational Navajo.* Flagstaff, Ariz.: Northland Press. Took some spellings from this volume.

Greenberg, Henry, and Georgia Greenberg. 1984. *Carl Gorman's World.* Albuquerque, N. Mex.: University of New Mexico Press. Interesting portrayal of the Native American artist and activist.

Haile, Father Berard, OFM. 1974. *A Manual of Navajo Grammar.* New York: AMS Press. Father Haile's research, first published in 1926, provides a graphic example of how difficult Navajo is to learn.

Kawano, Kenji. 1990. *Warriors: Navajo Code Talkers*. Flagstaff, Ariz.: Northland Publishing. Photographs of code talkers.

Kluckhohn, Clyde, and Dorothea Leighton. 1951. *The Navajo*. Cambridge, Mass.: Harvard University Press. A wonderfully detailed book studying Navajo history, everyday life, and ceremonies.

Leckie, Robert. 1957. *Helmet for My Pillow*. New York: Bantam Books Trade Paperbacks. First-person account of the war on Guadalcanal, New Britain, and Peleliu.

McClain, Sally. 2002. *Navajo Weapon, the Navajo Code Talkers*. Tucson, Ariz.: Rio Nuevo Publishers. (Originally published in 1994 by Books Beyond Borders.) An exhaustive study of the code talkers and their role in World War II. Beautifully executed.

Messenger, Charles. 1989. *Chronological Atlas of World War Two*. New York: Macmillan. Detailed information on WWII battles.

Paul, Doris A. 1973. *The Navajo Code Talkers*. Pittsburgh: Dorrance Publishing Company, Inc. Some good information on the code talker project.

Rogers, Everett M., and Nancy R. Bartlit. 2005. *Silent Voices of World War II, When Sons of the Land of Enchantment Met Sons of the Land of the Rising Sun*. Santa Fe, N.Mex.: Sunstone Press. New Mexico's part in the war: development of the atomic bomb, Navajo code talkers, the Japanese internment camp at Santa Fe, the New Mexico National Guard at Bataan.

Santella, Andrew. 2004. *We the People: Navajo Code Talkers*. Minneapolis: Compass Point Books. A brief accounting of the code talkers with many good photos.

Sledge, E. B. 1981. *With the Old Breed*. New York: Presidio Press. A great first-person account of the in-the-trenches fighting on Peleliu and Okinawa.

Steinberg, Rafael, and the Editors of Time-Life Books. 1978. *Island Fighting, World War II*. Alexandria, Va.: Time-Life Books. The war in the Pacific. Great synopses of individual battles.

van der Vat, Dan. 1991. *The Pacific Campaign, World War II, The U.S.-Japanese Naval War 1941–1945*. New York: Simon & Schuster. World War II Naval details.

Wall, Leon, and William Morgan. 2007. *Navajo-English Dictionary*. New York: Hippocrene Books. Also used this book for spelling Navajo words.

Ward, Geoffrey C., and Ken Burns. 2007. *The War: An Intimate History, 1941–1945*. New York: Alfred A. Knopf. Personal stories from soldiers and great photographs.

Waters, Frank. 1950. *Masked Gods, Navajo and Pueblo Ceremonialism*. Chicago: The Swallow Press. Lots of great history, beliefs, ceremonies.

NOVELS/STORIES

Alexie, Sherman. 2000. *The Toughest Indian in the World*. New York: Atlantic Monthly Press. Riveting collection of short stories (not Navajo).

Bruchac, Joseph. 2005. *Code Talker: A Novel About the Navajo Marines of World War Two*. New York: Penguin Group. Historical novel with good detail about Navajo life and WWII.

La Farge, Oliver. 1937. *The Enemy Gods*. Boston: Houghton Mifflin Company. Interesting descriptions of Navajo customs.

La Farge, Oliver. 1929. *Laughing Boy, A Navajo Love Story*. New York: Mariner Books, Houghton Mifflin Company. Winner of Pulitzer Prize in 1930.

MEDIA

Websites
AcePilots.com World War II ships

Archives.gov The National Archives

Armchairgeneral.com Battles in the HBO miniseries The Pacific

Blountweb.com World War II time line

DestroyersOnline.com The destroyers

Historylearningsite.co.uk History learning site

History.Navy.mil U.S. government website for Naval history and heritage (Navajo code)

Historyplace.com World War II in the Pacific

Ibiblio.org/hyperwar War and tactics

LOC.gov Library of Congress

Marines.mil: Official home of the United States Marine Corps

Military.Discovery.com Military channel website with videos

Militaryhistoryonline.com Webzine of military articles

Navy.mil Official website of the United States Navy

NebraskaStudies.org Website offering historical photos, documents, letters, maps, more

NPS.com National Park Service

Olive-drab.com Military information

Pwencycl.kgbudge.com The Pacific war online encyclopedia

SantaFeNewMexican.com Santa Fe newspaper

Tecom.usmc.mil U.S. government website for Marine history and museums

Thinkquest.org Oracle ThinkQuest Education Foundation

USGovInfo.about.com U.S. government information

USMC.mil U.S. Marine Corps

USMC.mil/unit/2ndmardiv 2d Marine Division

ww2gyrene.org World War II Gyrene, dedicated to the U.S. Marine 1941–1945

www-cs-faculty.stanford.edu Educational website

Magazines and Newspapers

Survey Graphic: Magazine of Social Interpretation 23:6 (June 1934), p. 261.

Chevron, the Marine Corps newspaper in San Diego, May 16, 1942, and July 4, 1942.

Films

500 Nations, a Jack Leustig film, Warner Home Video, 1995.

Band of Brothers, a Tom Hanks and Steven Spielberg film, Home Box Office Miniseries, 2002.

Guadalcanal Diary, a Lewis Seiler film, 20th Century Fox Home Entertainment, 1943.

The Pacific, a Tom Hanks, Steven Spielberg, and Gary Goetzman film, Home Box Office Miniseries, 2010.

The War, a Ken Burns film, PBS Home Video, 2007.

INDEX

Page numbers followed by "n" indicate notes.

Aaseng, Nathan, 104, 104n
Adams, Robert, 60, 61
"air" *(nitXch'l)*, 36
Air Force (U.S.), 236
Albuquerque, New Mexico, 217, 218, 235, 241,
    243, 253, 255
Allied forces, 164, 215
    See also United States of America
"all service" base, 236
alphabet and Navajo code, 102–103, 105–106,
    108, 110, 114
"always faithful" *(semper fi)*, 214
America. *See* United States of America
"Among the Oak Trees" *(Chichiltah)*, 20–21, 31,
    43, 51, 54, 58, 68, 73, 80, 84, 90, 218–219,
    233, 235, 255, 261, 266
Amphibious Corps, Pacific Fleet, 92
Angaur, 197–200, 201, 202
Apache tribe, 38
Apra Harbor, 179–181, 182
"April" *(tah-chill)*, 110
A "red ant" *(wol-la-chee)*, 103
Arizona, 2, 10, 31, 36, 38, 58, 89
"Arizona" tag, 132
Army (U.S.), 157, 160, 180, 198, 200,
    201–202, 205, 236
arroyo baths, 69
arthritis, 71
atabrine, 144

"auntie" *(Shimá Yázhí)*, 23, 24
Austen, Mount, 146, 153, 157
Australia, 13, 149–150, 152, 156, 164, 209
Axis powers, 86
    See also Japan

B, "bear" *(shush)*, 103
Bad Way ceremony, 223n, 223–227, 224n, 226n
Baker, Davey, 215, 215n
Baltimore-class cruisers, 14, 14n
Banzai (suicide attackers), 129, 133, 138, 141,
    166, 181–182, 183
Bataan Death March, 114, 208
Battle of Bloody Ridge, 16
Battle of Empress Augusta Bay, 164
Battle of Guadalcanal, 145
    See also Guadalcanal
Battle of Midway, 15, 114
Battle of Savo Island, 13–15
Battle of the Coral Sea, 114
Battle of the Java Sea, 114
"battleship" *(lo-tso)*, 110
battleships, 6, 6n, 12
"bazookas" *(ah-zhol)*, 178
"beer," 106
beer, military issued, 120, 148, 171
Begay, Charlie (code talker), 8, 110, 111, 121, 184
Begay, Jack, 245
Begay, Roy (code talker)
    Angaur, 198
    Chester worrying about, 213

Begay, *(cont.)*
  Guadalcanal, 11, 11n, 12, 17, 18–19, 20, 127,
    128–129, 130, 133, 134–135, 136, 138, 139,
    142, 143, 144, 148, 151, 152, 153, 155, 156,
    157, 158, 159
  Marine recruit, 87, 88, 89
  Navajo code development, 106, 111, 112
  New Caledonia, 121–122, 123
  Peleliu, 190, 203
Begay, Samuel (code talker), 111, 121
Begay, Thomas (code talker), 266
Beijing, China, 86
Benally, John (code talker), 103, 111, 121, 156,
  157
Benny, Jack (code talker), 111, 121
Betoli, 25, 26, 26n
  See also Nez, Chester (childhood and youth)
Bingaman, Jeff, 256
Biníshíit Baa. See Nez, Dora (Chester's sister)
Bitsie, Wilsie (code talker), 90, 110, 121, 123, 187
Black Sheep clan *(Dibé-lizhiní* or *Dibé-
  tXizhiní)*, 26, 239n, 239–240
"Bloody Nose Ridge" (Umurbrogol Mountain),
  194, 201–202, 205, 206, 206n
boarding school, 41–52
  alter boys, 60, 61
  babysitting by older schoolmates, 53–54
  beds at, 48, 54
  "big harvest" and, 42, 43
  birth dates, 49
  bullies, 53–55, 58
  Catholicism and, 60–62
  Checkerboard vs. boarding school, 54
  church attendance, 60–61
  classes, 55–57
  cowboy dreams, 59
  cultural heritage, erasing, 57, 62, 84, 104, 108
  dormitories, 47, 48
  "English" all the time, 1, 42, 43, 49, 50, 56,
    102, 149, 431
  "English" names assigned, 43–44, 49
  food at, 44, 45, 54–55, 57, 122
  forbidden areas, 47, 48
  "fried bread" helmets, 60
  girls (speaking to), prohibited, 48
  graduating from, 83
  haircuts, 46, 94
  hockey, 59–60
  humiliation of students, 56, 59
    kindergarten, 43, 55–56
    lice treatment, 46
    marbles, 57–58
    matrons, 46, 47, 49, 50, 51, 53, 54, 73, 83, 84,
      150, 234, 240
    nightmares at, 48
    punishments, 1, 49, 50, 56, 57, 102, 128
    religion, 19, 60–62
    runaways, 58, 59
    teeth brushing with soap, 50, 128, 150
    trading post at, 57, 58–59
    uniforms, 46, 47, 52, 54, 55
"bomb" *(a-ye-shi)*, 110
Bonis (Japanese airfield), 165
Bosque Redondo, 38
Boston Red Sox, 259
bottle feeding lambs and kids, 27
Bougainville, 163–175
bows and arrows, 37
Brown, Cosey (code talker), 111, 121
Brown, John (code talker), 111, 121
Brown, John, Jr. (code talker), 256
Budweiser, 8, 8n
Buin (Japanese airfield), 165
Buka (Japanese airfield), 165
bullies, boarding school, 53–55, 58
Bureau of Indian Affairs (BIA), 49, 74, 77, 79, 93
Burma, 114
Bush, George W. (President), 257–258
Bushido code (no surrender), 124, 173

C, "cat" *(moasi)*, 103, 112
camaraderie of code talkers, 97, 105, 110, 121,
  149, 151, 159, 172, 213
Camp Elliott, California, 92, 101, 111, 114, 121,
  156, 235–236
Camp Pendleton, San Diego, 90
cans from field rations used as alarms, 153
Canyon people, 239
Cape Esperance, 145
Cape Torokina, 163–164, 165, 166–167, 168, 170
Capital Rotunda, 256, 257
card playing, 119, 120
Carlson, Evans (Lieutenant Colonel), 110–111
Carlson's Raiders, 110–111
Carson, Kit, 38, 45
Cassidy, Hopalong, 59
casualties
  Bougainville, 169, 170

code talkers (Navajo code), 166, 181, 186, 258
  Guadalcanal, 16, 17, 142, 145, 148, 159, 162
  Guam, 182, 184
  Iwo Jima, 214
  Peleliu, 192, 194, 195, 197, 201, 205, 206, 207
Catron, Ethel Pearl (Chester's wife), 234, 239,
    239n, 240–242, 244, 246, 247, 250, 252, 255
cedar, 24, 24n
celebrity, Chester as a, 249–250, 262
Chamorro natives, 84, 179, 187
Changing Woman, 36, 223
Charley, Yolanda Jane, 262
Checkerboard, New Mexico, 1, 2–3, 9, 24, 24n,
    39, 76, 77, 105, 213, 229
Chee, John (code talker), 111, 121
Cherokee tribe, 230
Chiang Kai-shek, 86
Chichiltah ("Among the Oak Trees"), 20–21, 31,
    43, 51, 54, 58, 68, 73, 80, 84, 90, 218–219,
    233, 235, 255, 261, 266
"Chief," 148, 170, 197, 202, 203
China, 15, 86
Choctaw tribe, 91
Christmases, 61, 168
civil servant incident, 217–218
clans, Navajos, 26, 239n, 239–240
Cleveland, Benjamin (code talker), 112, 121
Clinton, Bill (President), 256
Coast Guard (U.S.), 236
"coastwatchers," 13
code black, 172
code talkers (Navajo code)
  alcohol problems of some, 243
  bodyguards assigned to, 208n, 208–209
  camaraderie, 97, 105, 110, 121, 149, 151, 159,
    172, 213
  casualties, 166, 181, 186, 258
  "Chief," 148, 170, 197, 202, 203
  Congressional Gold Medals, 256, 258, 259,
    265
  Congressional Silver Medals, 256, 259
  declassification of code, 249–250, 258
  errors in messages, handling, 139–140
  exhibit, Pentagon, Washington, D.C., 256
  friendly fire death of Harry Tsosie, 166, 181,
    186, 258
  heroes, code talkers as, 10, 256
  honored by Nixon, 250
  Honoring the Navajo Code Talkers Act, 256

  Japan learning about, 207–208
  jobs, difficulty in finding, 243
  Marines and, 214n, 214–215, 215n, 243
  Navajo Code Talkers Dictionary, 271–291
  pairs, working in, 139, 148, 156
  POWs and, 202–203
  promotion protocol for, 213
  recruits (new), 156n, 156–157, 162, 258, 259
  R&R for, 171
  success of, 131–134, 135, 136–137, 138–141,
    146, 150, 157, 159, 185, 188, 200, 214n,
    214–215, 215n
  tagged messages, 132
  training new recruits, 121, 156, 157
  transmitting, moving, 134, 135, 183, 193
  undocumented code talkers, 259
  uniforms, 259, 261
  walking code machines, 138
  See also Begay, Roy (code talker); Marines
    (U.S.); Navajo language; Nez, Chester (code
    talker); radios (TBX radios); Tsinajnnie,
    Francis (code talker); World War II; *specific
    code talkers*
code talkers (Navajo code), development, 101–115
  accuracy of code, 113, 132, 136, 140
  alphabet and, 102–103, 105–106, 108, 110,
    114
  dictionary of Navajo Code Talkers, 271–291
  double encryption, 103
  expansion of code, 113–114, 178
  Japanese mistaken for, 9, 112–113, 131, 132,
    199–200, 202–203, 203
  Johnston, Philip and, 90, 91, 92, 198
  memorization of code, 108
  military men, assigned to help, 109, 110, 111,
    121, 256, 256n
  military terms and, 100, 109–110, 114, 178
  months of year and, 110
  officers and, 109, 172, 188
  one-letter-one-word pattern, 114
  "original" code talkers, 1, 8, 8n, 10, 10n, 11n,
    89, 102, 106, 109, 110–112, 121, 230, 256,
    256n, 258, 259, 266
  personalities of, 110–112
  phonetic English spelling, 108
  pilot project, 92–93
  practicing code, 8–9, 106, 108, 109, 112–113,
    118, 119–120, 123, 178
  printing vs. script, 108

code talkers (*cont.*)
  secrecy of, 3, 9–10, 87, 88, 90, 93, 101, 106,
    120, 217, 218, 221–222, 233, 235, 237, 249
  Shackle code vs., 92, 113, 131–132, 136, 198
  testing code, 112–113, 131–132
  unbreakable code, 1, 3, 8, 8n, 10, 10n,
    101–115, 121, 256, 256n
Cole, Nat King, 232
Collier, John, 76, 77, 78, 79
Comanche tribe, 91
combat fatigue, 216
coming-of-age ceremony, 69
"commando," 181
Commission of Indian Affairs, 77, 79
community sense of Navajos, 79, 80
Como, Perry, 232
condition black, 112–113
condition yellow, 174
Congressional Gold Medals, 256, 258, 259, 265
Congressional Silver Medals, 256, 259
Connor, Howard (Major), 214
cookhouses, 250
Cooper, Gary, 160
cornmeal mush, 242, 242n
corn pollen and Navajos, 11, 25, 61, 65, 130,
  228, 246, 248, 259
Corn Pollen people, 239–240
corpsmen ("docs"), 195, 206
Cousins, Bob, 235
Coyote the trickster, 36
coyote threat to sheep, 28–29, 33
Crawford, Eugene (code talker), 10, 110, 121, 123
Crawford, Gene, 103
creation of the world, 36
Crosby, Bing, 232
"cruiser" *(lo-tso-yazzie)*, 110
cruisers, 14, 14n, 145, 164, 165
"cultural freedom" for Indians, 77n, 77–78
cultural heritage (erasing), boarding school, 57,
  62, 84, 104, 108
Curley, David (code talker), 111, 121
"Curse of the Bambino," 259

D, "deer" *(be)*, 103
daisy cutters, 138
Damon, Lowell (code talker), 111, 121
Darwin, Australia, 88, 152
declassification of Navajo code, 249–250, 258
Dennison, George (code talker), 111, 121

Depression (Great), U.S., 75, 76
"destroyer" *(ca-lo)*, 110
destroyers, 14, 145, 164, 165
development of Navajo code. *See* code talkers
  (Navajo code), development
dictionary of Navajo Code Talkers, 271–291
Diné ("the People"), 25, 28, 35, 36, 37, 38, 39,
  39n, 68, 91, 104, 219, 223, 240, 259
dive-bombers, 6, 6n
Dixon, James (code talker), 111, 121
"docs" (corpsmen), 195, 206
"Don't Sit Under the Apple Tree," 119, 158
"do or die," 132
Durrett, Deanne, 185, 185n
dust bowl in Great Plains, 76

"earth" *(nahasdzáán)*, 36
East *(ha'a'aah)*, 65
Empire of the Rising Sun, 124
  See also Japan
Empress Augusta Bay, 163, 165, 168
Enemy Way ceremony, 222n, 222–223, 250–252
"English" all the time, boarding school, 1, 42,
  43, 49, 50, 56, 102, 149, 431

Father (Chester's father)
  boarding school, 42, 45, 50–51, 56, 58
  code talker declassification, 249
  hogan, building Grandmother's, 63, 64, 65, 66
  homecoming (Chester's), 218, 220, 221, 222,
    223, 225
  Korean War and, 235, 236
  sheepherding, 26, 30, 31
  Sleeping Rock people, 240
  stories (great), 35, 36–37
  sweat lodge, 69, 70, 71
Fels-Naptha soap, 50, 128
"fighter plane" *(da-he-tih-hi)*, 110
First Man and First Woman, 23, 36–37
First Marine Division
  Guadalcanal, 6, 10, 13, 16, 132, 141, 147–148,
    151, 152
  New Caledonia, 123
  Peleliu, 189, 191, 198, 201, 202
  R&R for, 149–150, 151, 152, 156, 209
  See also Begay, Roy (code talker); Marines
    (U.S.); Nez, Chester (code talker)
flame throwers, 195
Fletcher (Admiral), 13–14

Fletcher-class destroyers, 14, 14n
Flores, David (Major), 259
Florida Islands, 14, 145
Fort Defiance School, Arizona, 38, 38n, 44–62, 80–81, 83–84, 88, 98, 229, 230, 241
Fort Sumner, New Mexico, 38n, 38–39
Fort Wingate, New Mexico, 84, 89–90
"49-er" party, 254, 254n
Fox tribe, 234
French dislike of Marines, 121
friendly fire death of Harry Tsosie, 166, 181, 186, 258
fry bread, 186–187, 234
Fryer, E. Reeseman, 79
Fuji Evening, 215

Galloping Horse, 157
Gallup, New Mexico, 31, 68, 173, 218
Gallup's Catholic Hospital, 246, 247
Gallup School, New Mexico, 83–84
Geiger, Roy (General), 197, 201, 202, 207
Germany, 86, 91, 121, 215, 217
ghosts *(chindi)*, 223, 224
GI Bill, 241
Gifu Ridge, 146, 152–153, 157
girl babies as highly valued, 247
"glittering fourth world," 36
goats as best friends, 24–25, 30
Golden Gloves tournament, 231–232
Good Life (Right Way), 5, 24, 61, 65, 72, 110, 219, 220, 223, 225, 243, 244, 246, 265
Good Way ceremony, 223, 223n, 224, 252
Goon (Japanese translator), 208
Gorman, Carl (code talker), 88, 95, 112, 121, 262
Gorman, Zonnie, 262
government employees ("Washing-done"), 74
Grable, Betty, 160
Grande Terre, 120, 121, 123
Grandmother (Chester's grandmother)
    boarding school and, 42, 45, 50–51
    clans and marriage advice, 240
    Great Livestock Massacre, 74, 75
    herd, building, 75
    hogan, building, 63–68
    homecoming (Chester's), 218, 219, 221, 222, 225, 226
    sheepherding, 27, 28, 31, 33
    stories (great), 36, 37–38, 67
Grants, New Mexico, 36

Gray, Charlie, 251
Gray, Johnny, 262
Gray, Raymond, 262
Great Depression (U.S.), 75, 76
Great Livestock Massacre, 39, 73–81, 266
Great Plains dust bowl, 76
grid system, field-testing, 195–196
Guadalcanal, 5–21, 127–162
    Austen, Mount, 146, 153, 157
    Banzai (suicide attackers), 129, 133, 138, 141
    Battle of Bloody Ridge, 16
    Battle of Guadalcanal, 145
    Battle of Savo Island, 13–15
    Bougainville training, 159
    burying bodies with tractors, 162
    capture strategy, 132
    casualties, 16, 17, 142, 145, 148, 159, 162
    crabs and crocodiles at, 153, 154, 155
    dog tags, 162
    dysentery, 143, 151
    fear of soldiers, 11, 20, 123, 156, 159
    first battlefield use of Navajo code, 133
    food, 7–8, 134–135, 160
    foot problems, 143
    foxholes, 18–19, 127, 128, 134, 144–145, 150, 153, 154, 160
    friendly fire, avoiding, 130–131, 135–137, 139, 140–141
    Gifu Ridge, 146, 152–153, 157
    "jungle rot," 143
    landing, 12–13, 16–18, 127
    malaria, 143–144, 148, 151
    Melanesian population of, 161
    "Midnight Charlie," 127
    mosquitoes, 143–144
    night attacks by Japanese, 127, 145
    radios (TBX radios), 19, 133, 134, 135, 138, 139, 157
    Slot, The ("Ironbottom Sound"), 14, 16, 145, 158
    South Pacific voyage to, 5–12
    sunbathing Marines, 158–159
    "Tokyo Night Express, The," 16
    training for Guam, 177–179
    training for Iwo Jima, 209, 221
    typhus, 143
    "walking fire in," 136
Guam, 87, 114, 177–188
Gutierrez, Benny and Sally, 244

Haile, Father Berard, 91, 91n, 102, 102n
Halsey, "Bull" (Admiral), 168
"hand grenade" (nimasi), 110
hand grenades, 97, 98, 127, 128
hand-to-hand combat, 98, 122, 170
hand-trembler, 222n, 222–223, 224
Harvard, 250
Haskell Indian Nations University, Kansas, 229–233, 234, 240
Haskie, Ross (code talker), 10, 10n, 109, 111, 121, 256, 256n
Hataathlii, Ned, 230
Hawaii, 236, 237
Hawthorne, Roy (code talker), 259
"hearing" Navajo, 104
Hellzapoppin Ridge, 167, 168, 170
helmets, uses of, 171, 181
Henderson, Lofton R. (Major), 15
Henderson Field, 15, 16, 146
Higgins boats, 13, 16, 17, 17n, 163, 191–192, 196
high explosive (HE) warheads, 178
Hirohito (Emperor of Japan), 215
Hiroshima, Japan, 215
Hisey, Henry, Jr., 185–196
hitting corporal incident, 95, 95n
hogan, building Grandmother's, 63–68
Holcomb, Thomas (Commandant), 92
Holy People, 35, 37–38, 62, 237
Holy Way ceremony, 252
homecoming (Chester's), 217–227
home memories, 11, 144, 153, 174
Honoring the Navajo Code Talkers Act, 256
Hoover Dam project, 76
Hopi Indians, 84
howitzers, 135–136
humor of Navajos, 112, 263
"hunger," 105
Hunt (Lieutenant), 18, 131–132
Hunter's Point, Arizona, 242, 242n
Hyakutake, H. (General), 16, 158, 170

Ichiki, Kiyono (Colonel), 16
"I do not like" (doo shil yá'át' ééh da), 251, 251n
"I Love You for Sentimental Reasons," 233
Ilthma, Oscar (code talker), 111, 121
Indian Reorganization Act, 77n, 77–78
Inoue, Sadae (Lieutenant General), 202
"Ironbottom Sound" (Slot, The), 14, 16, 145, 158
Italy, 86, 121

"I've Got Sixpence," 119
"I will return" (MacArthur), 207
Iwo Jima, 185, 209, 211–212, 214

"jackass" (tkele-cho-gi), 8–9
"January" (yas-nil-tes), 110
Japan
    American vs. Japanese soldiers, 124–125, 173
    atomic bombs dropped on Hiroshima and Nagasaki, 215, 217
    Banzai (suicide attackers), 129, 133, 138, 141, 166, 181–182, 183
    blue-white artillery tracers of, 20
    bombing of Tokyo, 215
    Bushido code (no surrender), 124, 173
    codes cracked by, 93, 115, 157
    code talkers mistaken for Japanese, 9, 112–113, 131, 132, 199–200, 202–203, 203
    dishonor of soldiers' families, 206
    divine right to rule world, 124
    earthquake of 1923, 86
    expansion of, 86, 87–88, 114
    14th Division, 194
    HakkoX ichiu (manifest destiny), 124
    invasion of China, 86
    learning about Navajo code, 207–208
    "Midnight Charlie," 127
    "missing," 206
    Naval masters, 145–146
    night attacks by, 127, 145, 175
    176th Army, 16
    Pearl Harbor attack by, 7, 13, 85, 86, 87, 121
    prisoners of war (POWs), Japanese, 186, 187
    "scalp" for Bad Way ceremony, 142, 224, 226–227
    Shinto religion, 124
    snipers, 167
    South Pacific dominance by, 1, 13, 114, 179, 200
    surrender of, 217
    tanks, 194
    "Tokyo Night Express, The," 16
    Tokyo Rose, 198–199
    unbreakable Navajo code, learning about, 207–208, 215
    underground systems built by, 190, 197, 200, 212
    World War I and, 85–86
    wounded, abandoning, 197

Yamato race, 124
Zeros, 18, 169–170, 201
    See also casualties; code talkers (Navajo code);
        Guadalcanal; World War II
"Japan" *(beh-na-ali-tsosie)*, 110
Japan, Sea of, 15
Johnston, Philip, 90, 91, 92, 198
Jolson, Al, 232
Jones, Buck, 59
Jones, James E. (Colonel), 92
"June" *(be-ne-eh-eh-jah-tso)*, 110
June, Allen Dale (code talker), 89, 112, 121, 256
junipers, 24, 24n, 43, 68, 70–71, 120, 219

Ka-bar knives, 94, 143, 153, 203
Kawaguchi (Major General), 16
Kieyoomia, Joe, 208
"kindness" *(hozoji)*, 225, 227
King, Jimmie (code talker), 207
kitchen duty, 120
Kluckhorn, Clyde, 224, 224n
Korean War, 235–237
Kotb, Hoda, 259
kunai grass, 144

Laguna people, 49
land craft, vehicle and personnel (LCVPs), 196
landing ship, tank (LSTs), 196
landing vehicles, tracked (LVTs), 191, 196
"Land of the Rising Sun," 15
    See also Japan
land vs. ship positions, 139, 140
Larry King Weekend (TV show), 259
Lawrence, Kansas, 230, 231, 233, 242
Leighton, Dorothea, 224, 224n
Leonard, Alfred (code talker), 111, 121
Leonardo da Vinci, 234
Lew Wallace Elementary School, New Mexico,
    241
"light" *('adinídíín)*, 36
"light complexion" *(Betoli)*, 25, 26, 26n
    See also Nez, Chester (childhood and youth)
lightning bolts as weapons, 37
"little man" *(Hachi Yázha)*, 239
"little mother" *(Shimá Yázhí)*, 23, 24
Livestock Massacre, Great, 39, 73–81, 266
Lockard, G. R., 185, 185n
Long Walk, 37–39, 45, 80, 266
Louis, Joe ("Brown Bomber"), 231

MacArthur, Douglas (General), 88, 164, 207
Mack, Ted, 233
mail call, 161, 203–205
Malay Peninsula, 114
manifest destiny *(HakkoX ichiu)*, 124
Manual of Navajo Grammar, A (Haile),
    91, 91n
Manuelito, John (code talker), 103, 111–112,
    121, 156, 157
Mariana Islands, 179
Marine Corps *Chevron*, 96–97, 97n,
    98–99, 99n
Marine Corps Recruitment Center in San
    Diego, 90
Marines (U.S.)
    abandoning ship drills, 95, 121
    age requirements of, 88
    basic training, 8, 9, 18, 90, 93–99
    cadence, counting, 97
    camaraderie, 97, 149, 151, 159, 172
    close-order drills, 96
    code talkers and, 214n, 214–215, 215n, 243
    communications school, 98
    cultural vs. physical challenges, 95–96
    dropping out, 89
    equipment issued to, 127–128
    food during basic training, 95, 120, 134
    German Shepherds and, 142–143
    "getting tough" test, 95, 95n
    hand-to-hand combat, 98, 122, 170
    heads shaved, 94
    hitting corporal incident, 95, 95n
    "jar-heads," 175
    Marine Corps MOS (Military Occupational
        Specialty), 114
    marksmanship of, 97, 138
    night-landing practice, 121
    obstacle course, 94
    Platoon 382, 9, 96–97, 97n, 98–99, 101
    points system for going home, 212–213
    prayers encouraged by, 10
    recruits, 83–99
    segregation of soldiers, 185
    shouting, 96
    survival training, 98
    swimming, 94–95, 108
    trust in Navajos, 185n, 185–186, 186n
    uniforms, 7, 94, 107, 117
    women in, 98

Marines (*cont.*)
  See also Begay, Roy (code talker); casualties;
    code talkers (Navajo code); First Marine
    Division; Guadalcanal; Nez, Chester (code
    talker); Second Marine Division; Third
    Marine Division; Tsinajnnie, Francis
    (code talker)
Massacre, Great Livestock, 39, 73–81, 266
matriarchal society, Navajos, 26, 31, 42, 44
matrons, boarding school, 46, 47, 49, 50, 51, 53,
    54, 73, 83, 84, 150, 234, 240
McCabe, William (code talker), 111, 121, 132
McClain, Sally, 186, 186n, 214, 214n, 215,
    215n
McDonald, Peter, 250
medicine bags, 10, 11, 129–130, 167, 266
medicines used in sweat lodge, 70–71
"medicine" vs. "mouth," 104
Melbourne, Australia, 152
Merrill (Admiral), 164
MGM Studios, 258
Michelangelo, 234
"Midnight Charlie," 127
military terms and Navajo code, 100, 109–110,
    114
milking ewes and goats, 26, 26n
"million-dollar" wounds, 183
Mix, Tom, 59
Model T Ford truck, 43, 45
monkeys, 169
monsters roaming the earth, 36, 37, 223
Morgan, Jake, 245
Morse code, 98
mortars, 135–136
mosquitoes, 122, 123

Nagasaki, Japan, 215
Nakagawa, Kunio (Colonel), 194, 202, 205
naming livestock, 25
Nanking, China, 86
narratives. *See* stories (great)
National Geographic, 259
National Park Service, 76–77
Native Americans
  alcohol not served to Indians, 8, 107, 231
  citizenship of U.S. and, 217–218
  identification card required for, 217
  petroglyphs, 254
  vote, right to, 1, 217, 218

World War I, using languages, 91
  See also Navajo culture; Navajo language
Navajo, The (Kluckhorn and Leighton), 224, 224n
Navajo Code Talkers (Aaseng), 104, 104n
Navajo Code Talkers Dictionary, 271–291
Navajo culture, 3–4
  allegiance declaration by Navajo Tribal
    Council, 84–85
  "allotments," 31
  all things should be respected, 251
  animals vs. money, 42
  ash, importance of, 65–66
  bears as relatives, 245–246
  boy babies, 247
  burials, 30–31
  clan affiliations, 26, 239n, 239–240
  clothing of, 220
  community sense, 79, 80
  compass points and, 65
  corn pollen, importance of, 11, 25, 61, 65, 130,
    228, 246, 248, 259
  dead, avoiding, 18, 19, 30, 31, 142
  Diné ("the People"), 25, 28, 35, 36, 37, 38, 39,
    39n, 68, 91, 104, 219, 223, 240, 259
  discipline, 50–51
  dry (sand) paintings, 220, 226
  east-facing doorway, 64
  education program promises to, 77, 78
  evil people as coyotes, 29
  expansion for reservation, 77, 78, 78n
  eye contact and, 95–97, 153, 239
  facial hair, 162
  "49-er" party, 254, 254n
  fry bread, 186–187, 234
  ghost of deceased *(chindí),* 18, 40
  girl babies as highly valued, 247
  graves, 30–31
  humor of, 112, 263
  incest, 240
  index finger pointing and, 155
  marriage, 240–241, 242, 265
  matriarchal society, 26, 31, 42, 44
  medicine bags, 10, 11, 129–130, 167, 266
  mourning, 31
  mutton, 42, 44, 45, 55, 58, 66, 67, 78, 220,
    234, 263
  oral tradition of, 39, 80, 108, 138
  owls as signs of trouble, 24, 48
  physical bodies of, 223–224

public-works jobs for, 77, 78
sheep as wealth, 75
smoking, 160–161
snowbanks for toughing children, 67
social gatherings, 68
spiritual bodies of, 223–224
"squash blossom" necklaces, 220
stepping over someone and, 251
suffering in silence, 180
time marked by seasons, 49
"trader," 91
"walking in beauty," 10, 219, 244
warrior tradition of, 6, 7, 87
witchcraft belief, 46–47, 161, 162
wool preparation, 51–52
See also Nez, Chester; stories (great)
Navajo culture, ceremonies
Bad Way ceremony, 223n, 223–227,
224n, 226n
Blessing Way, 144
coming-of-age ceremony, 69
Enemy Way ceremony, 222n, 222–223,
250–252
Good Way ceremony, 223, 223n, 224, 252
hand-trembler, 222n, 222–223, 224
Holy Way ceremony, 252
medicine men, 65, 224–225
morning blessings, 25, 130
pot drum, 226, 251
"putting up" a sing, 222, 222n, 225
Right Way (Good Life), 5, 24, 61, 65, 72, 110,
219, 220, 223, 225, 243, 244, 246, 265
sing ceremonies, 219–221, 222, 222n, 224,
224n, 225, 225n, 226, 226n, 227, 251
Squaw Dance, 225–226, 251
Navajo language
aspirated stops, 104
complexity, 91, 91n, 102, 103, 104–105
dialect differences, 103
glottal stops, 103, 104
hearing language difficulty, 104
learning in infancy, 91, 108–109
modulated voices, 96
painting pictures with, 105, 105n
pronunciation of, 91, 103, 104–105
tonal language, 103, 104, 104n
unwritten language, 91, 91n, 102, 102n
verbs, 104, 105
See also code talkers (Navajo code)

Navajo Nation (Navajo Reservation), 2, 2n, 31,
79, 88, 91, 105
Navajo National Park, 77
Navajo Tribal Council, 84–85, 87, 250
Navajo Tribal Fair, 250
Navajo Weapon (McClain), 186, 186n, 214, 214n,
215, 215n
Navy (U.S.)
Bougainville, 174–175
corpsmen ("docs"), 195, 206
Guadalcanal, 12, 14, 15, 145
Korean War, 236
Marines vs., 175
Pearl Harbor attack by Japan, 7, 13, 85, 86,
87, 121
Seabees, 168, 171, 182
"swab jockies," 175
Navy Crosses, 188
New Caledonia, 114, 117–124
New Deal, 76, 77, 79
New Guinea, 114, 164
New Mexico, 2, 10, 31, 36, 58, 89, 144, 218,
236, 245
"New Mexico" tag, 132
New York Yankees, 259
Nez ("very long" or "very tall"), 43–44
Nez, Chester (childhood and youth)
Betoli ("light complexion"), 25, 26, 26n
Checkerboard, New Mexico, 1, 2–3, 9, 24,
24n, 39, 76, 77, 105, 213, 229
"chips" (money of trading post), 52
clothing, 25, 52
food, scarcity of, 2, 7
friends, livestock, 24–25, 30, 67, 75
gratitude for boarding school, 80, 88, 89, 149
joining the Marines, decision, 87, 88
public school, 83–84
shearing sheep, 51
sheepherding, 23–33
slingshots, 28, 29–30, 226
"string game," 51
"summerhouse," 31, 36, 42, 47
sweat lodge, 69–72
toys, 29–30
trading post, 42, 52, 75
See also boarding school; Navajo culture
Nez, Chester (code talker)
Angaur, 197–200, 201, 202
baptism, killing fields, 18

Nez, *(cont.)*
  basic training, 8, 9, 18
  Bougainville, 163–175
  flying, first time, 188
  Guam, 87, 114, 177–188
  guard duty, 236
  Iwo Jima, 185, 209, 211–212, 214
  outperforming white peers, 9
  Peleliu, 189–197, 201–207
  points system for going home, 212–213
  promotion to corporal, 236
  reading letters out loud, 171, 204–205
  Reserves and, 234–235
  sharpshooter (pistol) qualification, 97
  shooting man vs. coyote, 129
  volunteering for Marines, 1, 7
  "wide open," liking, 106–107
  See also Begay, Roy (code talker); code talkers
    (Navajo code); Guadalcanal; Marines
    (U.S.); Nez, Chester (postmilitary life);
    Tsinajnnie, Francis (code talker)
Nez, Chester (family)
  Albert "Chubby" (Chester's son), 247
  Black Sheep clan *(Dibé-lizhiní* or *Dibé-*
    tXizhiní), 26, 239n, 239–240
  Charlie Gray (Chester's brother), 24, 28
  children and, 245–248, 252, 253–255
  Coolidge (Chester's brother), 23, 24, 28,
    30–31, 42, 44, 48, 55, 58, 69, 70, 71, 81,
    217, 218, 237
  death of children, 246–247, 254–255, 266
  death of Mother *(Shimá),* 30, 31
  divorce from Ethel, 252, 253–254, 265
  Emery (Chester's great-grandson), 261
  Ethel Pearl Catron (Chester's wife), 234, 239,
    239n, 240–242, 244, 246, 247, 250, 252, 255
  Georgann (Chester's first daughter), 246–247
  Grandfather, 64, 65, 66, 69, 70, 74, 75, 101,
    109, 218, 222
  Great-Grandmother, 37–38, 52
  Korean War and, 235, 236
  Latham (Chester's grandson), 255, 256
  Michael (Chester's grandson), 255, 256, 261
  Michael (Chester's son), 1–2, 247, 252, 253,
    255, 256, 258, 259, 261, 262, 266
  Mother *(Shimá),* 30, 31
  New Caledonia, 114, 117–124
  Old Auntie (Chester's aunt), 23, 26, 27, 28, 29,
    30, 32, 33, 51, 52, 63, 69, 75

  Ray (Chester's son), 247, 252, 255, 266
  Rita (Chester's daughter-in-law), 255, 256,
    259, 263
  Shawnia (Chester's granddaughter), 255, 256
  Stanley (Chester's son), 247, 252, 254–255
  telling family about enlistment, 101
  Tyah Chester "TC" (Chester's adopted son),
    247–248, 252, 255, 266
  Uncle, 24, 32, 63, 64, 69, 70, 219, 220
  wedding and white man's work, 239–244
  Young Auntie, 28, 33, 41, 51, 52
  See also Father (Chester's father);
    Grandmother (Chester's grandmother);
    Nez, Dora (Chester's sister)
Nez, Chester (personal)
  appearance of, 7, 112, 161–162
  basketball and, 231, 252–253
  bells, comfort from, 144
  blackouts, 255
  boxing career of, 231–232
  Chichiltah ("Among the Oak Trees"), 20–21,
    31, 43, 51, 54, 58, 68, 73, 80, 84, 90,
    218–219, 233, 235, 255, 261, 266
  civil servant incident, 217–218
  concentration skills of, 192–193
  death, never forgetting, 119, 141–142
  devastation, feeling sick from, 169
  diabetes, 266
  football and, 60, 230, 253
  friendships, 57, 58, 230, 231, 234
  home memories, comfort from, 11, 144, 153, 174
  humidity, trouble with, 119
  landscapes, 234
  memories of war and, 221–222, 223
  ocean, seeing for first time, 107–108
  painting skills of, 243
  prayers by, 10, 12, 20–21, 147, 149, 155
  proud, making family, 10, 11, 21, 33, 89, 99,
    158, 186, 218, 242, 249, 263
  secrecy of code talker and, 217, 218, 221–222,
    233, 235, 237, 249
  serving country vs. heroism, 10
  singing and, 119, 232–233
  soft-spoken man, 2, 19
  wounds of, 180–181, 183, 186
  Ye'ii mural painted by, 243–244
Nez, Chester (postmilitary life)
  artist education, 233–234, 243, 255
  Bad Way ceremony, 223n, 223–227, 224n, 226n

blessing the Red Sox by, 255, 256, 259
celebrations for, 261–263, 266
celebrity of, 249–250, 262
deer hunting, 245–246
Enemy Way ceremony, 222n, 222–223,
    250–252
Good Way ceremony, 252
Haskell Indian Nations University, Kansas,
    229–233, 234, 240
high school diploma, 229, 230, 233
Holy Way ceremony, 252
homecoming, 217–227
hunting, 245–246
interviews of, 259
legacy, 265–266
leg left amputation, 262, 266
nightmares about war, 216, 222, 223, 250, 252
saluting President Bush, 258
"scalp" of Japanese for Bad Way ceremony,
    142, 224, 226–227
speaking engagements by, 250, 259, 266
TV show appearances, 259
University of Kansas, 233–234, 241, 249
Veterans' Administration Hospital,
    Albuquerque, 243–244, 255
war experiences impact on, 213, 215–216,
    250, 252
white man's world and, 244
Ye'ii mural painted by, 243–244
Nez, Dora (Chester's sister)
    boarding school, 41, 42, 43, 44, 45, 55–56,
        58, 59
    Checkerboard and, 2–3
    Chester's children and, 253
    death of, 266
    Great Livestock Massacre, 75, 80–81
    helped by Chester, 235, 244, 255
    hogan, building Grandmother's, 66, 67
    homecoming (Chester's), 218, 222
    letters to/from Chester, 161, 204, 205
    sheepherding, 25, 30
    stories (great), 37, 39
Nez, Jack (code talker), 111, 121, 230
Nez Valley, 221
night attacks by Japanese, 127, 145, 175
nightmares about war, 216, 222, 223, 250, 252
Nimitz, Chester W. (Admiral), 164, 185
Nixon, Richard (President), 250
"no longer available" (ádin), 31

North (náhokos), 65
North Island Headquarters, 112–113
North Korea, 235
Notah, Roy (code talker), 157, 158, 159, 162,
    190, 198, 203, 213
Noumea Bay, 120

O (ne-ahs-jah), 132
Oka (Colonel), 152, 153
Oklahoma City, 231
"old mother, the" (Shimásáni). See Grandmother
    (Chester's grandmother)
Olive-drab.com, 206, 206n
Oliver, Lloyd (code talker), 111, 121, 256
Operation Cartwheel, 164
Operation Forager, 179
Operation Stalemate, 190
Operation Watchtower/Operation Shoestring,
    13–15
oral tradition of Navajos, 39, 80, 108, 138
    See also stories (great)
"original" code talkers, 1, 8, 8n, 10, 10n, 11n, 89,
    102, 106, 109, 110–112, 121, 230, 256,
    256n, 258, 259, 266
Orote Peninsula, 180, 182, 183
ouu (yes), 12
overgrazing, 76, 77, 77n

Pacific Ocean Areas command, 164
Padaock, Lawrence, 230
Palau Islands, 190, 198, 202
Palmer, Joe (Balmer Slowtalker) (code talker),
    111, 121, 156, 156n, 256
Palmer, Kermit, 256
Patch, Alexander (General), 149, 152, 158
Peleliu, 189–197, 201–207
Pentagon, Washington, D.C., 256
"People, The" (Diné), 25, 28, 35, 36, 37, 38, 39,
    39n, 68, 91, 104, 219, 223, 240, 259
Pete, Frank (code talker), 111, 121
Philippines, 88, 114, 198, 207
"picking up" an object, 104
Pima people, 49, 50
piñons, 41, 43, 63, 68, 120, 144, 155, 219,
    261–262
pistols, 94, 97, 236
Platoon 382, 9, 96–97, 97n, 98–99, 101
Pocatello, Idaho, 236, 237
"Point, The," 192

Point Cruz, 152
points system for going home, 212–213
porcupine meat, 32–33
practicing Navajo code, 8–9, 106, 108, 109, 112–113, 118, 119–120, 123
Price, Wilson (code talker), 10n, 109, 111, 121, 256, 256n
Pueblo tribe, 77, 243
Puller, "Chesty" (Colonel), 188, 191

R (gah), 132
Rabaul, New Britain, 14, 15, 163, 164, 168
radios (TBX radios)
    Bougainville, 166, 167, 172, 173, 174
    Guam, 180, 181, 182
    Marine recruits and, 98
    New Caledonia, 122–123
    Peleliu, 193
rattlesnake killing incident, 251
Red Cross, 187
"reduction," livestock, 75–76, 77, 78n, 78–79
Reeves, Dolph (Sergeant), 214, 214n
religion, boarding school, 19, 60–62
Richard, Freddie, 229, 230, 241
rifles, 94, 97, 98, 137–138, 235, 236
Right Way (Good Life), 5, 24, 61, 65, 72, 110, 219, 220, 223, 225, 243, 244, 246, 265
"Rock of Ages," 119
"roger and out," 132
Roosevelt, Franklin D. (President), 76, 88
Ross, Mrs., 241
runners (spotters), 133, 136, 138, 140, 141, 166, 193
Rupertus, William H. (Field Commander General), 191, 192, 201
Ruth, Babe, 259

Sac tribe, 234
safe area bounded by four sacred mountains, 35–36, 38
Saipan, 179
Salt people, 239
San Diego, California, 90, 106–107, 117, 217
San Francisco Naval Hospital, California, 213–214, 215–216
Seabees, 168, 171, 182
seasickness, 5, 117, 118, 120
Second Marine Division

Guadalcanal, 6, 10, 148, 149, 151, 152, 156, 157, 158, 159, 162
    See also Begay, Roy (code talker); Marines (U.S.); Nez, Chester (code talker)
secrecy of Navajo code, 3, 9–10, 87, 88, 90, 93, 101, 106, 120, 217, 218, 221–222, 233, 235, 237, 249
semaphore, 98
semper fi ("always faithful"), 214
September 11 terrorist attacks, 257
Shackle vs. Navajo code, 92, 113, 131–132, 136, 198
Shanghai, China, 86
sheep as wealth, 75
    See also Great Livestock Massacre
sheepherding, Checkerboard, 23–33
Shimásání. See Grandmother (Chester's grandmother)
ship vs. land positions, 139, 140
Shirley, Joe, 263, 266
Shizhé'é. See Father (Chester's father)
showering, 54, 160
sing ceremonies, 219–221, 222, 222n, 224, 224n, 225, 225n, 226, 226n, 227, 251
"singer" (hataathlii), 219, 220, 226
Singer, Tommy (code talker), 207
Sioux tribe, 230
Sixth Marine Regiment, 149, 152, 155–156, 157
60 Minutes (TV show), 259
"slant-eye" (beh-na-ali-tsosie), 110
Sledge, E. B., 207, 207n
Sleeping Rock people, 240
Slop Chute, San Francisco, 8, 106–107
Slot, The ("Ironbottom Sound"), 14, 16, 145, 158
Slowtalker, Balmer (Joe Palmer) (code talker), 111, 121, 156, 156n, 256
Smith, Holland (General), 185
snafu (situation normal, all fucked up), 164, 164n
Solomon Islands, 164
South (shádi'ááh), 65
South Korea, 235
South Pacific dominance by Japan, 1, 13, 114, 179, 200
South Pacific strategy of U.S., 13–14, 114
South Pacific voyage to Guadalcanal, 5–12
Spam, 122, 134, 142
speaking engagements by Chester, 250, 259, 266
spotters (runners), 133, 136, 138, 140, 141, 166, 193

Spruance (Admiral), 185
Squaw Dance, 225–226, 251
St. Michaels Catholic Church, Arizona, 241
"Star-Spangled Banner," 262
Stephenson, L. J. (Sergeant), 97
stories (great), 35–39
  bows and arrows, 37
  Changing Woman, 36, 223
  code talkers, 265–266
  Coyote the trickster, 36
  creation of the world, 36
  Diné (Navajo Nation), 35, 36, 37, 38, 39,
    39n, 68
  First Man and First Woman, 23, 36–37
  "glittering fourth world," 36
  Great Livestock Massacre, 39, 73–81, 266
  Holy People, 35, 37–38, 62, 237
  lightning bolts as weapons, 37
  Long Walk, 37–39, 45, 80, 266
  monsters roaming the earth, 36, 37, 223
  prayers for leaving safe area, 35
  safe area bounded by four sacred mountains,
    35–36, 38
  Sun, 36, 37
  underworlds, 36
  white settlers, fighting, 37–38
  See also Navajo culture
Strumm, George, 214, 214n
submachine guns, 94
success of Navajo code, 131–134, 135, 136–137,
    138–141, 146, 150, 157, 159, 185, 188, 200,
    214n, 214–215, 215n
Sugar Ridge, 183–184
suicide attackers (Banzai), 129, 133, 138, 141,
    166, 181–182, 183
sulfa drugs, 127–128
Sumner (Colonel), 45
Sun, 36, 37
Suribachi, Mount, 211
sweat lodge, 69–72

Takashina, Takeshi (Lieutenant General), 181
"tall man, the" *(D'ent Nez),* 44
  See also Father (Chester's father)
Tassafaronga Point, 145
TBX radios. *See* radios
teeth brushing with soap, 50, 128, 150
TennoX heika banzai, 129
testing Navajo code, 112–113, 131–132

Thinkquest.org, 105, 105n
Third Marine Division
  Angaur, 198
  Bougainville, 168, 171, 172
  Guadalcanal, 159, 162
  Guam, 179, 180–181, 182, 187
  Iwo Jima, 209
  Peleliu, 190, 191
  See also Begay, Roy (code talker); Marines
    (U.S.); Nez, Chester (code talker);
    Tsinajnnie, Francis (code talker)
Thompson, Nelson (code talker), 111, 121
Thorpe, Jim, 233
"Thundering Mexican, The," 42
Tinian, 179
Tiyan airfield, 184
tkele-cho-gi (J, "jackass"), 108
Today (TV show), 259
Tohatchi School, New Mexico, 43–44, 48, 56
Tokyo, Japan, 86, 215
"Tokyo Night Express, The," 16
Tokyo Rose, 198–199
Toll, Roger, 76
Topeka, Kansas, 231, 232, 233
"transport plane" *(atsah),* 110
transport ships, 6, 14
Tsinajnnie, Francis (code talker)
  Angaur, 198, 199, 200
  Bougainville, 163, 165, 166, 167, 168,
    169–170, 173
  Guadalcanal, 156n, 156–157, 158, 159, 160, 161
  Guam, 180–181, 182, 183, 187, 188
  Iwo Jima, 209, 213
  Peleliu, 190, 191, 192, 193, 195, 202, 203
Tsingtao, China, 85
Tsosie, Harry (code talker), 111, 121, 166, 181,
    186, 258
Tuba City School, Arizona, 84, 85, 87, 88, 89,
    101, 123
tuberculosis, 80, 81
Tumon Bay, 184
Turner, R. K. "Terrible" (Rear Admiral), 14
Two Wells Trading Post in Gallup, 58

Umurbrogol Mountain ("Bloody Nose Ridge"),
    194, 201–202, 205, 206, 206n
unbreakable code. *See* code talkers (Navajo code)
underground systems built by Japan, 190, 197,
    200, 212

Underhill, James L. (Colonel), 98–99
underworlds, 36
United States of America
    Air Force (U.S.), 236
    Army (U.S.), 157, 160, 180, 198, 200,
        201–202, 205, 236
    censorship of mail to/from military by, 204,
        205
    declaration of war against Japan, 86
    diversity of, 3
    Great Depression, 75, 76
    Japanese vs. American soldiers, 124–125, 173
    nationalizing Japanese assets in, 86
    Pearl Harbor attack by Japan, 7, 13, 85, 86,
        87, 121
    POWs treatment by, 187
    red artillery tracers of, 20
    September 11 terrorist attacks, 257
    South Pacific strategy of, 13–14, 114
    World War I, 85–86, 91, 137
    wounded, never abandoning, 197
    See also Begay, Roy (code talker); casualties;
        code talkers (Navajo code); Marines (U.S.);
        Navy (U.S.); Nez, Chester; Tsinajnnie,
        Francis (code talker); World War II
"United States of America" (Ne-he-mah), 110
University of Kansas, 233–234, 241, 249
Unsung Heroes of World War II (Durrett), 185,
    185n
USS Lurline (ocean liner), 117–120

Vandergrift, Alexander (General), 6, 16, 18, 131,
    149, 185
Veterans' Administration Hospital,
    Albuquerque, 243–244, 255
Vogel, Clayton B. (Major General), 92

Wake Island, 87
"walking in beauty," 10, 219, 244
Walley, Robert (code talker), 57, 58, 59, 60, 266
war experiences impact on Chester, 213,
    215–216, 250, 252
warrior tradition of Navajos, 6, 7, 87
"Washing-done" (government employees), 74
Washington, George (President), 258
"water" (tó), 36
wedding and white man's work, 239–244
West (e'e'aah), 65
Westerner, The (movie), 160

Where Two Waters Meet people, 239, 240
white settlers, fighting, 37–38
Willie, John (code talker), 111, 121
Window Rock, Arizona, 84, 88, 240, 241
Windtalkers (film), 258
witchcraft belief, Navajos, 46–47, 161, 162
With the Old Breed (Sledge), 207, 207n
"woman who fights a battle in a circle" (Binishiit
    Baa). See Nez, Dora (Chester's sister)
World War I, 85–86, 91, 137
World War II
    Allied forces, 164, 215
    atomic bombs dropped on Hiroshima and
        Nagasaki, 215, 217
    Axis powers, 86
    Bataan Death March, 114, 208
    Battle of Empress Augusta Bay, 164
    Battle of Guadalcanal, 145
    Battle of Midway, 15, 114
    Battle of the Coral Sea, 114
    Battle of the Java Sea, 114
    bombing of Tokyo, 215
    combat fatigue, 216
    "million-dollar" wounds, 183
    Operation Cartwheel, 164
    Operation Forager, 179
    Operation Stalemate, 190
    Operation Watchtower/Operation Shoestring,
        13–15
    surrender of Germany, 215, 217
    surrender of Japan, 217
    veterans and Korean War, 235
    See also casualties; code talkers (Navajo code);
        Guadalcanal; Japan; Marines; United States
        of America
"worst battle of South Pacific war," 190, 197,
    206, 207, 207n
Wuhan, China, 86

yá'át'ééh greeting, 251, 251n
Yazzie, Felix (code talker), 10, 10n, 109, 110,
    121, 156, 156n, 256, 256n
Yazzie, Robert, 230
Yazzie, William (William Dean Wilson) (code
    talker), 112
Ye'ii mural painted by Chester, 243–244

Z, "zinc" (besh-do-tliz), 108
Zeros (Japanese), 18, 169–170, 201